Business History

This major new textbook on business history brings together the expertise of two internationally renowned authors to provide a thorough overview of the developments in business—from just before the Industrial Revolution up to the globalization of businesses today.

Business History is global in scope and looks at the major players—Europe, the USA, and Japan—as well as emerging economies, such as China and India. Focusing mainly on "big business," Amatori and Colli critically analyze "the firm" and its interaction with the evolution of economic, technological, and political systems at the micro- and macro-levels.

This outstanding textbook is an exceptional resource for students on economic and business history courses, as well as for practitioners interested in broadening their understanding of business.

Franco Amatori is Professor of Economic History and Head of the Institute of Economic History at Bocconi University, Italy. He specialized in business history during his time at Harvard Business School, USA, and has written extensively on Italian and international business history.

Andrea Colli is Associate Professor in Economic History at Bocconi University, Italy. He has published several books in fields such as the structure and evolution of SMEs, and the role of family firms in modern economic growth. In 2008, he was awarded the Harold Williamson prize for the most promising mid-career business historian, by the Business History Conference.

Business History
Complexities and comparisons

Franco Amatori and Andrea Colli

Routledge
Taylor & Francis Group

LONDON AND NEW YORK

First published 2011
by Routledge
2 Park Square, Milton Park, Abingdon, Oxon OX14 4RN

Simultaneously published in the USA and Canada
by Routledge
711 Third Avenue, New York, NY 10017

Routledge is an imprint of the Taylor & Francis Group, an informa business

British Library Cataloguing in Publication Data
A catalogue record for this book is available from the British Library

Library of Congress Cataloging in Publication Data
Amatori, Franco.
Business history: complexities and comparisons/Franco Amatori and
Andrea Colli.
    p.cm.
Includes bibliographical references and index.
1. Business—History. 2. Business—History—Cross-cultural studies
    I. Colli, Andrea. II. Title.
HF351.A63 2011
338.709—dc22   2010044471

ISBN: 978–0–415–42396–0 (hbk)
ISBN: 978–0–415–42397–7 (pbk)
ISBN: 978–0–203–81790–2 (ebk)

Typeset in Times New Roman
by Book Now Ltd, London

Printed and bound in Great Britain by
TJ International Ltd, Padstow, Cornwall

Contents

Illustrations

Tables

Figures

Acknowledgments

This book is the outcome of a combined 40-plus years of teaching at Bocconi University in Milan as well as periodic stays at other European institutions including Pompeu Fabra in Barcelona and the Stockholm School of Economics.

The interest our students showed for the topic of this volume as well as the constructive interaction we've always enjoyed with them have been a fundamental encouragement for us. Equally stimulating have been the occasions when we've met and discussed with colleagues in contexts such as the European Business History Association (EBHA) to which we feel a strong attachment for both personal as well as professional reasons. Hubert Bonin, Ludovic Cailluet, Albert Carreras, Youssef Cassis, Margarita Dritsas, Patrick Fridenson, Matthias Kipping, Christopher Kobrak, Ioanna Pepelasis, Mary Rose, Harm Schroeter, Philip Scranton, Keetie Sluyterman, and John Wilson are some of the EBHA friends who have helped to shape our ideas on business history.

Many colleagues and friends read the manuscript, in part or in its entirety, and we are grateful for their thoughtful observations. They include Giuseppe Berta, Brian Cheffins, Nicola Crepax, Michele D'Alessandro, Daniela Felisini, Paola Lanaro, Elisabetta Merlo, Corrado Molteni, Giandomenico Piluso, Francesca Polese, Franco Russolillo, Harm Schroeter, and Luciano Segreto. Silvia Conca, Robert Grant, Matthias Kipping, and Pierangelo Toninelli came together for a lively discussion and seminar at Bocconi; their critical and constructive observations are a sign of the solidarity that exists between scholars and we, too, have tried to get the maximum benefit from their insights.

Our young Bocconi colleagues, Veronica Binda and Mario Perugini, worked nonstop to give us the kind of help that every scholar would like to receive from a research assistant.

Marilena Merlanti provided constant organizational support, while (thanks to a generous grant we received from Bocconi) Amanda Herbert and Brigitte Pocta worked at editing our English into something that really works. In this respect, the contribution of Maggie Dufresne has been so fundamental.

In the last months of revising this work, we realized that our manuscript needed the input of the most critical of scholars. Luckily, Lou Galambos is not only a great business historian but also a real friend. It is thanks to his tireless efforts that this project has come to a satisfactory conclusion.

Franco Amatori and Andrea Colli
Milan, September 2010

Part I
Relevant issues

1 Introduction

This book is about modern economic development (Kuznets, 1971) as observed through the study of one of its most important actors, the business firm. In the wake of the Great Recession of 2008–2010, most of us have been thinking a great deal about businesses and their impact on our societies and economic opportunities. We add to those thoughts a perspective on the evolution of the firm, the primary social organization in the capitalist system. We know this is not all that can be written about business history, but we are certain that it is a crucial segment of our economic past and present.

Our volume is composed of 24 chapters. After we set the stage in this introduction, we explore some of the theoretical arguments that provide the foundation for our narrative. Chapter 2 focuses on the relationship between various economic theories of the firm and the history of business. In Chapter 3, we examine these issues via the firm's leader—the entrepreneur—as this topic has been analyzed by historians, economists, and other social scientists.

With Chapter 4, we switch gears and begin a diachronic description and analysis of business evolution. Chapters 4–6 are dedicated to firms in the preindustrial era and their main characteristics during the First Industrial Revolution. Here, our reference country is England, as this is the country in which this truly revolutionary process started.

We then shift our focus in Chapters 7 through 9 to the United States, a leading economy during the Second Industrial Revolution. It was this period, with its mass production, that serves as the starting point of the times in which we live now. This section is organized with a chapter about the infrastructures (especially railways) that made possible this new form of production. This will be followed by another chapter that gets to the core of the problem by analyzing the issues of technology and organizational change. Then we will follow up with a chapter on the national developments within this broad technological paradigm both in front-row nations such as the United States, the United Kingdom, and Germany, as well as in latecomers such as Russia, Japan, and Italy (from our perspective, France fits midway between the two groupings).

At the beginning of Chapter 10, our focus is once again on the United States. The next two chapters offer us an opportunity to examine how the Second Industrial

Revolution developed in the interwar period. In Chapter 10, we discuss the origins of the M-form (the multidivisional enterprise). Then we will expand the scope by considering the debate on managerial capitalism in the United States and Europe.

In Chapters 11 and 12, we enlarge the international perspective, considering convergences and differences between the United States, Europe, and Japan. Many of these differences are related to the importance of cartels, the predominance of family-headed enterprises, the active presence of the State, and the different roles played by workers in societies that do not adopt the American "Fordist model." From Europe, we will then go on to consider Japan and the origins of the Japanese "miracle" in the post-World War II period.

We examine the passage from the Second Industrial Revolution to the beginning of the Third Industrial Revolution—the Information Age—in Chapters 13–18, where we also discuss global competition in a divided world. The world becomes increasingly global in part because, at the beginning of the Third Industrial Revolution, electronics and jet transportation shrank space. Nevertheless, the world was still sharply divided by the presence of two opposing political systems: capitalism and communism.

Chapter 13 is important because it outlines the early stages of the Third Industrial Revolution. In the next three chapters, we examine what happened to business between the 1950s and the 1980s. We analyze the rise and decline of the American model, the failure of the Soviet Union, Japan's outstanding economic growth, and the challenge that the Land of the Rising Sun presented to the United States and its leading position in the world economy. We then return to Europe, considering the fundamental research done at Harvard Business School as well as that of management scholars Richard Whittington and Michael Mayer on the evolution of strategies and structures in the "Old Continent." Here, we address the Italian case and the industrial districts that for Italy (but not only for this country) were an important aspect of economic growth in the 1970s and 1980s. Looking again outside the leading industrial nations, we treat convergencies and divergencies, comparing, for instance, businesses in Argentina and South Korea. From the perspective of business history, the concepts of a Third World and developing countries are less useful than they have been to scholars in other disciplines.

The final section of this volume provides an examination of the era of "boundless globalization" (the version that was created with the fall of the Berlin Wall and thanks to the Internet). This brings us up to current times. In Chapter 19, we analyze an essential actor in this global scenario, the multinational firm. We enter into the very heart of the Third Industrial Revolution in Chapter 20, as we consider its forms of enterprise and the technological tools that foster new styles of company organization.

In this context—one dominated by globalization and the Third Industrial Revolution—in Chapters 21 and 22, we examine the surprising American recovery versus the slower development that characterized Europe and Japan. The Japanese problems are particularly telling because the nation's strengths became, in an era of globalization, its major weaknesses.

Of course, we would be remiss if we did not briefly survey the recent changes in business in China and India (Chapter 23). The former differs from the other Asiatic models because of the system's ability to play across the technological spectrum from labor-intensive sectors to high-tech ones, its recent openness to the activities of multinational companies inside its borders, and the actions of the State (especially those concerned with the liberation of the so-called "animal spirits" from the legal constraints that were typical of all communist regimes). What appears to be especially relevant in the case of India is the nation's capacity to transform the heritage of British colonialism into a positive force, the capacity to grow from a very ancient culture into an ultramodern scientific center at the service of enterprises (Bangalore), and, finally, the strong ethical inspiration that guides many of its entrepreneurs. When we consider its subtle lights and shadows, the Indian experience makes us confident of a better future.

Our volume ends with Chapter 24 that offers an overview of the settings of the firm, the technology, and the local contexts for business—three variables that play a central role in our general framework for a new narrative of the role of business in economic growth. We briefly explore some of the implications, for business, of the changes in the global political economy induced by the Great Recession of 2008–2010. But we leave to others an elaborate exposition along these lines, hoping that they will take into consideration the long-term historical perspective on the firm that our book provides.

Following this quick summary as regards the volume's contents, let us now try to single out some issues that the reader will find throughout the work.

Micro and macro developments

We can observe throughout the history of business the strong relationship between the two, a relationship that becomes clear in the efforts we make in providing context and also because, *de facto*, in our narrative, the main character is the large enterprise that often dominates its industrial sector. As a result, a single company's fate can often be directly related to the wealth of the nation where the firm is based. In this volume, our unit of analysis will be national economic systems with one exception, post-World War I Europe, where many of the Western European nations shared a number of common features that stand out most clearly when compared with the United States.

Industrial revolutions

These are sharp transitions in technological paradigms that were determined by aspects such as technical skills, scientific knowledge, forms of energy, and capital intensity. Many actors contribute to them. Among these was the enterprise, so that a long-term technological paradigm is at the same time both exogenous and endogenous to the firm. Technical progress is cumulative, but there are also substantial discontinuities.

Entrepreneurs and managers

We define entrepreneurs as persons who innovate, take risks, grab opportunities, and, above all, make decisions at the highest level. The most important are those who are able to synchronize their firm's activities with the form of the Industrial Revolution with which they are involved. From this point of view, there are different levels of entrepreneurship, and there is a typology of entrepreneurs.

Managers, instead, are individuals who, over the course of acquiring theoretical and practical experience, have developed a precise, often firm-specific, functional know-how. Typically, they have autonomy in a significant segment of the company's activities, usually inside a framework designed by the entrepreneur.

Markets

We are concerned mainly with national markets. They are determined by factors such as the number of inhabitants and per capita income. It is true that a company may also look toward international markets, as have many British, German, and Japanese businesses. But for most firms for most of the history we examine, it has usually been the domestic market, at least for a medium or large nation, that is the more reliable point of reference. Very important for a market is its dynamicity, more so than its absolute size.

Cultures

Culture is the attitude of a nation toward economic activity and economic change. It helps us understand the British entrepreneurs' propensity to risk during the First Industrial Revolution, the United States' search for order around 1900 (a search that favored the advent of big business), the marriage between science and technology in Germany in the same period, and Japan's unique form of radical, probusiness nationalism.

State

This entity plays various roles in our tale. In many contexts, the State served as a guarantor of the legal framework. In others, it was also a supplier of physical and intangible infrastructures. It can be a regulator, entrepreneur, and opponent, as well as a central or sector-specific planner.

Forms of enterprise

They are defined by their general design, by their size, by their strategies, and by their interrelationships. A crucial aspect of any enterprise is the relationship between headquarters and the operating units. The various forms of enterprise (the unitary form, the multidivisional, the conglomerate, and the holding company) are, theoretically, neutral as to the economic performance. The important thing is to clarify the way they have worked in specific historical settings; how they have or have not allowed the technical and organizational potential of the firm to develop. It is extremely important to recognize that inside each national economic system there is a community of companies (i.e., companies with different strategies and different dimensions) that is operative.

Varieties of capitalism

This is the intersection between the economy and its institutions. It determines the regulation of competition, the relationship between finance and companies, the nature of industrial relations, and the structure of the society's welfare systems. As for the forms of enterprise, it cannot be said that there is one typology of capitalism that is absolutely superior to the others.

Change and how it is unforeseeable

A lesson we can draw from our history is the volatility of the relative positions of the different nations and the fact that it is extremely difficult to make forecasts about international competition. What works in one phase does not necessarily work in the following one. Who would ever have imagined in 1800 the decline of the United Kingdom at the middle of the nineteenth century, the rise of the United States and Germany around 1900, the decline of the United States after the 1960s, the rise and decline of Japan in the last four decades, or the huge growth of China after the end of the Maoist period?

Post-Chandlerism

Any scholar who reflects on the state of business history invariably uses an adjective to define the present phase as post-Chandlerian. For some, this seems reasonable just because Alfred Chandler (1918–2007), the world's leading business historian, passed away and is no longer writing books and articles (something that he did practically until his final days). For others, his passing has provided a type of liberation because they perceived Chandler as an obstacle to progress in the discipline.

With his adamant persistence on industrial big business as the engine of economic development, Chandler placed some scholars in a predicament. They found it difficult to explore other aspects of business history because Chandler was the scholar who gave academic and scientific status to business history. Before him, the discipline was isolated, of little note to historians or economists; it was trapped in the middle of a battle between those accusing or defending the "robber barons" and those publishing a series of soulless company histories. Chandler's distinctive methodology (with its sharp focus on the entrepreneurial actions that gave birth to big business and a comparison of the structural changes in hundreds of companies) made it possible to develop generalizations that were indispensable reference points not only for business historians but also for scholars in other disciplines. *Strategy and Structure* (a comparison of companies) became almost a "bible" for students of management. *The Visible Hand* (a comparison of sectors) was almost as useful for institutional economists and lawyers interested in issues related to antitrust. *Scale and Scope* (a comparison of nations) emphasized the importance of organizational capabilities for building the wealth of a nation and reassured the evolutionary economists about some of their most important concepts.

For Chandler, the essential task of entrepreneurs was to give birth to an extended managerial network. His work thus enabled him to reconcile Max Weber, the pioneering sociologist of bureaucracy, with Joseph Schumpeter, the preeminent student of entrepreneurship. Chandler's framework emphasized the centrality of technology, making some sectors more "equal" than others: they are the sectors that can exploit the economies of scale and scope, giving birth in this way to the big businesses that came to dominate the world's leading economies in the Second Industrial Revolution. Technology was seen as both a constraint and an opportunity that could not always be grasped, an affirmation that left plenty of room for historical research.

While our history builds on the Chandlerian paradigm, we bring into our story a number of elements that Chandler either ignored or left for other historians to explore. Thus, we give substantially more emphasis, than he did, to the political context for business activity, both in a negative (as with antitrust) and a positive sense (as with State entrepreneurship and demand for innovative products). We also give more emphasis to globalization. We carefully consider culture as an independent variable, and we look beyond the giant, integrated firm into a present that includes more emphasis on business networks and specialization of function. Nor do we minimize, as Chandler did, the instability and social problems that can arise from developments like the Great Recession of our time. In this way, we hope to do credit to a neo-Chandlerian framework that links the technology, entrepreneurs, markets, culture, and State actions that impact the businesses central to our ability to produce the goods and services that constitute the wealth of all of our nations.

Further reading

F. Amatori and G. Jones (eds.), *Business History Around the World*, Cambridge University Press, New York, 2004.

A.D. Chandler, Jr., F. Amatori, and T. Hikino (eds.), *Big Business and the Wealth of Nations*, Cambridge University Press, Cambridge, 1997.

G. Jones and J. Zeitlin (eds.), *The Oxford Handbook of Business History*, Oxford University Press, New York, 2007.

S. Kuznets, *Modern Economic Growth: Findings and Reflections*, Nobel Prize Lecture, 1971. http://nobelprize.org/nobel_prizes/economics/laureates/1971/kuznets-lecture.html

N.R. Lamoreaux, D.M.G. Raff, and P. Temin (eds.), *Learning by Doing in Markets, Firms, and Nations*, University of Chicago Press, Chicago, 1999.

T. McCraw (ed.), *The Essential Alfred Chandler: Essays Toward a Historical Theory of Big Business*, Harvard Business School Press, Boston, 1988.

Appendix

Table 1.1 Fortune 500 companies, 2009

Country	Number of Global 500 corporations
Britain	26
Canada	14
China	37
France	40
Germany	39
India	7
Italy	10
Japan	68
The Netherlands	12
South Korea	14
Spain	12
Switzerland	15
United States	140

Source: http://money.cnn.com/magazines/fortune/global500/2009/index.html. Last accessed October 6, 2010.

2 Business history and theories of the firm

A "new" unit of analysis

Since the First Industrial Revolution, the business enterprise has been one of the most prominent units of analysis for understanding modern economic growth. From the early nineteenth century, business enterprise increasingly has been identified with the "factory." That was the British way of organizing production, a form of organization and related technology that spread throughout the European continent. Thanks to this innovation, Europe began to experience a consolidation of economic and political power that reverberated around the world. As peripheral countries became involved with this style of industrialization, they began to experience the same struggles over control, the same social and political transformations, and the same surges of growth that had carried Britain to a leadership role in the international economy of that day.

At the outbreak of the First Industrial Revolution, near the end of the eighteenth century, capital and labor concentration was not a novelty. In fact, during the preindustrial period, large concentrations of workers were already employed in shipbuilding, mining, and construction. In the textile field, merchants relied on a large number of cottage laborers, while the scale-intensive phases of the production process were performed in centralized plants run by entrepreneurs who often hired specialized workers. So the "factory" itself was not new. What was new was the special combination of a centralized operation with a more efficient technology. The new factories (normally located away from urban centers) used water and then steam power to mechanize production. Specialization of function and the related division of labor called for new forms of labor discipline. Thus was created a highly productive and increasingly efficient style of business, which became the basic "building block" of the early industrial economies.

These complex phenomena stimulated many streams of commentary and analysis, which dealt with the origins, structure, and function of the industrial enterprise. This chapter contextualizes, within a historical perspective, some of the various "theories of the firm."

The varied nature of the firm

When you see the expression "theory of the firm," you immediately think of classical and neoclassical economics from Adam Smith to the present day. We will discuss those theories later, but it is important to recognize that the "firm" and its "theories" have been of interest to many disciplines other than economics and management studies. They have also been the source of debates about legal rights, and especially the issue of the firm's legal identity. The shift from craft production—carried out by skilled and unskilled individuals and based on the identification between the household and the workplace—to the factory sparked a radical transformation of the juridical status of the production unit itself.

As a consequence, terms such as *company* or *corporation* started to be associated with a new organizational structure that came to have its own legal status. This was independent from that of the single individuals involved in the different steps of the production process. During the past century, the growth of firms has brought about further substantial legal transformations, with new juridical and organizational forms emerging to cope with the increasing complexity of the firm's activities. The individuals and groups within these "firms" cooperated strategically but competed as regards resource allocation and the distribution of returns. These activities and the organizations in which they took place became a focus for scholarly work across many fields. It has been, for instance, one of the main fields of study for sociologists who are deeply interested in the analysis of the clusters of individuals and relationships that constitute society's social systems. Building on the bureaucratic organizational theories of Max Weber, Talcott Parsons' functionalism, and the more recent analyses of conflict and social evolution, they have improved our understanding of the firm's internal operations and external relations to the market and other forms of authority. Recently, other scholars have probed the relationships between business organizations and the values and other social institutions of the society in which they operate. The role of individuals has also become a source of investigation for anthropologists and cognitive psychologists concentrating on the processes through which knowledge spreads across an organization and society as a whole.

Statics and the neoclassic perspective

The primary perspective on the firm in economics is provided by neoclassical theory, a static form of analysis that treats business behavior in a particular slice of time. It is important to understand the basic assumptions that are employed in this theory. In this scenario, the representative firm enjoys perfect information and operates efficiently at the lowest point of the marginal cost curve. It is a price-taker, with few possibilities of influencing the markets or the industry in which it operates. Technology is exogenous, and the contribution of the economic actors within the firm is not relevant to the theory. This abstract universe can be complicated by comparing it with another slice in time (Time 1 and Time 2), but in both cases, the analysis is static. It does not tell you how you get from Time 1 to Time 2 or Time 3. The representative enterprise is the small–medium business that performs only a limited number of functions. Some examples of firms that come close to those analyzed in neoclassical theory are the single-phase, scarcely integrated businesses in the cotton industry and those in the early British metal-working districts.

The neoclassical firm operated in a highly competitive, price-oriented system. There were a high number of production units in the industry, very little functional integration, and an absence of proprietary technologies. Technical knowledge and other information could be obtained freely or at a very low cost.

The neoclassical perspective is thus particularly relevant to the business history of the First Industrial Revolution. As will be described in the next chapters, this first industrial transformation did not suddenly produce the kind of large, integrated, capital-intensive corporations that we are familiar with today. It did produce a radical technological breakthrough, but the technologies were largely general purpose, not expensive, and easily appropriable. The process of innovation was determined by micro, incremental innovations that were primarily generated in the workplace. Some of them were immediately diffused through a process that has been defined as "collective invention." This process was similar to a twenty-first-century open-source system in which usually incremental innovations circulate freely among users, and each user contributes to the increase of the overall stock of knowledge.

Broadly speaking, this kind of firm was not inclined toward growth, because its increase stopped at the average size determined by the lowest point in the cost curve. Moreover, the ways in which this growth was achieved and the resources that were involved were off bounds according to the theory. So too was the distribution of power within and outside the firm, neither of which were considered to be relevant to this form of economic analysis. The theory dealt mainly with perfect competition and monopoly, and since the firm's internal structure was inside the "black box," it was not involved in the analysis.

Dynamics in a business history perspective

By contrast, business history inherently has a *comparative and dynamic dimension*: firms are seen as complex units that evolve over time and have considerable differences in their structures and internal dynamics. Still, historians can generalize about these organizations. Although the firms may operate in many different countries and have distinct patterns of ownership and organization, firms in the same industry usually share some relevant characteristics such as capital and labor intensity.

Another analytical dimension is *dynamism*. The firms of greatest interest to business historians tend to increase their size over time. This happens in capital-intensive industries, characterized by scale economies, as well as in some labor-intensive industries. Given a certain technology, one expects to find that firms expand until the point at which, in the language of neoclassical economics, marginal returns start to decrease. Nevertheless, in the real world, growth is not a mechanical process, subject only to economic calculations. Firms may continue to grow, seeking greater market shares, even though their returns on capital are declining. They may also voluntarily curb their growth by limiting their size to avoid the problems associated with expansion. In addition, firms react differently to the exogenous and endogenous technological changes that trigger the major spurts of dynamism that influence the method, speed, and direction in which firms develop patterns of growth. For instance, the new information technologies of recent years provide incentives for internal growth and further integration, given the lower incidence of information costs on management activities. But for some firms, these same technologies encourage subcontracting and outsourcing. All the phases of this dynamic process (continuity and discontinuity, expansion, stagnation, and decline) are relevant to the analyses of business scholars.

Finally, *relational complexity* has to be considered. The process of economic growth in the past two centuries has created extremely complicated organizations with significant internal and external relationships. The iron-smelting furnaces of the first half of the nineteenth century and the Carnegie steelworks at the beginning of the twentieth century operated in close temporal proximity to each other. Nonetheless, the differences between them from technological, organizational, and occupational points of view are striking. Technological imperatives had a great deal to do with the growth experienced in the iron and steel industry and other industries. But other significant variables contributed to the intensity and direction of expansion, and these help to explain the continued existence and success of small-sized firms. Moreover, the mix of these variables is different across time and space. For this reason, firms display different patterns of growth according to their varying geographical contexts and periods. Given a certain technology, the growth of the firm is frequently determined by the dimensions and dynamism of the consumption market. Two other important elements determining the firm's expansion can be the efficiency of the financial markets in channeling necessary resources to the firm and the presence of legal frameworks that protect the firm's assets and facilitate trade. All these developmental elements interact. Technologies and markets are very sensitive to changes in legal systems and financial markets, and these dynamic elements can force the business enterprise to adapt and adjust.

The evolution of firms can be linked to the cultural patterns and institutional elements of different societies. Technology fosters the process of growth, but cultural patterns still play a considerable role. Where the cultural perception of large-sized firms is negative, firms may adopt some technologies instead of others. To some extent, this helps to explain the differences in the internal structure of industries across the world and in different contexts. In food and beverages, for instance, standardization and mass production are accepted in some cultures and not in others. In the case of beer, radical differences of opinion still exist today between the United States and Continental Europe. This affects not only technological standards but also the strategic behavior of the actors in the sector. In other cases, the preferred financial market structure may have direct consequences on the availability of resources. Fundamental differences in terms of the quality and quantity of financial resources can be detected among financial markets. Some are primarily based on banks' intermediation, and in others, there is a strong emphasis on the efficiency of the stock exchange as a way to channel resources to business. Legal systems can be the outcome of institutional and cultural heritages, and this can explain the completely different approach toward regulation of collusive practices among firms in the United States and Europe. History is a key instrument to use in analyzing these differences, and a business history perspective helps us to understand both the constraints placed on firms and the general framework within which growth processes take place.

"Large" firms in practice and theory

Many years ago, the Austrian economist Joseph Schumpeter challenged the neoclassical approach to the firm. Schumpeter's thought was characterized by two features. The first was the "competitive habit" of the firm as the main driver of economic growth, due mostly to entrepreneurial action. Second, Schumpeter believed that disequilibrium was more important than homogeneity among firms. In his last works, he emphasized the role of the corporation as the most powerful agent of change and growth.

This radically new subject, the Schumpeterian corporation, challenged the neoclassical concept of the "standard firm." Schumpeter was interested in the innovative role of the firm, and the way in which this innovation was carried out under the direction of the entrepreneur. Less emphasis was placed on what actually happened inside the firm (its organizational structure). In the end, Schumpeterian firms grew active by exploiting their superior abilities and innovating and strengthening their competitive positions. In doing so, they were the main agent of change in modern economies, but still, they remained largely in "black boxes."

This changed after World War II, when the bulk of our "new" theories about the firm were developed. From the 1950s to the early 1960s, some scholars (often with very different backgrounds) became interested in the triumph of the large, vertically integrated, multidivisional and multinational "managerial corporation." This kind of organization was in part responsible for America's economic leadership in the period after World War II. Comprehension of the mechanisms governing the large corporation was thought to be extremely important to understand the "mystery" of economic growth. For the first time in history, a close relationship was established between the "micro" level of the firm and the macroeconomic level in which scholars explored "the wealth of the nation."

In many sectors, the optimal size of the firm seemed now to be very large, and industry structures tended toward oligopolistic rather than perfect competition. The influential management thinker Peter Drucker dedicated one of his first books, *Concept of the Corporation* (1946), to the emergence of this style of big business. Drawing on his knowledge of General Motors, he described in detail this new economic actor. Drucker said that big business could best be understood by looking at its technological foundations, at the human effort that went into the efficient coordination of its multitude of individuals, and at the social impact this institution had in modern capitalism.

The new theoretical approaches dealt with several issues. The first involved developing an understanding of the determinants and dynamics of the firm's growth, both on a national and international basis. The second was related to their behavior policies (later known as strategies). The third involved the optimal architecture of the firm. The last issue was the main interest of scholars focusing on the roles, patterns of behavior, and dynamics of the individuals inside these organizations. This influential cadre of scholars included Herbert Simon (1960)[1] as well as Richard Cyert and James March (1963).

Now more and more attention was devoted to technology as the principal driver in the process of growth. Product and process innovations made the expansion of the scale of production more appealing and sometimes compulsory. Some industries were still characterized by traditional production techniques, but the most important sources of growth were the mass-production, mass-distribution industries central to the Second Industrial Revolution. American business historian Alfred Chandler (1962, 1977, 1990) emphasized the effects of this technologically determined transformation on the successful firm's organization. Chandler analyzed the entrepreneurial and organizational responses to this technological shift. In doing so, he launched the scholarly study of one of the most important issues in the theory of the firm, that is, the interactive relationship between the strategy and the basic structure of the firm.

Chandler implicitly considered technological change as an exogenous force that had a decisive impact on business's entrepreneurial choices. In his perspective, technological regimes or paradigms—an array of scientific, technological, and research principles producing the dominant trajectories (e.g., scale intensity or the tendency toward mechanization)—determine the activity and competitiveness of enterprises and their "optimal" organizational structures. Other scholars—industrial economists as well as business historians—emphasized the endogenous nature of technological progress and of the innovative activity that increasingly took place in the R&D laboratories of the large firms. This latter line of reasoning moved the analysis into a vast array of other entities such as universities, associations, and governments. When technology became something generated primarily inside the business enterprise, it became knowledge particular to the firm, a strategic resource, and often one of the firm's major competitive advantages.

Among the first who pointed scholars toward this explanation of the process of growth in the modern firm was the American economist Edith Tilton Penrose (1959). In her seminal book, *The Theory of the Growth of the Firm*, Penrose brought out a new issue in the theory of the modern enterprise and provided a new foundation stone for what became social evolutionary theory. According to Penrose, firms are a "stratification" of resources and competencies; the modern firm is an organization that learns, and eventually knows, "how to do things." The process of growth is explained by the firm's ability to best exploit its physical and human capabilities. Over time, the corporation itself evolves and creates new knowledge and gains capabilities applicable to a multitude of industries. The idea of an organization that is able to learn and pursue a growth process through the use of its competencies has become a cornerstone of modern theories of the firm. Today, when we think of the firm, we inevitably consider its role in organizational learning and the creation and employment of knowledge.

Building both on Schumpeter's ideas about innovative activity inside the modern bureaucratic organization and on Penrose's idea of internally developed knowledge and competence, two American economists, Richard Nelson and Sidney Winter (1982), introduced the concept of routines. They regarded routines as the way in which organizations are able to remember successful behavior to maintain their leadership positions. Routines are one of the theoretical foundations of the evolutionary theory of the firm, which characterizes an economic process that is not determined solely by rational choices and individual and institutional objectives. Economic agents (and firms among them) are characterized by bounded rationality, cumulative learning based on experience, and trial-and-error processes. They try to reduce uncertainty by employing routines that lead to "path dependence." This explains the widespread resistance to change on the part of individuals and organizations. As business organizations became very large, complex institutions, a crucial role in their development became the flow of knowledge and information inside the organization itself. More than a price-taker with a cost-minimizing structure or a creature of an entrepreneurial initiative, firms were considered as actors able to influence deeply the environment surrounding them. They were characterized by complex internal dynamics and had an ability to evolve and adapt much as living organisms do.

In this framework, learning and knowledge accumulation is crucial in explaining the successful and unsuccessful behaviors of organizations. Competitiveness depends on the ability of the management to understand and fully exploit the bulk of resources accumulated inside the firm itself. This resource-based view is another important tenet derived from Penrose's theory of the growth of the firm.

The idea that "modern" firms can act as storehouses for competence and competitive advantage breaks away decisively from the neoclassical view and gives rise to another set of theories that focus on the internationalization strategies of large firms. After World War II, US-based corporations became the largest investors worldwide in production facilities. In 1960, only one year after Penrose published her growth theory, Stephen Hymer (1960) advanced a convincing explanation of the multinational enterprise's pattern of expansion. Hymer posited that competitive advantage could be developed on the domestic market and then exploited abroad. Hymer's analysis of the US multinational expansion was further developed by other scholars in international business, including John Dunning. In the second half of the 1970s, Dunning offered an explanation of the international activity of firms based on a mix of competitive (ownership) advantages that were developed on the domestic market and the advantages present in the host country (for instance, a productive and skilled workforce). There were also "internalization advantages"—that is, the advantages of maintaining knowledge and added value activities inside the boundaries of the firm, instead of selling them on the market.

During the early 1960s, another important field of research was developed by Robin Marris, who published *The Economic Theory of Managerial Capitalism* (1964). In his sharp analysis, the growth of the firm is explained through managerial self-interest. Managers want to expand the borders of the firm to gain more resources and more control over existing resources. This behavior clashes with the shareholders' interests that are more oriented toward performance and returns rather than growth. The rate of growth of a firm is therefore the result of something similar to a political bargain among managers and shareholders. This theory of managerial capitalism is important for at least two reasons. First, Marris's analytical effort made sense of the intense diversification process that had erupted in the US corporate landscape during the 1960s and early 1970s. This brought about a large wave of mergers and a significant conglomeration process in many of the largest American corporations. Second, Marris created the basis of what became a prominent debate in the theory of the firm, a debate over principal–agent relationships (i.e., agency theory).

The 1970s and 1980s: agency theory and transaction cost economics

The power of corporate managers generated by the separation of ownership from control began to be challenged at the beginning of the 1970s. The world economic crisis and the growing competitive pressure from European and Japanese firms emphasized the directors' lack of ability to generate enough resources and profits to finance both growth and reasonable returns to shareholders. The conflict between managers and shareholders frequently became tense.

In 1976, two American scholars, Michael Jensen and William Meckling, jumped into the resulting debate when they published (*Journal of Financial Economics*) their "Theory of the Firm: Managerial Behavior, Agency Costs and Ownership Structure." They emphasized the "principal–agent" problems that can arise between stockholders (who own most of the firm's equity and are called principals) and managers (who own only a small fraction of the firm's equity and are called agents). The agency theory, Jensen and Meckling developed, considers the firm as a "legal fiction which serves as a nexus for contracting relationships." Their "firm" is characterized by the "existence of divisible residual claims on the assets and cash flows of the organization," and this explains the need to align, either through the market or by means of legal instruments, the personal interests of the subjects (principals and agents) who sign this contract. Jensen and Meckling's theory of the firm is noteworthy it was developed in a period characterized by significant challenges to the large, diversified, managerial corporation, a style of firm no longer considered effective by many theorists and (and maybe above all) by practitioners. At the beginning of the 1980s, two McKinsey consultants, Tom Peters and Robert Waterman, published a book that had a considerable influence on the ensuing managerial debate. *In Search of Excellence: Lessons from America's Best-Run Companies*[2] lauded a managerial philosophy exalting "core competencies" more than diversification.

The idea of the firm as a "legal device" to solve problems arising from the interaction of various economic actors was the source of another extremely influential stream of studies that attempted to explain the existence of the firm itself: *transaction cost theory*. The origins of transaction cost theory date back to a provocative article by Ronald Coase published in 1937, entitled "The Nature of the Firm."[3] Coase's fundamental questions were as follows: why do firms exist? And why is it necessary to internalize some transactions inside the legal boundaries of a firm instead of leaving them to the market? His answer was that these transactions were internalized due to inefficient markets. In Coase's words, firms are "islands of conscious power in this ocean of unconscious cooperation like lumps of butter coagulating in a pail of buttermilk." He believed that their origins and characteristics lay in the need to contain the costs of transacting in the market.

Coase's basic ideas were further developed by Oliver Williamson in a series of research first summarized in the influential book *Markets and Hierarchies* (1975). According to Williamson, transactions involve the costs related to searching and monitoring. In a framework in which economic actors are characterized by limited knowledge and bounded rationality and inclined to act as free-riders, the more idiosyncratic resources are, the higher their transaction costs will be. This system generates strategic alternatives, making it convenient to internalize certain types of transactions, rather than resorting to the market. Internalized transactions may include those that are systematically repeated or those that involve strategic assets that ensure the firm's existence.

Transaction cost theory has had a powerful impact both on the study of the firm and on business history. Its conceptual framework helped us to understand a wide array of historical events, from the rise of the factory system during the First Industrial Revolution to the growth strategies through vertical integration of the large industrial corporation. Finally, transaction cost theory provided an interpretation of the persisting efficiency of production systems that were alternatives to mass production. These included, for instance, industrial districts in which small, specialized producers benefited from external coordination guaranteed by a local system of shared values. This drastically lowered transaction costs and thus eliminated the need for vertical integration.

"From one to many": theories of the twenty-first century firm

The goal of all of these theories of the firm was to interpret and understand the origin and the dynamics of the dominant form of industrial organization during a large part of the twentieth century. But on the eve of the new millennium, different styles of organization and different theories of the firm emerged. According to the new ideas, Third Industrial Revolution technologies (electronics and telecommunications) had a pervasive impact on the firm's structure and its dynamics. New coordination forms in the production process were becoming more important. Networks of independent, specialized producers (especially those who clustered around specific tasks and projects) had the necessary flexibility to cope with the new technologies and their products.

Richard Langlois (2007) maintains that expansion of these twenty-first century markets was due to the globalization process, and that during the last two decades this process set off a further specialization of production units. The new technologies of the information age made the coordination process among firms easier and essentially lowered transaction costs and uncertainty. As a result, the role of large integrated managerial firms became less important, whereas the coordination of the production process by market forces increased. Indeed, the transformation of the coordination mechanisms has been fostered in many industries by the diffusion of modular processes and products. Many of the products were characterized by different components that related to one another with standard interfaces. Thus, single parts can be developed by individual, independent producers carrying out the innovation process inside relatively small modular firms. After a hundred years of integration, we may well be moving toward the disintegration of the large corporation. This transformation is, however, far from complete, and in our current economic setting (like that of the previous century), the large firm in industry and services is still central to business and the history of business.

Notes

1 H. Simon, *The New Science of Management Decision*, Harper & Row, New York, 1960.
2 T. Peters and R. Waterman, *In Search of Excellence: Lessons from America's Best-Run Companies*, Harper & Row, New York, 1982.
3 R. Coase, "The Nature of the Firm," *Economica*, 4 (16), 1937, pp. 386–405.

Further reading

A.D. Chandler, Jr., *Strategy and Structure: Chapters in the History of the American Industrial Enterprise*, MIT Press, Cambridge, MA, 1962.
A.D. Chandler, Jr., *The Visible Hand: The Managerial Revolution in American Business*, Belknap Press, Cambridge, MA, 1977.
A.D. Chandler, Jr., *Scale and Scope: The Dynamics of Industrial Capitalism*, Harvard University Press, Cambridge, MA, 1990.
R. Cyert and J. March, *A Behavioral Theory of the Firm*, Prentice-Hall, New Jersey, 1963.
P.F. Drucker, *Concept of the Corporation*, John Day, New York, 1946.
J. Dunning, *Economic Analysis and the Multinational Enterprise*, Praeger, New York, 1974.
S.H. Hymer, *The International Operations of National Firms: A Study of Direct Foreign Investment*, Ph.D. dissertation (1960), published posthumously, MIT Press, Cambridge, MA, 1976.
M.C. Jensen and W.H. Meckling, "Theory of the Firm: Managerial Behavior, Agency Costs and Ownership Structure," *Journal of Financial Economics*, 3 (4), 1976, pp. 305–360.
R.S. Kroszner and L. Putterman (eds.), *The Economic Nature of the Firm: A Reader* (3rd edition), Cambridge University Press, Cambridge, 2009.
R. Langlois, *The Dynamics of Industrial Capitalism: Schumpeter, Chandler, and the New Economy*, Taylor & Francis, London, 2007.
R. Marris, *The Economic Theory of Managerial Capitalism*, Macmillan, London, 1964.
A. Marshall, *Principles of Economics*, Macmillan, London, 1890.
R.R. Nelson and S.G. Winter, *An Evolutionary Theory of Economic Change*, Harvard University Press, Cambridge, MA, 1982.
E. Penrose, *The Theory of the Growth of the Firm*, John Wiley & Sons, New York, 1959.
H. Simon, *Administrative Behavior: A Study of Decision-Making Processes in Administrative Organizations*, Free Press, New York, 1947.
O.E. Williamson, *Markets and Hierarchies*, Free Press, New York, 1975.

3   Entrepreneurship

An elusive phenomenon

Over the past two decades, we have heard a great deal about entrepreneurship and the business leaders who are identified in the media as successful *entrepreneurs*. It is not too difficult to find the sources of this appeal. In the context of intense global competition, we would all like to learn the secrets of innovation. Many of the large corporations we thought were being successfully run by a new breed of highly paid managers–bureaucrats have suddenly collapsed. Others—said, rather mysteriously, to be too large to fail—have turned to the public sector for financial first aid. At the same time, we have rediscovered the entrepreneurially based small- and medium-sized business. Whether they were leading small start-ups or reorganizing and reorienting giant firms as Jack Welch did at General Electric, the innovators of this generation seemed in the public imagination to be larger than life, different than the rest of us. This is true even when innovators failed or slipped into corruption as did the fabled Michael Milken. Some started their firms in a garage with hardly any working capital. Others were able to tap the world's burgeoning sources of investment. In either case, they appear to have been a major force in creating a great wave of innovation in industries such as electronics and information-communications, industries that in turn have brought the world into the era of globalization.

Entrepreneurship seems so central to the wealth and competitiveness of a nation that, in all advanced countries, there is a tendency to codify it, both for instructional purposes and for industrial policies. In the United States, hundreds of colleges and business schools offer academic programs or centers dedicated to entrepreneurship. No reputable business school in America or abroad would now advertise a program that did not have special training for budding entrepreneurs.

Notwithstanding its acknowledged centrality in the economic process, entrepreneurship is an elusive phenomenon, a concept very difficult to define clearly, a concept so protean that it is virtually impossible to categorize it in a mathematically formalized discourse. It appears in organizations of different sizes: it can be found in large corporations as well as in small retail shops. It can present itself under various forms. You may discover that it is a motivating force behind a scientist who assigns economic meaning to his or her lab activity. It was also found in the old-time peddler who was particularly skilled in selling his wares, just as today it might appear in the highly educated manager who oversees a large corporation utilizing techniques learned in business school. And, of course, it is what pushes the impetuous, instinctive type who seeks to anticipate demand and to build an economic empire. Entrepreneurship can be a long, day-by-day accumulation or it might just present itself in a dramatic leap ahead.

Understandably, there is confusion in the language and the generally diffused concepts utilized when we talk about entrepreneurship. This same uncertainty and confusion can be found in the academic community. So much so that a well-respected economist such as William Baumol wrote, "The entrepreneur is at once one of the most intriguing and one of the most elusive in the cast of characters that constitutes the subject of economic analysis."[1] Another economist, as well as historian, Mark Casson, recognizes that entrepreneurship "means different things to different historians."[2] While acknowledging the uncertainty and confusion, we can perhaps clarify matters by starting with a simple litmus test: entrepreneurship always involves the individual or joint capacity to create something new that has a positive economic impact. The innovations have been as varied as their sources. Some are well known and others obscure. But all play an important role in the capitalist system.

Hero, invisible entity, and ordinary man

When we use the term "hero" in a discussion on entrepreneurship, the work of Joseph Schumpeter immediately comes to mind. Schumpeter was not alone in this regard. He was part of an intellectual climate typical of the German-speaking part of the world at the turn of the twentieth century. In this setting, numerous distinguished scholars were attentive to innovation and the role culture played in fostering entrepreneurial action on a social scale. Just think of giants such as follows:

- **Max Weber**, the father of modern sociology, who described the entrepreneur as the beholder of an "instrumental rationality," which makes him capable of linking systematically his goals (the pursuit of economic gain) with the most proper means (pervasive attitude to calculation);
- **Werner Sombart**, who in *Der Moderne Kapitalismus* stressed the elitarian aspect of the entrepreneur, whose vital energy and creativity brings to life economic factors that otherwise might be considered deadweight—factors such as labor and capital lingering beyond the denomination of property rights or their formal position in a company;
- **Friedrich Nietzsche**, whose influence reached its height in the first decade of the twentieth century when Schumpeter was in Vienna formulating his theories. Nietzsche underscored the difference between those who are far ahead of the conventional wisdom of their times and those who only adapt to it. He thus stressed the role of individuals who follow a path that does not appear rational; they are moved by an unusual willpower. This concept is very similar to that of the Schumpeterian entrepreneur whose behavior is

very distant from an abstract and utilitarian rationality. He is moved by an unbound energy, an interior force that cannot be controlled. For these individuals, wealth is not the goal. Instead, they aspire to social ascent and are encouraged by the joy of creating, the pleasure of victory over their competitors, and the awareness of their role as heads of organizations that sometimes turn into economic empires.

Certainly, no one more than Schumpeter placed the entrepreneur at the center of the stage of the economic system. His entrepreneur was the engine of growth. In the intellectual construction of the Austrian economist, the entrepreneur was so central that, when his role was taken over by a slow-moving bureaucratic organization, the entire capitalistic, bourgeois system degenerated into a bureaucratized socialism. Innovation was fundamental. It meant new products, new methods of production, new markets, new sources for raw materials or semimanufactured goods, or the establishment of a new organization such as the creation of a monopoly or the breaking up of an old one. Innovation, seen as the justification of the entrepreneur's formidable profits, did not adapt itself to the current demand but imposed its output on the market. Innovation signified change, disequilibrium, and "creative destruction"; it was not synonymous with invention but was instead the materialization of new ideas on an economic level.

In this vision, the entrepreneur is a sort of "translator" who strives to take advantage of the long technological waves singled out by Kondratieff. From 1786 until 1842, the wave was characterized by swarms of innovation in the textile and metallurgy sectors; from 1843 through 1897, it was animated by innovations clustered in railways and closely related activities; and from 1897 until the outbreak of World War II, it was evident in sectors such as electricity, chemicals, and automobiles, all of which experienced rapid expansion.

Technological innovation, considered as an independent variable, was crucial for the Schumpeterian hero who was, above all, a man of production. Not necessarily a risk taker nor even an owner, this kind of businessperson kept a sharp eye on the opportunities for innovation. What counts in the Schumpeterian framework is the function of innovation performed by a single capitalist, by a salaried manager, by a team, or even by a political entity. In an era of harsh challenges to the bourgeois capitalistic system, Schumpeterian entrepreneurship (seen as an endogenous advantage of this economic and social order) was and still is today a very effective apologia of it.

Another concept of economic process can be found in classical and neoclassical economics. One can think of this as a spectrum, with Schumpeter at the right extreme and Adam Smith at the left. On the extreme left side, entrepreneurship is *de facto* deemed as irrelevant. Such an assertion is important because we are talking about the mainstream of economic theory. It was Joseph Schumpeter in his *History of Economic Analysis* who observed that, by reading Smith's *Wealth of Nations* or Ricardo's *Principles*, we get the impression that the economic process goes ahead on its own. In Adam Smith's work, the most important function of the businessman was to supply capital while David Ricardo stressed even more the automatic nature of economic movements. Of course, the founding fathers of economic science looked at the skills in business as important factors for the success or the failure of single initiatives, but those skills were hardly influential when the economic process was considered as a whole. So too with Karl Marx: notwithstanding the eulogy of the industrial bourgeoisie contained in his *Manifesto*, Marx was ever faithful to the logic of classical analysis. He denied any relevance to a subjective factor such as the entrepreneur. Central to the Marxian paradigm was the social relationship that binds capitalists and workers.

Entrepreneurship is even more neglected by the highly successful neoclassical paradigm based on the concept of market equilibrium. Here, the firm is the locus where productive factors are turned into goods by way of mechanisms that are by definition well-known and foreseeable. Uncertainty exists in exogenous variables such as the price of the good that will be sold or of the specific productive factors to be used. In this framework, the entrepreneur only needs to choose the most efficient production function and check that the "ingredients" are consistently assembled.

"Economic theory and the entrepreneur have never made easy traveling companions." This is the initial affirmation of an essay dedicated to this topic by J.S. Metcalfe, a statement that appears to be true even when mainstream theory is used to explain the phenomenon of growth.[3] In this case, entrepreneurship is regarded as a "residual," something that cannot be measured with the usual tools of the economist who is attempting to explain an increase of productivity. In this way, Edward Denison—while trying to single out the sources of growth of the United States in the period 1900–1960—mentioned factors such as technical progress, human capital, resources reallocation, and institutional change as sources of increasing productivity. He rejected entrepreneurship because he considered it to be automatically included in the various inputs.

We believe that there is, in fact, a middle ground between Schumpeter and the classical and neoclassical traditions. Fortunately, not all mainstream economists have completely disregarded the entrepreneur. Even when attributing a relevant role to him or her, they do not mention heroic virtues and do not consider only the peaks, the truly outstanding innovations. Instead, they stress abilities that are relatively diffused, including the ability to face aleatory plights. This is what stands out in the *Traité d'economie politique* written at the beginning of the nineteenth century by Jean-Battiste Say, a Protestant from the French town of Nantes. Say was both a professor of economics and a textile manufacturer. He described the decisive trait of entrepreneurship as the power to unify different elements—for instance, the workers, owners, and financial supporters—behind the visionary goal of product creation.

Alfred Marshall, too, one of the fathers of the neoclassic school with his *Principles of Economics*, located entrepreneurship inside the area of business management. He did this even though he distinguished the entrepreneurial role dedicated to fundamental decisions from a managerial one characterized by a delegated power. In Marshall's framework, the entrepreneur was not an exceptional personality; rather, he was portrayed in his daily activity, well embedded in the company, aiming to keep the system going after the charismatic founders have ceased their activity.

Some contemporary economists have underlined the psychological dimension of entrepreneurial actions. Israel Kirzner belongs to the "Austrian School," which generally follows the ideas of Ludwig Von Mises and Frederic Von Hayek on the relationship between economics and knowledge. Kirzner viewed alertness as the entrepreneur's essence. Alertness is described as the ability to recognize the opportunities that arise in markets from a misallocation of resources. For this purpose, it is necessary to possess creativity, imagination, and the ability to anticipate events and identify the right sources of knowledge about market data. Another who stresses the relationship between economics and psychology is Mark Casson, who defines the most relevant talent of an entrepreneur as his ability to make effective decisions regarding the coordination of scarce resources. The entrepreneur (whom Casson sees as an individual and not as a team) is one who unifies the roles of the capitalist, the owner, and the manager and is distinguished from them by his special ability to perceive situations in which it is possible to reap profits.

For all of these scholars, however, the entrepreneur is really "one of us," a somewhat ordinary person performing an ordinary function in the capitalist system. He or she may be "different" because of gifts of courage, leadership, promptness in seizing opportunities, or well-developed judgment, but this individual, like all others in the system, lacks the outstanding characteristics so important to Schumpeter.

Entrepreneurship and organizations

Several times we have mentioned the involvement of an entrepreneur in an organization. This is a common occurrence. In the vast majority of cases, the entrepreneur is required to create or reorient an enterprise to make sure that his ideas materialize and are sustained. This leaves him or her with a set of physical and human resources linked by hierarchical relationships. The connecting tissue of the enterprise can be found in management's intermediate layer, between the workers and the entrepreneur whose impulses were transmitted to the entire organization and who controls the realization of those ideas. This is especially the case for the sectors most relevant for a nation's economic competitiveness, sectors in which successful organizations frequently grow at astonishing rates.

This creates the entrepreneurial paradox: the organizations with their bureaucratic rules and routines can easily undermine the entrepreneur's vision. This was the famous argument of Joseph Schumpeter in his 1941 work *Capitalism, Socialism, Democracy*, an argument in which—as we have already seen—the Austrian economist anticipated the inevitable decline of the bourgeois-capitalistic system. Bureaucracy and government intervention, he said, would stifle the vital force that had driven the system ahead and given capitalism its justification.

It was in the United States, the land of managerial capitalism, that the rise of large organizations had the strongest impact on studies in the first half of the twentieth century. Consider Taylor's *Principles for Scientific Management* (1911), Berle and Means' *The Modern Corporation and Private Property* (1932), Burnham's *The Managerial Revolution* (1941), and Whyte's *The Organization Man* (1956). Each of these significant works stressed the centrality of the organization and the long, slow decline of the nineteenth-century forms of entrepreneurship. In this vision of capitalism's evolution, the auditors conquered the entrepreneurs. Organization signified the routine, whereas entrepreneurship was associated with creativity; one stands for conformism, whereas the other suggests deviance; one promotes stability, whereas the other is for change. The crisis of the large corporation in the 1970s forced many to conclude that perhaps Drucker had been wrong and that managerial capitalism might have to give way now to a new and as yet undefined system of political economy.

William Lazonick revisited the competition between different capitalisms and found, in the success of the triumphant Japanese company of the 1980s, an ability of the ruling class to involve in the innovating process all components of a modern bureaucratic company, starting from the shop floor. Lazonick focused most of his attention on middle management. Others searched for similar solutions to the bureaucratic phenomenon. Drucker, adapting to the new environment, came up with the idea of "intrapreneurship" and "corporate venturing." Rosabeth Moss Kanter in her study of innovative organizations[4] sought a mobilization of the entrepreneurial resources of middle management within a new type of framework that "contains vague assignments, overlapping territories, uncertain authority and a mandate to work through teams rather than to act unilaterally."

That innovation comes from *within* the corporation and not through a top-down process is an opinion shared by a wide array of management scholars. They believe that how strategies are *formulated* is not as important as how they *materialize* in reality (i.e., in a disorderly sequence to which many actors—particularly front-line managers—participate). In ex-post descriptions and in the firm's organizational charts, it will thus be difficult to reconstruct the true path of entrepreneurship, especially because we like to generate highly rational explanations of organizational and individual behavior. But we cannot deny that innovation frequently arises from a progressive and sometimes serendipitous process of learning.

Learning cannot, of course, be the only ingredient of innovation. There are situations in which patient learning is not adequate; for example, in times of a deep crisis, an overemphasis on learning can end up damaging what is working well and bring about undesired consequences. So, organizational learning— learning by doing—is vitally important, but it needs to be framed in a system dominated by the capacity to provide direction and to make crucial decisions. In this roundabout way, we find ourselves back to the issue of entrepreneurial leadership.

The need for decision-making capability at the top of large organizations was fully understood by Alfred Chandler, who had an unusual gift for merging business stories with generalizations that stimulated dialog with economists, sociologists, legal scholars, and other social scientists. In all of his major books, Chandler emphasized the description and analysis of entrepreneurial decisions in bureaucratic settings. In his first important work, *Strategy and Structure* (1962), he carefully distinguished the functions of an entrepreneur from those of a manager. Although the former had the responsibility of allocating resources at the highest levels in the company, the latter stayed within the resource and conceptual framework created by the top executives, the true entrepreneurs of the new order. Unlike Kanter and others, Chandler did not emphasize the innovations that moved from the bottom or middle up in the organizations he studied. Nonetheless, Chandler said that one of the essential tasks of the entrepreneur was to create, staff, and perfect the managerial hierarchy. This internal network was essential for the successful functioning of the large corporation and an indispensable tool of growth and economic competitiveness in the age of the Second Industrial Revolution.

A return to the animal spirits

The late Robert D. Cuff, writing in 2002, explained why Harvard University's Research Center in Entrepreneurial History shifted its focus from the "Carusos of economic life" to entrepreneurship within organizations. Cuff singled out external and internal factors. The former have to do with the general climate that emerged from the US national mobilization in World War II, which emphasized the importance and the pervasiveness of large-scale organizations. Then the government and the general society came to appreciate—as did Peter Drucker—the capacity of huge but flexible organizations such as General Motors to respond to wartime demands. Internally to business history, there was a desire, influenced in part by sociologists such as Talcott Parsons, to write a nonjudgmental "scientific" history. This was a difficult goal to reach if, at the center of the stage, there were the exceptional personalities of larger-than-life entrepreneurs.

These two elements shed light on the fact that, for almost 30 years (1950s–1980s), the main unit of analysis for American business history was corporate entrepreneurship. This choice also had a significant influence on business historians in many other countries. But, as Cuff pointed out, times were changing and a new vision of the entrepreneur emerging. This vision returned in many ways to the heroic personalities central to the original Schumpeterian theory. The historical context called for a change:

> Reagan in the White House; intensified global competition; disillusionment with American managers and management education; fascination with the Silicon Valley phenomenon; changing forms of business organization, including the growth of alliances, networks, "virtual corporations" and so forth; renewed appreciation of small business as a source of employment; the media cult of the entrepreneur—a wide range of factors external to the field can help to account for the change.[5]

Thus, the entry on entrepreneurship prepared in 1980 for the *Encyclopedia of American Economic History* by Jonathan R.T. Hughes chose to emphasize the following foundations of the phenomenon: free ownership of land, maximum flexibility in transactions, stability of the legal framework, limited social control, and the frontier squatter as progenitor of the Schumpeterian entrepreneur. The distance from the Chandlerian model of the executive entrepreneur was remarkable indeed. The individual, heroic entrepreneur returned as the main character in the advancement of business. The most compelling issue for historians was, in this formulation, finding out how the entrepreneur was able to break down constraints created by lesser mortals. No longer was the business historian charged primarily with identifying the social factors that channeled innovative actions. In the array of social sciences, which historians are attentive to, sociology had to be complemented by psychology, organizational analysis by a study of personality theory.

Conclusions: entrepreneurship in history

Whatever definition and/or representation we give to entrepreneurship, we cannot avoid including it as a vital part of our modern economic, social, cultural, and political systems. According to some authors, entrepreneurship shapes those systems. For others, it is a variable that depends on the terrain in which it operates. In his wonderful book on preindustrial Europe,[6] Carlo Cipolla coped with this problem, as he dealt with the topical subject of productivity. It was not satisfactory, Cipolla said, just to correlate the increases of production with those of physical inputs. Nevertheless, the idea of naming that "plus" factor the entrepreneur and then conceiving of it as a "creative reaction of history," as Schumpeter did, was not convincing to this historian. According to Cipolla, the Austrian economist made the mistake of reducing a whole to a part that in this specific case is the entrepreneurial activity. "This is an important and necessary element but I don't think," Cipolla wrote, "it is enough."

For Cipolla, it was the "human vitality" of an entire society that at a certain point could enter into the game with a decisive effect, sparking "the creative reaction of history." In this way, the residual (as seen by the mainstream theorists mentioned earlier in this chapter) remains mysterious, explained only by "intangibles," in their turn the fruit of a collective social process.

Cipolla picked up on Emile Durkheim's notion of the "collective effervescence" that occurs when the intensity of social interaction reaches such a peak as to overflow into the diffusion of innovation. Durkheim took as an example of this condition the Renaissance or the French Revolution. The Swedish sociologist Richard Swedberg—trying to translate this elaboration into contemporary economic terms—mentioned the first stages of the Industrial Revolution in England, the period around 1900 in the United States, and the more recent history of Silicon Valley.

Assertions such as these have encouraged some social scientists to measure the phenomenon of entrepreneurship. One example is provided by the sociologist Paul H. Wilken, who wanted to understand the impact of entrepreneurship on national economic development. Wilken singled out four variables: O (opportunities), Y (economic growth), X (noneconomic factors), and E (entrepreneurship). Basing his work on secondary sources, Wilken considered the case of development in nineteenth-century Great Britain, France, Germany, Japan, the United States, and Russia, arriving at the apparently odd result that, in both the United Kingdom and the United States, entrepreneurship had a very low impact. The problem with this attempt at quantification was that it was very difficult to draw clear lines between the variables. The economist James Foreman Peck, instead, preferred to measure entrepreneurship in France during the Second Empire using sophisticated statistical methods such as data envelopment analysis (DEA) and stochastic frontier analysis (SFA). He focused entirely on the creation of new enterprises and their performances.

Certainly, these studies make important contributions, but in each case, they bring us back to economic history, to the growth process, and in particular to the emergence of the modern firm. We can, we believe, still learn a great deal from careful historical study and analysis. Collective biographies will be helpful, as will the Chandlerian methodology of organizational history. Pushing ahead in these ways, we might not be able to grasp Protheus, but we could surely watch him from up close.

Notes

1 W.J. Baumol, *Entrepreneurship, Management and the Structure of Payoffs*, MIT Press, Cambridge, MA, 1993, p. 2.
2 M. Casson and A. Godley, "Entrepreneurship and Historical Explanation," in Y. Cassis and I. Pepelasis Minoglou (eds.), *Entrepreneurship in Theory and History*, Palgrave, New York, 2005, p. 25.
3 J.S. Metcalfe, "The Entrepreneur and the Style of Modern Economics," in G. Corbetta, M. Huse, and D. Ravasi (eds.), *Crossroads of Entrepreneurship*, Kluwer Academic Publishers, Boston, 2004, p. 33.
4 R.M. Kanter, *The Change Masters*, Simon & Schuster, New York, 1983.
5 R. Cuff, "Notes for a Panel on Entrepreneurship in Business History," *Business History Review*, Spring 2002, n. 76, p. 130.
6 C. Cipolla, *Before the Industrial Revolution*, Metheun & Co. Ltd., London, 1976.

Further reading

W.J. Baumol, R.E. Litan, and C.J. Schramm, *Good Capitalism, Bad Capitalism, and the Economics of Growth and Prosperity*, Yale University Press, New Haven, CT, 2007.
Y. Cassis and I. Pepelasis Minoglou (eds.), *Entrepreneurship in Theory and History*, Palgrave Macmillan, London, 2005.
M. Lynskey and S. Yonekura (eds.), *Entrepreneurship and Organization: The Role of the Entrepreneur in Organizational Innovation*, Oxford University Press, Oxford, 2002.
R. Swedberg (ed.), *Entrepreneurship*, Oxford University Press, Oxford, 2000.

Part II

The company between the preindustrial era and the First Industrial Revolution

4 Preindustrial manufacturing

The factory system of the eighteenth and nineteenth centuries drastically realigned the political economy of Europe, but neither entrepreneurship nor the capitalist enterprise actually began with the First Industrial Revolution. Long before the era dominated by British factories, businessmen were already developing new combinations of capital, labor, and natural resources (usually expressed as "land") in order to provide customers with the goods and services they needed. The pace of change was relatively slow. But change was taking place in all sectors of the European economies, including manufacturing. There were of course important differences between the pre- and postindustrial revolution styles of manufacturing. The differences were closely linked to the demographic, economic, and social structures of preindustrial European societies—structures, populations, and patterns of commerce that had long shaped the form in which the production of goods and services was carried out (Cipolla 1976).

Preindustrial Europe: general features

Preindustrial Europe was not a homogeneous entity, although all the European countries had certain aspects in common. The primary sector pervaded: according to some calculations, 80 to 90 percent of Europe's total gross domestic product (GDP) came from agriculture, and the vast majority of the population (probably as much as 70 percent) worked directly in farming. Most of the workforce was made up of farmers and their families, all of whom worked land that was passed from generation to generation. Mobility was relatively low, as were levels of urbanization. Some cities—including Paris, London, and Naples—reached considerable size, but they resembled "icebergs" floating in a vast sea of farms, country villages, and small towns.

While tradition was powerful throughout, these economies were certainly not static. Their growth rates, which varied, were not comparable with what followed the outbreak of the Industrial Revolution, but all were changing. The total population of Europe increased from around 57 million in AD 1500 to 132 million by the end of the eighteenth century. According to Angus Maddison's calculations,[1] the annual rate of growth of the Western European population from AD 1000 to 1500 was around 0.16 percent and 0.26 percent from AD 1500 to the beginning of the nineteenth century. In these same periods, the annual growth rate of gross national product (GNP) was 0.3 and 0.4, respectively, much lower than the results registered in the years after 1820, when growth started to surpass 1 percent per year.

These figures are symptomatic of relatively rigid, pyramidal societies with highly unequal distributions of income. Although there were some improvements in agricultural techniques (draining of swamps, for instance), the production of food was increasing slowly, along with the population. Society's purchasing power lay almost entirely in the hands of a very small, very wealthy percentage of the total population, that is, those who owned and controlled the agriculture and industry.

As the preindustrial European economy depended almost exclusively on agriculture, it was heavily susceptible to the deep fluctuations characteristic of this sector. Bad weather and debilitating wars caused unpredictable downturns. Malnutrition left populations vulnerable to disease, and the periodic famines, as well as war, had devastating effects on population growth. After the fifteenth century, following a brief period of successful diffusion of new techniques in agriculture, some Europeans were able to build up crop surpluses. But the surpluses were limited to those areas that were climatically and geographically favorable, and even there, the lifesaving surpluses were irregular.

Cultural and social factors, as well as the relatively rigid and unequal political and economic systems, had powerful negative effects on the level of aggregate demand, but during the three centuries preceding the Industrial Revolution, this began to change. The economy gradually became more dynamic; here, one can point to important innovations in agriculture and actually speak of a first "Agricultural Revolution." Europe as a whole was starting to experience the initial short steps toward a long-term process of cumulative economic growth. The resulting rise in aggregate demand encouraged the development of long-distance trade, which was also facilitated by technical improvements in sailing ships and shipbuilding. There were, as well, positive changes in what some scholars have called "institutional efficiency" (North and Thomas 1973): starting in the medieval period, legal contracts such as the *commenda* and the *compagnia* (designed to handle complex and/or risky transactions in distant markets) made for easier and safer long-distance financial transactions. Financial markets had also become more efficient, thanks to the introduction of innovations such as the bill of exchange and the banknote.

Predictably, European dynamism appeared in some places (Britain, northwestern continental Europe, and the north of Italy) more than others. The "new agriculture" and the revolution in trade and institutional modernization took place in a few advanced areas, leaving the *peripheries* static, stagnant, and vulnerable to devastating economic collapses.

Manufacturing typologies

The putting-out system

In the rural arena where autarchy prevailed, manufacturing created enterprises that took different forms depending on the location of the activity, the industry, and the degree of specialization of the labor force. It is especially important to differentiate between those activities located in the countryside and those performed in urban areas.

The nature of the countryside economy had an important influence on the form and nature of the firm itself. The peasant world consisted of small households in which families of peasants and, less frequently, artisans ran productive activities with sporadic contacts with the market. Some areas consisted of relatively closed economic systems that were based on self-consumption and an almost total absence of market transactions and specialization. Thus, the countryside was an important repository of surplus labor. The rural poor usually dedicated a significant part of their working time to activities outside the primary agricultural sector. Manufacturing work offered an alternative to temporary emigration, particularly when extra income was required.

The presence of a cheap, flexible, and docile workforce encouraged manufacturers to push their operations into the countryside. To do so, they developed the *putting-out system*, based on a hierarchical, but flexible, architecture. At the top was a "master," or a "merchant-entrepreneur," who was the owner of the raw materials (*circulating capital*). This person usually coordinated a network of *cottage workers* who performed some phases of the production processes (e.g., spinning and weaving in the textile field) in their homes. The merchant-entrepreneur directly controlled the activities with higher capital intensity or increasing returns to scale. The putting-out system was in use in many industries, but above all in textiles where it was easy and relatively efficient to break down the separate functions in the production process.

Apart from the ready use of a cheap labor force, the putting-out system was efficient because of its flexibility. The network of laborers, sometimes in the hundreds, on which the merchant-entrepreneurs relied, could be quickly enlarged or shrunk according to fluctuations in demand. These accommodations could be made at no cost to the merchant-entrepreneurs. As the production unit was located in the household, the workers were in effect supplying the enterprise with cheap, easy-to-maintain fixed capital. In textiles, for example, the workers used and owned their hand-operated, wooden looms.

There were of course some hidden costs in this system. As with any decentralized organization, there were agency and transaction costs, which increased proportionally with production growth. The merchant had almost no control over either the quality of his product or the efficiency and reliability of his laborers, who were paid on a piece-rate basis (i.e., according to the quantity of items produced). According to some scholars, rudimentary technologies were handled easily by cottage workers, but there was little incentive to improve the technology. The system could, as well, have delayed and maybe even prevented the introduction of the more advanced production techniques associated with the factory system.

Craft production in the countryside and urban settings

Although the putting-out system and the domestic, decentralized networks were the most common ways of organizing the production of consumer goods, craft production played a lesser but nonetheless important role. Craft work, which was characterized by a higher level of sophistication, employed skilled laborers in industries with relatively high value added. There was a higher degree of specialization and capital intensity among, for instance, metalworkers, cobblers, gunsmiths, and tanners.

Often these industries were located near the source of raw materials and where energy—in the form of water, wind, wood, or coal—was cheap and easily available. Consequently, clusters of skilled craftsmen set up highly specialized production systems in particular geographic areas, sometimes in the countryside and sometimes in urban locations.

High value-added activities tended to be located inside towns and villages. In the urban areas, these industries existed alongside the tertiary sector (i.e., domestic services, bureaucracy, and administration) and generated a consistent and significant portion of the society's production and income. The internal organization of the "representative" production unit was quite simple and based on a rigid hierarchy. The master, with some apprentices, managed all of the processes of production in a shop of which he was the owner. His workplace was often connected to his household. The apprentices learned the secrets of the profession on-the-job, and after a long training period, they were able to become masters themselves and start their own businesses.

In cities, the craft system was typically limited to the production of high value-added items such as gold and jewelry, hats, leather, and shoes, as well as other durable goods that were produced either for the urban market itself or sold directly to powerful customers such as the king, the government, the aristocracy, or the army. In the larger urban areas where the market was more substantial, some of these craft shops developed a more numerous workforce and a higher degree of complexity. But for the most part, craft shops were very simple organizations. Because the master owned the fixed capital and the raw materials, he was solely responsible for marketing the goods and performing other business functions associated with the commercialization of the products. He generally paid his workforce on a piece-wage basis.

The master and the shop were normally part of a complex organization, the *guild*, that was based on particular types of work. One of the most common of these in preindustrial European cities was the Goldsmith's Guild. Guilds, which were relatively rigid organizations, were based on detailed sets of written rules. The rules determined the quality and quantity of the goods produced in a given city. Guilds also set the prices that masters could charge, resolved conflicts between members, controlled internal regulatory standards, organized apprentice training, and judged the process by which apprentices were promoted to master status. Monitoring costs were reduced because guilds legally required their members to live within city limits.

The main goals of the guild system varied according to the location and to the guild's particular political agenda. Guilds had many advantages: they were quasi-enterprises that organized labor and capital, regulated craft activities, and managed human capital formation and quality control. They were successfully able to monitor both the skills of the labor force and the production standards of their industry. They accomplished this mainly by restricting entry into the labor market through their long-term training process. This in turn helped to lower the customers' information costs. The guild system was based on the single shop, characterized by a low degree of specialization among its extremely skilled members. The guild system provided these craft producers with a degree of protection and stability in an economy in which few were protected from sharp fluctuations in income.

But as long scholarly debates have established, these benefits were overshadowed by several important disadvantages. Like most monopolies, the guilds restricted production and demand by maintaining relatively high prices. They normally inhibited technological innovation by controlling techniques of craft production. Because the guild system was conservative, innovation was discouraged. The introduction and diffusion of technological improvements was a threat, as was especially the case in England, where the factory system eluded guild control by moving outside city walls. Where the guilds succeeded in establishing monopolies within the town walls, they artificially shrank the supply of skilled labor and kept prices high. Under the pressure of economic change, the guild system began to weaken in Europe during the seventeenth century and was abolished nearly everywhere by the end of the eighteenth century.

It is important to remember, however, that the guild system comprised a limited fraction of the manufacturing activity of preindustrial Europe, which meant that it had a limited impact on the economy as a whole. In addition, the existence of a form of "institutional agreement" meant that the guild did not influence organization at the shop-floor level. There, masters had a higher degree of control than in the putting-out system and were able to establish the quantity and selection of items they were to produce. They did not depend on a merchant-entrepreneur and dedicated almost all their working hours to manufacturing, which was their primary occupation. Labor division on a systematic scale was not the *modus operandi* of a guild master's shop. The apprentice was by definition trained in "all the secrets of the job," as was commonly said, with a "general purpose" approach. The master himself had to demonstrate his ability to manage the entire production of a single item. Consequently, division of labor when it did exist was based on the worker's age and status rather than the individual skills any single worker possessed. Despite the fact that guild membership could range from several hundred to even thousands of members, the production unit remained small.

Compared with the putting-out system, guilds were more inclined to constrain output. Theoretically, higher volumes of production could be achieved at the single-shop level simply by adding units of labor. However, this was not possible because of guild rules that regulated how many apprentices each master could train. At an aggregate level, increased production volumes could be reached by admitting more masters to the guild. But the guilds leaned against creating this kind of competition. Because guild craftsmen produced largely for the wealthiest part of society or for the Crown, consumption patterns for the entire society were not significantly impacted by guild controls. Thus, the system could insulate itself, to a considerable degree, from the fluctuations in demand that were characteristic of the rest of European society.

"Big business" before the Industrial Revolution

Large-scale enterprises with large numbers of workers and high capital intensity existed before the Industrial Revolution. "Manufactories" was a term commonly used to describe a concentration of laborers working in the same place, "under the same roof." Can these precursor firms be compared with the big businesses that followed centuries after? Some scholars have argued that the rise of the factory was a consequence of the concentration of large numbers of workers in firms like the manufactories. The factory system, they contend, cannot be traced to the technological shifts of the First Industrial Revolution. As they point out, many of the large, preindustrial plants developed relatively sophisticated methods of reporting and accounting, both of which were introduced to manage their complex production processes.

As Sidney Pollard underlines in his study of the genesis of modern management, however, these large, preindustrial concerns, which were often protected by royal patents and operated as monopolies, were more the exception than the rule. Moreover, in many of them, only a very small portion of their employees were actually working "in" the plant. The majority were "out" because they worked at home (Pollard 1965: 50). As a result, the percentage of people employed in manufactories was probably slightly lower than in domestic industry, which was the most common form of organizing preindustrial production. One particularly telling example provided by Pollard is the Austrian imperial woolen factory in Linz, which in the 1770s was employing about 26,000 workers. But only 750 weavers were clustered in the town, whereas the rest of the workforce was made up of domestic spinners scattered throughout Austria, Bohemia, and Moravia.

In other manufactories, the workforce was more concentrated. For instance, in the iron smelting, shipbuilding, and construction fields, it was not possible to operate economically either on a small scale or from a workshop or household (Mokyr 2002). In mining, the nature of the activity itself forced a concentration of workers in a single place. Some of the phases of production in the textile industry (like dyeing or calico printing) also had to be performed in centralized plants. These, for the most part, were either totally or partially owned by the merchant. A similar combination of systems existed, where centralized production was linked to the putting-out system; the central shop in some cases provided semi-finished goods that were eventually dispatched to cottage workers. For example, in metalworking, merchant-entrepreneurs used ironmasters to manage the building and operating of smelting plants. These highly skilled men were helped by some apprentices. Blacksmiths, who operated at home under the putting-out system, then completed the work.

A "compromise between the domestic system and the need to produce away from home"[2] can be seen in other kinds of large firms as well. In shipbuilding and construction, several thousand workers often were employed under the same roof, but the organization and nature of this type of work was still decentralized. These firms could operate efficiently, thanks to an aggregation of several "teams of skilled artisans or a cluster of small craft shops each performing a specific task."[3] Given the status of the technology, these "firms" were not able to realize scale economies by increasing the volume of production. They were in this regard like batch producers today. In shipyards, for instance, the only way to produce more vessels was by adding additional units of labor, that is, hiring more artisans.

It was important that most of these preindustrial large firms enjoyed a privileged and monopolistic position. When not directly interested in the business, the government or more often the Crown granted patents to private entrepreneurs. This protection was given in order to stimulate the establishment of factories and plants specializing in the production of particular types of goods. There were various motivations for this strategy, ranging from the necessity to secure the supply of "strategic" items (as in the case of ships and weapons) to the pursuit of mercantilist policies that aimed to limit the purchase of high-value goods produced abroad. One telling example is the origin of Saint-Gobain, which today is one of the world leaders in the production of glass and special materials. Founded in 1665 by the French Minister of Finance Jean Baptiste Colbert under the name of *Manufacture royale de glaces de miroirs*, the company was run by private entrepreneurs, financed in part by the State, and enjoyed royal privileges. The main purpose of its establishment was to reduce French imports of glass from Venice, in particular mirrors, a very high value-added product.

As this brief survey suggests, large plants and centralized production facilities existed as independent forms of manufacturing in only a few cases. Most often, the central organization complemented the much more diffuse putting-out system. Where there was a concentration of employees, coordination and organization were extremely rudimentary because these plants were made up of groups of craftsmen, rather than a coordinated assembly of skilled or unskilled workers. For the most part, manufactories were thus organizations ancillary and complementary to the prevailing pattern of production based on the *domestic system*, rather than a fundamentally different way of coordinating capital, resources, and labor.

Notes

1 Angus Maddison, *The World Economy: Historical Statistics*, OECD, Paris, 2003, tab. 8a.
2 J. Mokyr, *The Gifts of Athena: Historical Origins of the Knowledge Economy*, Princeton University Press, Princeton, NJ, 2002, p. 123.
3 Ibid., p. 122.

Further reading

C.M. Cipolla, *Before the Industrial Revolution: European Society and Economy, 1000–1700*, Methuen, London, 1976.
P. Malanima, *Pre-Modern European Economy: One Thousand Years (10th–19th Centuries)*, Brill Academic Publishers, Leiden, 2009.

J. Mokyr, *The Gifts of Athena: Historical Origins of the Knowledge Economy*, Princeton University Press, Princeton, NJ, 2002, p. 123.

D.C. North and R.P. Thomas, *The Rise of the Western World: A New Economic History*, Cambridge University Press, London, 1973.

S. Pollard, *The Genesis of Modern Management: A Study of the Industrial Revolution in Great Britain*, Harvard University Press, Cambridge, MA, 1965.

S. Pollard, *Peaceful Conquest: The Industrialization of Europe 1760–1970*, Oxford University Press, Oxford, 1981.

J.L. Van Zanden, *The Long Road to the Industrial Revolution: The European Economy in a Global Perspective, 1000–1800*, Brill Academic Publishers, Leiden, 2009.

Appendix

Table 4.1 Sectoral contribution to the gross national product in modern Europe and in the European Union (%)

	Europe 1500–1800	*European Union 2000*
Agriculture	60	2.2
Manufacturing	20	28.1
Services	20	69.7

Source: Adapted from Paolo Malanima, *Uomini, risorse, tecniche nell'economia europea dal X al XIX secolo*, Bruno Mondadori, Milan, 2003, p. 248.

Table 4.2 Components of gross national product in modern Europe and in the European Union (%)

	Modern Europe	*European Union 2000*
Consumption	85–90	58
Investment	5–10	21
Government spending	5	21

Source: Adapted from Paolo Malanima, *Pre-Modern European Economy: One Thousand Years (10th–19th Centuries)*, Brill Academic Publishers, Leiden, 2009, p. 249.

Table 4.3 Sectoral distribution of workers in developed market-economy countries, except Japan

	Total working population (millions)	*Sectoral distribution (%)*		
		Agriculture	*Manufacturing*	*Services*
1750	53	approx. 76	approx. 13	approx. 11
1800	56	74	16	11
1913	155	40	32	28
1950	210	23	37	40
1970	287	10	38	52

(Continued)

Table 4.3 (Continued)

	Total working population (millions)	Sectoral distribution (%)		
		Agriculture	Manufacturing	Services
1980	331	7	34	58
1990	374	5	29	66
1995	388	5	27	68

Source: Own elaboration based on Paul Bairoch, *Victoires et deboires: histoire économique et sociale du monde du XVIe siècle a nos jours*, Gallimard, Paris, 1997.

Table 4.4 European (Russia excluded) and global socioeconomic transformation, 1300–1990. Some indicators

		c. 1300	c. 1700	1900	1990
Total population (millions)	Europe	60–90	95–110	285	499
	World	370–530	630–740	1,640	5,280
Per capita GDP (in 1960 dollars)	Europe	150–180	170–200	560	3,110
	World	160–180	160–190	300	1,150
Life expectancy at birth (males)	Europe	23–30	26–35	45	72
	World	22–28	25–33	31	62
Farmers in the workforce (%)	Europe	76–83	76–80	50	11
	World	76–83	76–83	72	49
Percentage of urbanization[a]	Europe	9–11	11–13	38	70
	World	9–10	10–11	16	43
Iron production[b]/per capita	Europe	0.5–1.5	1.0–2.0	80	390
	World	0.5–1.5	0.5–1.5	25	143
Energy consumption[c]/per capita	Europe	250–400	300–450	1,500	4,400
	World	200–400	250–400	400	2,020

Source: Own elaboration based on Paul Bairoch, *Victoires et deboires: histoire économique et sociale du monde du XVIe siècle a nos jours*, Gallimard, Paris, 1997.

Notes
a   % of total population living in cities of more than 5,000 people.
b   1990: crude steel.
c   Equivalent in kilos of coal.

5 Enterprises and entrepreneurs of the First Industrial Revolution

The First Industrial Revolution transformed the world economy, gave business leadership to Great Britain, and launched the world's first long-term change in population dynamics. According to Angus Maddison's historical statistics, the annual average compound growth rate of Great Britain's population from 1820 to 1870 was 0.79, compared with (Western) Europe's average of 0.69. Great Britain's per capita gross national product (GNP) growth rate during the same period was 1.26, compared with the continental rate of 0.96 (Maddison 2003: tab. 8a and 8c). In terms of GNP growth, only tiny Switzerland and Belgium did better than Britain, with Germany and France lagging behind. Later, of course, the continental powers caught up. If one measures growth over the so-called "long" nineteenth century, from 1789 to 1914 (Aldcroft 1994), Great Britain, Germany, Belgium, and France were all growing fast and at almost the same rate (with a nearly 1.2–1.3 percent average yearly growth rate of GNP).

The prosperity of the leading European nations and their Western offshoots opened up a significant gap between the developed and the undeveloped world, where growth rates were much lower. Compared with contemporary rates of economic growth, and especially with those of rapidly developing economies such as China's, the statistics for Europe may not seem especially remarkable. However, if you compare them with those of the preindustrial world, which relied extensively on the agricultural sector, the numbers are quite impressive. A seemingly small difference in the *rate of growth* between Great Britain and the rest of Europe and between Europe and the rest of the world constituted a truly revolutionary transformation with formidable consequences for the economic and political relations between nations and regions.

The British exception

What made Great Britain's economic performance so outstanding during the decades following the Napoleonic Wars was not just the rate of economic growth. What was outstanding was also the way in which Britain's growth took place and made it different from the rest of Europe and the world. For the first time in history, the main source of the "wealth of the nation" was to be found outside agriculture and its related commerce. Now the heart of the economy was manufacturing. The real difference between Great Britain and the other countries was in the contribution of this rapidly expanding macrosector to gross product and value added, and the resulting redistribution of the workforce. According to Crafts' estimations (1985: tab. 3.6), the percentage of the British male labor force employed in agriculture in 1760 was approximately 53 percent, compared with the European norm of 66 percent. The percentage of income derived from the British primary (agricultural) sector was 37.5 percent, whereas the European average was 46.6 percent. Eighty years later, agriculture in Britain employed slightly more than one-quarter of the male workforce (against a European norm of over 55 percent), whereas the primary sector only contributed 25 percent of total income (in Europe the percentage was nearly 40 percent). During the same period in Belgium, France, and Germany—three of the most economically advanced European nations—the percentage of the labor force employed in agriculture was still either at or above 50 percent. In the words of Crafts (1985: 69), "a fundamental redeployment of resources had taken place by the 1840s when Britain had an employment structure quite unlike the rest of Europe."

Continental Europe eventually followed the British pattern, but the pace of growth varied from country to country and sometimes the transition to manufacturing was considerably delayed. By the end of the nineteenth century, the percentage of the labor force working in agriculture had fallen to less than 50 percent in Belgium, Germany, Denmark, the Netherlands, Switzerland, and France. In the peripheral European countries—such as those in the Mediterranean areas and in Scandinavia—agriculture continued, however, to be the main source of employment.

As each country experienced this transformation, its degree of export specialization increased. This was accomplished through the more efficient use of its factor endowments, as well as the judicious use of available technologies. Thanks to an unprecedented degree of openness of the world economy, new countries were able to follow the British example, and by the mid-nineteenth century, some of them became leading exporters in manufacturing. By the beginning of the twentieth century, the percentage of exports (by value) in total manufacturing output was more than 70 percent for Great Britain, Switzerland, and Germany and about 60 percent for France. The peripheral nations still lagged far behind, with only 20 to 25 percent of their manufactured goods going into exports.

For the first time in history, a number of European countries enjoyed a stable position in the international market, thanks to their productive specialization in manufacturing. They were now able to finance large imports of goods produced in other countries or regions. This was particularly evident in Great Britain, where the process of economic specialization (in cotton and wool textiles, metalworking, and mechanics) was well advanced and the economic relevance of agriculture correspondingly reduced. In a society in which land holding and tenant farming had long been the basis of the social and political system, this was a truly revolutionary change.

Structural change and the British competitive advantage

The structural transformations that changed the rates of growth, patterns of development, and competitive advantages for European countries were rooted in radical transitions both at the "meso" level—that is, that of industries—and at the microlevel of firms.

In manufacturing, product innovations and new ways of organizing the production process accelerated the rate of growth in particular industries. New technologies were especially important in some branches of textiles, mining, metalworking, and light mechanical equipment, all of which became core industries in the British transformation. Water power continued to be the primary source of energy for many decades, but it was supplemented increasingly by the steam engine, a powerful example of a general-purpose technology with a broad range of applications. The introduction and diffusion of the steam engine—together with an increase and improvement in the use of water power—provided manufacturers with cheap and efficient energy. In the case of the steam engine, for the first time in history nonanimated energy could be transferred relatively easily from one place to another. This had an impact on efficiency and the reduction of location costs. According to Joel Mokyr (1990), during the second half of the eighteenth century approximately 2,500 steam engines were built in Great Britain, 1,000 of which were used in mining.

In textiles, and particularly in cotton manufacturing, technological innovations in both spinning and weaving improved the industry's productivity enormously. Efficiency more than tripled in textiles during the last quarter of the eighteenth century. According to Nick Crafts' estimates, between 1700 and 1760 cotton's real output grew at an average of 1.37 percent per year. From 1760 to 1770, this figure jumped to nearly 5 percent and to an outstanding 12.76 percent for the decade from 1780 to 1790 (Crafts 1985: 23). The same phenomenon could be observed in iron, steel, and coal, where innovations in the smelting process and extraction techniques increased both the output and productivity of the entire sector. Iron real output growth per year increased from 0.60 percent in the first half of the eighteenth century to nearly 6.5 percent per year from 1790 to 1801. Meanwhile the quality of the products was improving. Similar effects were achieved in the mechanical industry, which started to flourish during the same period.

The cluster of innovations characterizing the early phase of the First Industrial Revolution in Britain could be traced to a series of factors that were economic, cultural, institutional, and legal. Britain already had a strong commercial sector with significant capacity for distributing goods and extending credit. There was as well an "industrial enlightenment," that is, a cultural climate generally favorable to science, innovation, experimentation, and new practices. This created a positive framework for inventors, technicians, and entrepreneurs who were willing to make profits by putting into practice the "useful knowledge" they had developed or learned from others (Mokyr 2002).[1] The legal protection of intellectual property (patents) also added an incentive for invention and innovation.

By 1851, the year of the Great Exhibition at the Crystal Palace in London, Britain was undoubtedly the most advanced industrial nation in the world. Following a century of significant innovation in its core industries, Britain, the so-called workshop of the world, offered a powerful example of how to achieve comparative advantage. The British, who took Adam Smith's lessons seriously, exported manufactures and imported the food and raw materials that could be produced cheaper elsewhere (Crafts 1985: 142). In 1780, the ratio of exports to gross industrial output was nearly 22 percent in Britain, and this figure rose 20 years later to approximately 34.5 percent (Berg 1994: 119). During the first half of the nineteenth century, manufactured goods consistently accounted for 80–90 percent of British exports. The most important products continued to be textiles (woolen and cotton) and metals. In the case of cotton, more than half of the industry's gross total output was sold abroad, and during the first half of the nineteenth century, exports of cotton goods came to constitute nearly half of all British exports. Also interesting is the dynamic pattern of increasing foreign trade in metals. The share of all metal industries in exports of manufactured goods increased from 12 percent at the end of the Napoleonic wars to more than 25 percent in the 1850s (ibid.: 122). The main shift was in the composition of metal exports: finished metals gradually gave way to machinery and engineering products, the high-tech products of that age. Britain was building a powerful export sector while it was offering to sell to other nations the machinery and methods that were providing its competitive advantage.

From macro to micro: entrepreneurs and enterprises

Leading the way into and through what anthropologist and historian Karl Polanyi has called the "great transformation" were entrepreneurs of the sort we discussed in Chapter 3. They came in all shapes and sizes, with wildly skewed social origins and levels of professional training. Entrepreneurs were thus found in almost every social class. In general, countries with more fragmented social structures such as Britain and the Low Countries, and to a lesser extent Germany, offered the most favorable environments for the development of entrepreneurial initiatives. The composition of what has since been labeled "the entrepreneurial class" varied from country to country, according to an array of institutional, historical, and cultural factors. In many cases, culture and institutions appear to have made the difference, especially when they provided a good framework of available financial resources or legal protections of intellectual property, as was the case in England. Social values and cultural attitudes that approved of individual initiative also helped encourage the kind of behavior that fostered innovation. Other kinds of incentives, including social acceptance of the entrepreneurial status and nationalism, could also encourage entrepreneurship. For many, entrepreneurial status provided a powerful instrument of upward social mobility, something relatively new in degree in most European societies.

In the British "entrepreneurial crowd" of the First Industrial Revolution were those artisans and masters who transformed their shops into factories and enlarged the range of their business activities from local to regional, then national and even international levels. Significant is the case of Josiah Wedgwood, one of the most famous British entrepreneurs. Born in 1730 into a family of masters and artisans in the pottery industry, he successfully transformed the small, traditional family business into a formal, carefully organized firm characterized by a division of labor, high volumes of production, and modern marketing techniques. This allowed Wedgwood and his partners to establish a leadership position in the pottery industry throughout Europe.

In addition to artisans, the new entrepreneurial class included a large number of former shopkeepers and merchants, the same "merchant-entrepreneurs" who were the most dynamic component in preindustrial manufacturing. For these individuals, their business metamorphosis was the result of upstream integration aimed at establishing control over the most crucial phases of the production process and value chain. This practice was common in textiles where more and more merchants and "clothiers," as they were called, mixed their marketing activity with their direct control over production. One of these merchant-manufacturers, James Walker of Wortley, had under his control more than 20 looms, half of which were in his own house and the rest in laborers' homes.

On occasion, entrepreneurs came from social classes not normally associated with this style of risky business. Many noblemen and landowners looked suspiciously at the process of change but others mixed business opportunities with traditional activities. These men continued to manage large estates while promoting investments in mining or building capital-intensive infrastructure (canals, toll roads, and later railways) that would provide a necessary link to new markets. The Duke of Bridgewater invested his capital and entrepreneurial energies during the 1760s in building an important canal to carry coal from his estates to Manchester. Other members of the aristocracy became, like the Duke of Bridgewater, the driving forces of initiatives which needed a substantial capital investment.

Much further down the social scale was an instrument-maker like James Watt. He set himself, as did others similarly situated, to exploit the results of his research. Watt and others could patent their inventions and sell them through commercial partnerships. Watt's use of the efficient system of intellectual property protection allowed him to succeed in developing the steam engines so important as industry outgrew the sources of waterpower. The help of investors involved as financial partners allowed him, and many others, to raise the capital necessary to transform their inventions into important innovations.

The company of the First Industrial Revolution: ownership, control, and management

The Industrial Revolution not only led to the emergence of a more diverse array of business people but also necessitated finding and managing a quantity of fixed assets and a labor force that were normally larger—and in a growing number of cases considerably larger—than they had been in the past. New technologies and the enlargement of markets revolutionized the unit of production, which in turn opened up new challenges and choices for the entrepreneurs.

It is nevertheless inappropriate to overemphasize the extent of these increases in the scale of activity and in the organizational and managerial complexity, or to claim that they were the experience of the "average" factory in the First Industrial Revolution. This is especially true if it is compared with what happened during the truly capital-intensive Second Industrial Revolution. Although it was crucial to the history of economic development, the factory of the First Industrial Revolution was relatively small and usually retained only a few dozen employees. Its most important features were those related to ownership structure and to the organization of the production process. The relatively small size of the factory meant that necessary financial resources could, in many cases, be provided by individuals of moderate wealth and good connections. The main consequence was that ownership and control of the company generally remained in the hands of the founders and their families. In the absence of the joint-stock company (introduced in England only starting in 1856) and other systems of limited liability, the "partnership" became the legal device that allowed for the association of other individuals with the company's founder/owner. The partner(s) usually provided the firm with additional capital.

These organizations could, with decent leadership, adapt rather easily to new systems of manufacturing. Given the average dimension of the production unit and the complexity of the new technologies employed during the First Industrial Revolution, the bureaucratic structures of companies, even if largely "new," were relatively elementary. Management and ownership rested with the founder/owner and this person sometimes delegated tasks to other family members or partner(s). More often, however, the support provided by some "foremen" was sufficient. These individuals were responsible for organizing the factory's working hours and timetables, managing workers' behavior inside the factory, and ensuring the proper use of machinery and raw materials. These foremen were almost never asked to manage autonomously the production process. As a rule, the entrepreneur was responsible for almost all the crucial company functions, from strategic decision making to day-to-day management.

The company of the First Industrial Revolution: characteristics of the production process

The new technologies employed in the leading sectors generated few scale effects and throughput economies. In the case of textiles, for example, innovations tended to cluster around single stages of the production process (e.g., spinning), without changing the manner in which the products moved through the entire process from raw material to finished cloth. Innovation in one stage of the process, for example the various technical changes in spinning machines, created bottlenecks and pressured the firms to introduce innovations in weaving. Although this "innovation plague" encouraged innovation over the long term, it did not necessarily foster integration in the various stages of production. In the case of textiles, the production process thus remained fragmented. Even if thoroughly mechanized, it was carried on within separate, functionally distinct units. In metallurgy, too, and foremost in machinery, a disconnected process of production, separated into phases, was the rule.

Many entrepreneurs (whether alone or in partnership) had multiple factories under their control. If these factories operated in stages, it was possible to achieve some degree of vertical integration. But this type of business integration was of a legal rather than technical nature. The lack of coordination between the stages of production was also fostered by the tendency for similar units to cluster in the same geographic area. There were proximity advantages: these included benefits derived from having a fast flow of goods and services, as well as a plethora of skilled workers (the best vehicle for the dissemination of knowledge and innovations). Geographical proximity allowed companies to lower the cost of information and share knowledge more efficiently.

Relatively small production units characterized by simple cost structures were seldom able to have any influence on price levels. They operated in a setting characterized by continuous flows of information and knowledge and were thus the real version of the "representative enterprise" described by the British economist Alfred Marshall (see Chapter 2). This type of firm and industry could be found in famous territorial clusters such as the textile area around Manchester, the metalworking district of the Midlands, and Sheffield with its cutlery industry.

Marshall put considerable emphasis on the "collective strength" that companies derived from clustering in "industrial districts" in which knowledge circulated relatively freely and innovations could seldom be kept secret for long. News traveled fast in an industrial district, where technological and market information was "in the air." Industrial districts with these features could be found almost everywhere in Europe during the diffusion of industrialization. Often, their emergence was linked to manufacturing activities that had flourished in the preindustrial period but were now being transformed by new technology and new forms of business organization. Even in the era of the factory, however, such previous forms of manufacture as the putting-out system and the artisan shop had not disappeared entirely. But now these older forms of manufacture had to adjust to the competition of the low-priced, standardized goods pouring out of the new organizations in the manufacturing sector.

Trade and markets

The transformation of production forced a difficult redefinition of distribution and marketing functions. What emerged were forms of business for marketing and sales that were not historically associated with the activities of the merchant-entrepreneur. To manage relationships with the market, it was now necessary to build efficient networks of agents, representatives, or even independent but associated merchants. This allowed businesses to push sales beyond the narrow limits of the local market. There was greater specialization now in the wholesale and retail branches of many businesses. Creation of a suitable sales network introduced a number of other issues: an increase in transaction costs and the management of necessary relationships with other independent actors. Frequently, close relatives were employed as sales managers or representatives to solve the agency problem, but even a family network did not always ensure success in distribution on the larger scale required by the factory system.

Specialization followed, as it usually does when the volume of trade grows. The general tendency was for "big" merchants to act as mediators in long-distance transactions. For manufacturers seeking to enlarge their distribution and sell in markets characterized by high information asymmetries, the relationships with these merchants could create difficulties. Important merchants did not routinely accept exclusive commercial relationships because they considered producers to be mere suppliers. The merchants, who frequently wanted to be present in the market with their own brands, enjoyed a substantial degree of bargaining power over their manufacturers.

Increases in the size of the market and the degree of functional specialization during the First Industrial Revolution amplified the tensions between merchants and manufacturers. One outcome of this growing conflict was the emergence of strategies of downstream vertical integration. However, the intermediation of merchants was often necessary, especially when entrepreneurs could not afford the large investments required for the development of long-distance distribution networks. Vertical integration was thus justifiable only if it was strategic for the producer either to preserve control over the market or to strengthen his brand name.

Finance

Artisans, merchants, nobles, and engineers—all these individuals faced challenges when they decided to create new ventures or expand their existing enterprises. Frequently, they had to devise different, more complex organizations. This was a new challenge to those familiar with the business practices of the preindustrial period.

The first challenge was the one that every business faces (especially today): that of finding the capital necessary to finance the day-to-day activities of the business. Frequently, entrepreneurs needed funds for fixed assets as well as working capital. Although hardly comparable with the huge amounts of capital required to start up corporations during the Second Industrial Revolution, the funds that were needed to start a manufacturing business in the early nineteenth century were still a significant barrier to the entrepreneur. At this stage, the crucial task for the innovator was to efficiently exploit multiple channels of funding in the short and long term. Personal wealth, capital of family and close friends, and local credit were all tapped to fund the enterprise. Family wealth, often embodied in real estate or derived from commerce, was coupled with other income-generating activities, such as pledge loans, to generate enough money to finance entrepreneurial activity. Personal wealth was used not only in the start-up phase but also to keep the business running and to finance expansion. Real estate and other property were important forms of collateral that occasionally allowed an entrepreneur with a solid local reputation to raise funds from banks and other individuals. Frequently, entrepreneurial activity in manufacturing was only one component of a local portfolio of diverse investments that could include all three of the major macroeconomic sectors of agriculture, industry, and commerce. This was a rudimentary form of risk diversification and stemmed from the high uncertainty of the general environment in which this entrepreneurial activity was taking place.

On a local level, small credit was another important source of finance in the early stages of this "great transformation." Geographical proximity was essential, as it improved the lender's knowledge of the borrower and of the personal wealth that might be provided as collateral. Local banks and a dense network of individuals eager to lend out their personal wealth after guarantees and mortgages also channeled necessary resources to entrepreneurs. Before the birth of modern financial institutions that were devoted exclusively to the financing of large-scale manufacturing initiatives, local banks provided crucial support to entrepreneurial endeavors. Ploughed-back profits were also used to finance innovation. Family-controlled packages of investments allowed some lucky entrepreneurs to determine almost autonomously the destination of these personal resources. Whatever the nature and the quantity of these funds, it is necessary to recognize that this type of financing never reached the level characterized by the capital- and technology-intensive Second Industrial Revolution. In that regard, the links between the preindustrial and the early industrial era were still very strong.

Note

1 J. Mokyr, *The Gift of Athena: The Historical Origins of the Knowledge Economy*, Princeton University Press, Princeton, NJ, 2002.

Further reading

D.K. Aldcroft and S.P. Ville, *The European Economy, 1850–1914: A Thematic Approach*, Manchester University Press, Manchester, 1994.

M. Berg, *The Age of Manufactures: Industry, Innovation, and Work in Britain, 1700–1820*, Fontana Press, London, 1985.

N.F.R. Crafts, *British Economic Growth during the Industrial Revolution*, Oxford University Press, Oxford, 1985.

J. Kocka, "Entrepreneurs and Managers in German Industrialization," in P. Mathias and M.M. Postan (eds.), *The Cambridge Economic History of Europe, Vol. 7: The Industrial Economies. Capital, Labour and Enterprise*, Cambridge University Press, Cambridge, 1978.

A. Maddison, *The World Economy: Historical Statistics*, OECD, Paris, 2003, tab. 8a and 8c.

J. Mokyr, *The Lever of Riches: Technological Creativity and Economic Progress*, Oxford University Press, New York, 1990.

P.L. Payne, "Industrial Entrepreneurship and Management in Great Britain," in P. Mathias and M.M. Postan (eds.), *The Cambridge Economic History of Europe, Vol. 7: The Industrial Economies. Capital, Labour and Enterprise*, Cambridge University Press, Cambridge, 1978.

S. Pollard, *The Genesis of Modern Management: A Study of the Industrial Revolution in Great Britain*, Penguin Books, Harmondsworth, 1968.

Appendix

Table 5.1 Labor productivity in cotton: hours necessary to process 100 pounds of cotton

	Hours
Indian hand spinners (eighteenth century)	50,000
Crompton's mule (1780)	2,000
100-spindle mule (*c.* 1790)	1,000
Power-assisted mule (*c.* 1795)	300
Roberts' automatic mule (*c.* 1825)	135
Most efficient machines today (1990)	40

Source: Adapted from Christopher Freeman and Francisco Louçã, *As Time Goes By: From the Industrial Revolution to the Information Revolution*, Oxford University Press, Oxford, 2001, p. 155.

Table 5.2 United Kingdom's share of the following world figures (%)

	1750	1800	1830	1860	1880	1900	1913	1995
Population	1	1.6	2.1	2.2	2.4	2.5	2.5	1
Activities								
Total manufacturing production	1.9	4.2	9.5	19.9	22.9	18.5	18.4	3.9
Cast iron and raw iron production[a]	3.6	16.7	74.7	52.3	42.6	21.6	13.2	1.7
Raw cotton consumption	0.3	4.5	15.9	46.8	32.3	25.2	18.5	1.3
Anthracite production[b]		63	71	57	49	30	22	1.6
Trade								
Total export	13	19	18	20	16.5	14.6	13.8	4.8
Merchant fleet (tons)[c]		42	29	28	32	45	38	7
Stock of capital abroad[d]			42	50	49	48	42	11.7

Source: Own elaboration based on Paul Bairoch, *Victoires et deboires: histoire économique et sociale du monde du XVIe siècle a nos jours*, Gallimard, Paris, 1997.

Notes
a   Since 1913, crude steel.
b   Probably around 45–65%.
c   Probably around 13–20%.
d   Since 1913, direct investments.

Table 5.3 Professional origin of entrepreneurs in Southern Wales[a]

	Known entrepreneurs	Managed furnaces	Merchants	Other sectors	Industrial managers	Iron-masters	Other
1806	47	48	24	2	1	18	2
1823	35	67	18		2	11	4
1830	41	104	17	2	3	16	3
1839	30	110	13	2	4	7	4

Source: Pierre Leon, *Histoire économique et sociale du monde*, Vol. 3/2, A. Colin, Paris, p. 478.

Note
a   Thanks to the exploitation of coal and iron ore mines, Wales in general, and Southern Wales in particular, was at the forefront of the Industrial Revolution.

6 Technology, society, and the factory system

The setting

In the factories of this new economy, entrepreneurs combined fixed capital (in the form of buildings and machines) and working capital (raw materials, labor, and semifinished goods) to produce large quantities of standardized goods for domestic and foreign markets. Although organizational differences existed across geographic areas, there were significant structural homogeneities in the various factories. The combined impact of all of these businesses on the European and world economies leaves no doubt that this was a revolutionary development with implications that would spread far beyond the economies involved and would reverberate through the politics and social alignments of the nineteenth century. Both Karl Marx and Joseph Schumpeter well understood that those reverberations would continue to change dramatically all the nations that experienced industrial development.

Modern factories were different from previous workplaces and methods of production. First, the factory gathered a significant number of workers under one roof, many more than had been the norm in any place of business in the past. Neither arsenals nor shipyards employed so many workers, and neither had to coordinate their activities or make use of machinery in the factory style. Craft and domestic manufacturers rarely exceeded the size of an enlarged family.

A second break with the past was the clear separation between units of production and consumption. Contrary to the way that business had operated in the past, the factory system required that workers gather in one centralized place where an energy source (water or sometimes steam power) ran the plant's machinery. Ingenious systems of pulleys and axles made it possible to run a large number of machines from a single water wheel or engine.

The third feature of the factory was the specialization of labor. Each worker was assigned a small number of tasks, in some cases only one, in the style made famous by Adam Smith's description of the pin factory. Machines were specialized, as well as the workers. Employees seldom had the satisfaction of seeing a completed product through the entire manufacturing process. Instead of producing an entire boot, the worker would spend all of his days making only the soles or uppers for a standardized piece of footwear. Specialization was a characteristic of entire factories as well as individual tasks. The new technologies encouraged the specialization of the single production unit, as well as the enlargement of the market, as Smith sharply noted.

The mechanization of various stages of the production process was a distinctive characteristic of the modern factory. It was this mechanization that caused many contemporary observers to express amazement about, or to be appalled by, the "noisy hells." The machines at work were much more sophisticated than the tools used by the craftsmen and guild masters and were certainly more complicated than the rudimentary looms used by farmers weaving in their homes for the merchant-entrepreneurs. The new factory machines were complex from a technical point of view and thus required the presence of workers specialized in the maintenance of the machinery. These new machines were also expensive. At this stage, investment in fixed assets started to be a relevant constraint. On a far greater scale than in the past, the employee could no longer afford to be the owner of the means of production. Additional organizational problems arose when it became clear that in some cases a regulated system of training and supervision was required to ensure proper use of the machinery.

Although it is not possible to talk of "energy intensive" production processes in the case of the First Industrial Revolution, the machines used in this period certainly required more energy than in the past. This energy had to be cheap and almost continuously available, and therefore it necessarily had to be produced by nonanimated sources. These needs were often met by locating the factory in areas where it was possible to benefit from power derived from water wheels situated on rivers, streams, and waterfalls. This created a location constraint that often permanently affected the geography of industrial basins. The steam engine, which turned heat into immediately disposable energy, helped to mitigate some of these constraints. In an effort to reduce costs and avoid problems caused by coal shortages, manufacturers often employed a mix of new and old methods of energy production.

The factory system spread rather quickly through the British economy and then diffused more slowly throughout Europe. Unpleasant as factory work was, the new jobs quickly drew workers out of agriculture, just as cheap, standardized goods drove more expensive bespoke work into smaller market niches. There was little question as to the superior efficiency of the factory system, although there were some who clearly preferred the earlier, preindustrial economy. For some, agriculture still seemed to be a more manageable and rewarding style of life. To others, the social, economic, and psychological impact of the factory on the workers (sometimes now identified as "wage slaves") seemed intolerable.

The factory system: the impact on society

As European countries pushed into the process of industrialization and began to adjust to the new technologies and systems of production, a series of radical changes took place in their economic systems and social structures.

At a macroeconomic level, most of the major changes involved the rate of economic growth (both in aggregate terms and at the level of the single countries involved), the amount and quality of international trade, and the relative contributions of agriculture and manufacturing to gross domestic product (GDP) and employment.

At the microlevel, the spread of new technologies and organizational forms generated a variety of issues that employers were forced to confront. Some of these problems soon garnered such general interest that governments became involved in their management. The factory system required the creation of new kinds of capital-intensive functional structures of production. The owners experimented with various solutions in terms of architecture and factory layout. They also experimented with new ways to properly organize and discipline their workers—largely a commuter population. Individuals of different ages, backgrounds, and genders were now brought together in the limited workspace of factories and, in order for the production process to run smoothly, employers attempted to enforce behavioral rules.

From the perspective of the worker, employment in the factory system often meant a radical transformation of lifestyle. Whether they came from artisans' ranks or from the countryside, they had to quickly adjust their habits to the unusual rhythms imposed by the new technologies. Simultaneously, workers had to undergo an often dramatic and difficult process associated with urbanization. The relative freedom that characterized both peasants' and artisans' working lives, in terms of choosing working hours and leisure time, was replaced by clocks, bells, and shift work that took place both night and day. Bosses had to prevent factory workers from leaving the workplace during crop harvests. Employers also struggled to change some of the work patterns that had characterized artisans' lives, such as the institution of "Saint Monday," the extension of Sunday's rest through Monday.

Unlike previous forms of production, the factory introduced carefully defined and relatively rigid roles and hierarchies. The machines now dictated the worker's schedule and called for constant application of his or her attention. This was completely different from the organizational systems that had characterized traditional societies. This change, which was not implemented on a systematic basis as it was during the Second Industrial Revolution, created tensions for workers everywhere. As their lives changed, many factory workers had to cope with a new range of mental and physical problems. They were often forced to commute long distances to work or had to adapt to life in crowded dormitories, all without the degree of protection and emotional security that had previously been ensured by extended families and local communities. These precarious working conditions were only part of the problem. It was often difficult to integrate "foreign" workers into the exclusive and hostile local communities in which the factories were located.

In these and many other ways, the First Industrial Revolution indelibly affected the history of western European development. From the social and cultural point of view, the uneasy life and sharp transitions workers experienced in the machine-oriented world of the factory system were more important than the wealth generated by this more efficient system of production. As modern industrial society first emerged from the transition to the factory system, it was not at all clear that this new society would improve the lives of the bulk of the population experiencing these profound societal and cultural changes.

Managing the transformation

As the social structure of preindustrial European society began to crumble, entrepreneurs in different places and at different times experimented with a wide variety of solutions to the problems stemming from the abrupt social changes they were creating. Some owners simply ignored the problems their factories generated. Others who were more sensible tried to address these problems directly. Increasingly, factories were equipped with lodgings and dormitories for workers who lived a long distance away. Shops were built, so that workers could easily buy necessary items, including food and clothing. "Factory villages" were created close to large plants and, in general, were built with the financial help of the entrepreneurs themselves. In Britain, philanthropic industrialists had since the eighteenth century been building close communities of workers clustered into "model villages." They not only provided their workers with housing and services but also tried to diffuse a culture of sobriety and work commitment. One significant example is Saltaire, founded by leading wool industry entrepreneur Titus Salt in 1853 in West Yorkshire. The village, which was surrounded by Salt's five mills, included houses, schools, recreation areas such as a library and a concert hall, and other facilities for the workers' families. When it worked well, this system strengthened the personal and individual relationship between the entrepreneur and his workers and is well described by the term "paternalism."

Where the process of industrialization rapidly imposed urbanization on a large number of peasants and countryside workers, as happened in many European countries, the creation of communities was seen as a way to keep alive some of the values and traditions of the peasant world. This included the trust and respect due to the landlord. At Crespi d'Adda, a factory village built around a cotton factory in the north of Italy at the end of the 1870s, this entailed the creation of a cohesive new community in which it was possible to find everything needed for everyday life, including opportunities for recreational and educational activity. At Crespi d'Adda, which took its name after the surname of the entrepreneurial family that owned the factory, the community included the workers' houses, some villas for the management, a church, a cemetery, a grocery store, a hospital, and public baths. The owners had a large house resembling a medieval castle surrounded by a park.

With or without "castles," company towns and villages were built around factories throughout Europe and America. In many, the company and the founding family held a leading role in the social and civil life of the town. One example is the French town of Le Creusot, where in the 1840s, the Schneider family established a steelwork employing a large part of the local population. The family participated actively in the local social, civil, and political life and provided the town with schools, a hospital, and lodgings for blue- and white-collar workers.

The liberal generosity expected of elite aristocrats in the preindustrial period was thus replicated by some entrepreneurs during the Industrial Revolution—but with a new twist: the personal, individual relationships between nobles and their poor laborers or between mercantile fathers and sons, which had characterized preindustrial society, were recreated during the Industrial Revolution without the involvement of guilds, unions, or professional associations.

Paternalistic relationships between entrepreneurs and workers were established almost everywhere. They gained the most strength in areas where local and national institutions were weak and unprepared to manage the processes of change and social conflict that accompanied the Industrial Revolution. This kind of paternalism turned out to be a particularly effective method of control. It was so efficient that, in various forms, it remained in use well beyond the age of the First Industrial Revolution and could be found in almost all industrialized countries.

As the Industrial Revolution uprooted traditional European social structures, it created a new social class, the industrial bourgeoisie. This class soon began to assume economic and political leadership in local, regional, and even national societies. The newly empowered industrial bourgeoisie began to institute governmental rules that were aimed at mitigating the harshest aspects of the factory system. Starting in Britain and Germany, where this type of legislation was first introduced, new laws regulating the employment of women and children were passed. In some cases, forms of compulsory insurance and mutuality spread across Europe.

The industrial bourgeoisie attempted to introduce a moderate redistribution of the benefits of the industrialization process, mainly in terms of better living conditions but also through social development. They promoted cultural programs that in many cases had positive benefits for society as a whole. Industrialists were thus able to assume, according to the definition provided by Italian Communist Antonio Gramsci, a "hegemonic" role in industrial society. They consolidated their power while in many cases they were also able to reduce areas of conflict and social clashes. They sought stable new social relations that would enable them to get on with industrial progress without social and political struggles over authority and the distribution of income and wealth.

Why the factory?

Alas, even the most socially aware of the new entrepreneurs could not avoid all the problems of industrialization. Many workers were offended by the paternalism and the controls of the new system, controls that seemed always to favor the capitalists and their enterprises. There was a longing to return to an earlier day when individuals and families, not machines, controlled the tempo of life. Some workers were determined to fight back against the factory system or to at least regain a measure of control over their occupations. This set in motion labor struggles and political movements that would extend through the nineteenth and twentieth centuries and are still with us today in the Great Recession.

Joseph Schumpeter was mindful of those struggles and the implications they would have for modern industrial capitalism. In his great paradigm of modern capitalism, the entrepreneurs, the innovators who brought in the factory system, were merely taking advantage of new technology and new ways of organizing work that would be more efficient and would ultimately bring great benefits to society. The economic pie would get bigger, as it certainly did during the First Industrial Revolution. Schumpeter said this would happen because the new forms of doing business would drive the old forms out of the markets through "creative destruction."

That was surely taking place, but the process was not as simple and complete as Schumpeter described it. Previous forms of manufacturing were not always quickly abandoned. Factories were adopted at varying speeds by each industry, according to the type of business, its stage in the production process, the input's relative cost, and even local labor practices and cultures. During the First Industrial Revolution, different types of firms could coexist. Smaller, specialized shops succeeded alongside centralized factories that practiced scale-intensive and mechanized processes. It is important to recognize how complex the transition from older forms of manufacturing to factory production was in the eighteenth and nineteenth centuries. In cotton textiles, merchant-entrepreneurs were quick to invest in new spinning technologies; this centralized the upstream stages of the production process while maintaining a wide network of subcontractors in weaving and finishing. The putting-out system endured in the cotton industry, partially because the process for mechanizing spinning was discovered before that for weaving, and the weaving could continue to be performed cheaply by a well-trained agricultural labor force. Weaving mills, therefore, employed only a few dozen "internal" workers but employed several hundred who worked at home.

Once a mechanical form of weaving was developed, the textile entrepreneurs consolidated vertically in a manner well explained by transactions cost theory. Through integration, businessmen could better coordinate their operations and control their costs and the quality of their products. Then economies of scale once again came into play, encouraging the businessmen to supplement water with steam power, so that they could keep their mills running on regular schedules. As the scale of operations increased, the machinery became more sophisticated and expensive. For instance, automatic looms required substantial investments and scrupulous maintenance, often by skilled mechanics. Although it provided solutions for many problems, the factory system also created new ones: for maintaining expensive machinery, in delegating authority, in reporting, and in defining entirely new economic roles and procedures. No longer able to use a piece-work system, mass producers had to learn how to maintain discipline in a workforce that frequently did not give its paternalistic employers the respect or systematic effort the bosses thought they deserved.

Marxist historiography provides a different historical paradigm for analyzing the spread of the factory system. According to Marxist theories, entrepreneurs concentrated the workforce in a single location in order to exert a closer control over the workers and to achieve a more efficient exploitation of their labor. As the entrepreneurs now owned the means of production and controlled the workplace, they could progressively introduce new machinery (as they did in weaving) and lower their labor costs per unit of output. Here, at last, was the creation of the true proletariat with class interests inherently opposed to those of the bourgeoisie. Specialization of function further reduced the skill levels of the workers and gave the businessman even greater opportunities to exploit their labor. The fruits of economic progress were thus denied to the working class who would ultimately be unable to buy industrial goods. This, Marxist theory indicated, would create a final great crisis for the capitalist system.

From Schumpeter's perspective, of course, the factory system was a successful innovation, one of the truly epochal innovations that generated entrepreneurial profits and thus encouraged others to change the way they did business. All, in this view, would benefit as the economy became more efficient. Consumers would have cheaper products. Workers would have new jobs and the money they needed to buy the cheaper consumer goods. Managers would of course continue to have problems that called for continued innovation. Managing the production process through the division of labor required a form of knowledge, a kind of "software" necessary to produce standardized goods in large quantities. This in turn would call for new methods of distribution, new forms of marketing and sales, and new forms of financing enterprise. All would require the new type of knowledge that was radically different from that used before, which had been largely based on practical know-how and not on codification or implementation of general principles. The Industrial Revolution thus profoundly transformed the European training system. While apprenticed workers had learned their trade on the shop floor or at home, the factory became the primary place for the transmission of the most important forms of knowledge, those related to the use of the new machine technologies.

As the factory system grew, it would create the new wealth that Schumpeter lauded as well as the kinds of conflicts that Marx thought were central features of capitalism in any form. Labor as well as capital would develop new forms of organization suited to the new system. The older forms of business organization would gradually decline in importance as the factories established their dominance of national and international markets. The centralization of production met the requirements of the new technologies and allowed factory owners to better manage their labor forces. They now had greater control over the output and quality of their goods. These features made the factory not an occasional complement to decentralized craft production but the most widespread organizational device in industrial society.

Further reading

R.C. Allen, *The British Industrial Revolution in Global Perspective (New Approaches to Economic and Social History)*, Cambridge University Press, Cambridge, 2009.
P. Hudson, *Industrial Revolution*, London, Hodder Arnold, 1992.

D. Landes, *The Unbound Prometheus: Technological Change and Industrial Development in Western Europe from 1750 to the Present*, Cambridge University Press, Cambridge, 1969.
J.F. Wilson, *British Business History, 1720–1994*, Manchester University Press, Manchester, 1995.

Appendix

Table 6.1 Inanimate energy—world production of inanimate energy (equivalent to electricity in million megawatts per hour)

Year	Coal	Charcoal	Oil	Fuel	Gas	Hydroelectric energy	Total
1870	1,628	30	8	–	–	8	1,674
1880	2,511	58	43	–	–	11	2,623
1890	3,797	97	109	–	40	13	4,056
1900	5,606	179	213	–	75	16	6,089
1910	8,453	271	467	–	162	34	9,387
1920	9,540	394	1,032	14	254	64	11,298
1930	9,735	493	2,045	78	575	128	13,054
1940	10,904	798	3,037	83	867	193	15,882
1950	11,632	902	5,439	163	2,088	332	20,556
1960	14,472	2,184	11,159		4,971	689	33,475

Source: Own elaboration on Carlo Cipolla, *Before the Industrial Revolution: European Society and Economy 1000–1700*, 3rd ed., Routledge, London, 1993, p. 217.

Table 6.2 Capacity of all steam engines (thousands of horsepower)

	1840	1850	1860	1870	1880	1888	1896
United Kingdom	620	1,290	2,450	4,040	7,600	9,200	13,700
Germany	40	260	850	2,480	5,120	6,200	8,080
France	90	270	1,120	1,850	3,070	4,520	5,920
Austria	20	100	330	800	1,560	2,150	2,520
Belgium	40	70	160	350	610	810	1,180
Russia	20	70	200	920	1,740	2,240	3,100
Italy	10	40	50	330	500	830	1,520
Spain	10	20	100	210	470	740	1,180
The Netherlands	–	10	30	130	250	340	600
Europe	860	2,240	5,540	11,570	22,000	28,630	40,300
United States	760	1,680	3,470	5,590	9,110	14,400	18,060
World	1,650	3,990	9,380	18,460	34,150	50,150	66,100

Source: Own elaboration on D.S. Landes, "Technological Change and Development in Western Europe, 1750–1914," in H.J. Habakkuk and M.M. Postan (eds.), *The Cambridge Economic History of Europe. The Industrial Revolutions and After: Incomes, Population and Technological Change*, Cambridge University Press, Cambridge, 1965, p. 449.

Part III
The birth and consolidation of big business

7   Infrastructures

The emergence of the large firm: the origins of discontinuity

In the last quarter of the nineteenth century, large corporations began appearing in some of the most advanced industrialized nations. Over a relatively short period of time, they were destined to become multiunit, multifunctional, multiproduct, and multinational entities. The arrival of these large and complex organizations meant that, for the first time in history, it was necessary to adopt some form of governance via salaried managers (nonowners) who had specific technical skills.

Before the Industrial Revolution, there were a few examples of large corporations of these dimensions. In most cases, they were banks, overseas companies such as the East India Company (created by the English during the reign of Elizabeth I), or state manufacturers. Even though the "giants" of preindustrial capitalism could be extremely potent, it was possible for a few managers and clerks to direct their activities because the number of operating units and the quantity of transactions were small by modern standards.

As we have seen in the previous chapters, business began to change in dramatic ways as industry was transformed. The use of new sources of energy (like fossil fuels), the use of steam in production processes, the introduction of new machinery, and the expansion of the factories represented significant benchmarks in the history of mankind. As two astute observers noted, the bourgeoisie in the First Industrial Revolution had "accomplished wonders far surpassing Egyptian pyramids, Roman aqueducts, and Gothic cathedrals; it has conducted expeditions that put in the shade all former Exoduses of nations and crusades."[1]

But the large firm as we know it today was not born because of the changes that occurred in England at the end of the eighteenth century. The productive factories were still of somewhat limited dimensions in all the sectors typical of the First Industrial Revolution. The cost, as well as the uncertainty, of transportation constrained companies attempting to extend their market range. The typical firm still employed a relatively small number of workers, especially compared with the normal workforce in the twentieth century. For example, the typical cotton mill in Manchester in the 1830s usually gave work to less than 200 people; by the beginning of the 1970s, there were 401 companies in market economies around the world that each employed more than 20,000 persons. By the same token, the manufacturing capacity of the early industrial firm was much more limited than would become the norm a century later. In the 1840s, very few English ironworks produced more than 10,000 tons annually; by the 1980s, the minimum amount necessary for an efficient integrated cycle steel plant in Japan was approximately 6 million tons per annum. Even the substantial increases in production and trading in the first decades of the 1800s did not give rise to a significant concentration of economic activity. In the early nineteenth century, firms continued to be concerned with a single function and a single product while neither ownership structures nor internal organization was significantly different from preindustrial times. As historian Sidney Pollard explains, there was so little business administration in early industrialization that there was not a managerial theory associated with the Industrial Revolution.[2]

The fundamental prerequisites for the emergence of modern big business and its managerial hierarchy were advances in technology and markets that finally permitted firms to reach dimensions and complexity that were previously impossible to imagine. It was the large variety of processes (in production, machinery, electricity, and chemicals) that came about in the United States and Western Europe after 1870 that became the decisive element in the growth of large corporations. This turning point would not have been possible without accompanying changes in communication and transportation systems. It was the radical transformation brought about by steam navigation, by railroads, by telegraphs, and telephones that made it possible for firms to reach a much larger market, in a much more extensive area. Firms were able to count on more solid relationships with both suppliers and clients; they could organize their internal operations on a more regular schedule. With this kind of foundation, a firm could grow in size. The subsequent transformation led to important changes in decision-making processes and internal structures, changes that were essential aspects of management in the modern large corporation.

The diffusion of networks of transportation and communication

The second half of the nineteenth century witnessed a remarkable growth in communication and transportation networks. New developments such as the telegraph and the telephone permitted an ever faster, efficient, and extensive exchange of information. The telegraph machine, invented in 1844, was already in use for commercial purposes 3 years later. Inventions and improvements, combined with attempts at regulatory standardization and harmonization, allowed for the creation of a genuine international system for telegrams, meaning that it became possible to communicate news rapidly and over great distances. Their low costs and the speed with which these networks could be installed led to a rapid diffusion. In the United States, for example, by 1861, there were 50,000 miles of telegraph lines; two decades later this number had grown to 291,000, at which point, according to census data, almost 32 million messages were sent each year. The telephone, invented by Bell in 1877, at first was intended to be a complementary tool for telegraph machines, and its use was limited almost exclusively to local conversations, primarily in the United States. In a short period of time, however, the telephone revealed itself to be better than the telegraph: communication was quicker, and it was now possible to transmit 100–200 words per minute rather than the 15–20 words that could be sent in a telegram. The telephone had an additional advantage with the fact that it did not require the presence of an operator in loco.

The telegraph and the telephone helped facilitate communications in a world increasingly brought together by miles of railways and steam navigation. Even though much progress had been made in manufacturing since the medieval era, at the beginning of the 1800s transportation systems lagged behind. As French historian Fernand Braudel noted, Napoleon and Caesar were separated by eighteen centuries, but the speed (or a more appropriate choice of words, the slowness) with which they moved was not really that different![3]

The arrival of the railroads changed things decisively. Older forms of transportation, which were slower and less reliable, became obsolete. Stagecoaches disappeared, tolls were eliminated, and road traffic was reduced to moving short distances and with frequencies and regularity comparable with the railroads. Until the middle of the nineteenth century, only about 15,000 miles of railway had been laid in Europe. In the two decades between 1850 and 1870, the system expanded to almost 70,000 miles of tracks. The English system of railways, which was launched in the 1820s, was 70 percent completed by 1875. As the rails in Europe's principal nations became more extensive, the railway firms became the first big businesses in those nations, which were industrialized or in the middle of the path to industrialization. In England, the leading industrialized nation, the railway companies were the first enterprises of truly large dimensions. In 1850, when only a handful of industrial firms had a capital of more than 500,000 pounds, there were 19 railway companies each with capital in excess of 3 million pounds.

In Germany, the railways' impact was even more significant, not only for its more extensive coverage but also, above all, for the fact that the rapid expansion of railroads was intrinsically linked to the country's industrialization. The increasing financial needs of the railways gave birth in the 1850s to the universal bank (which, as we will see in Chapter 9, was one of the most important protagonists of industrial growth in Germany). Railroads also were the major client for industrial sectors such as metallurgy and machinery. In a short time, these industries, too, became key players for the nation. Even in countries such as Italy, where industrialization proceeded slower, the first big business was a railway called "Strade ferrate meridionali," better known as Bastogi, the name of its founder. In Italy, too, the railways helped to create a national market and a growing demand for the products of new sectors such as metallurgy and machinery. There was an important indirect effect for the companies that supplied the railways in Italy when they were nationalized in 1905. Many spent part of the indemnities they received from the State to finance the rise of the electric industry.

Innovations in transportation and communications that originated in Europe quickly found their way across the Atlantic Ocean, especially to the United States where distances between urban centers and the other territories called for a more extensive railway network. In 1860, when Great Britain had slightly more than

9,000 miles of tracks, the United States already had 30,000. Twenty years later almost 16,000 miles of track had been laid in Great Britain while the number for the United States had already reached more than 93,000. When the US network was complete around 1910, America had more than ten times as many railroad tracks as Britain (240,000 vs. 20,000). The installation of telegraph lines in the United States and Europe's most advanced nations also proceeded very quickly. As tracks were put down, telegraph lines were installed since they were a fundamental component of a rapid, safe, and efficient train system.

At the same time, coal and steam were revolutionizing water transportation. The first steamship for commercial purposes, the *Claremont*, was powered by a motor invented by James Watt. Starting in 1807, it plied the busiest American waterway, traveling the Hudson River between Albany and New York City. In 32 hours, the *Claremont* covered the same route on which earlier forms of transportation took six times as long. Until the middle of the nineteenth century, there were very few steamships, but in the 1850s, steam power worked a revolution in oceanic shipping. The new steamships were reinforced with iron; they were more reliable, traveled at faster speeds, and had greater capacity than ships powered by sails. Before the steamship, traveling westward from Europe toward the United States usually took between 3 weeks and 3 months. With the steamships, the same trip could be made in 10–15 days. Thanks to the additional progress made in steam technology, ships that traveled coastal waterways and rivers in both Europe and the New Continent gave the nations that relied on these forms of transportation still more positive results.

Networks of communication and transportation and the prerequisites for the birth of big business

It took a fair amount of time to construct those networks of communication and transportation extending across nations and international borders. The same can be said about the development of the skills necessary to administer them and the creation of institutions that could guarantee their consolidation over time. As they emerged, these new infrastructures became the decisive elements shaping the emergence of the modern form of big business both in the United States (where the first large corporations were established) and in the most advanced nations of Europe.

Railroads, in particular, played a critical role in the process by opening larger, more extensive markets, by rendering it necessary to find new forms for financing, by favoring the development of organizational capacities and managerial hierarchies, and by representing the first checkpoint for modern industrial relations and regulation policies.

Trains and markets

The railroads offered a means of transportation that became a fundamental component in large-scale production and distribution of goods and was a prerequisite for the emergence of big manufacturing firms and modern commercial institutions. There were three fundamental characteristics that made a significant difference between this means of transportation and that which had preceded it: speed, regularity, and reliability. Trains offered a fast means of moving both merchandise and people. Their advantage was tied to the extended diffusion and interconnection of trains, particularly as seen in the case of the United States where great distances had previously been covered by water or wagon transportation. The railroads revolutionized travel times. By 1857, the route between New York and Chicago could be covered in 3 days; previously it had taken 3 weeks.

By constructing networks of rail tracks and telegraph lines, companies were finally able to exploit a truly national market and quickly meet the needs of customers in every corner of the country. Firms now had a big incentive to increase manufacturing capacity. In marketing and sales, they now were ensured regular and reliable transportation. The railroad could guarantee a reliable service for shipping large quantities of goods, with a precise timetable that was normally not affected by meteorological conditions. Previously, the distribution of goods was conditioned by the weather and had to rely on the force of animals and men or energy sources such as wind and water flows. It was impossible to foresee the duration or intensity of these conditions, which made it difficult for firms to invest in larger factories or increase production. Steam locomotives contributed to reducing unitary costs for transportation of goods. In the same amount of time it took a ferry to navigate a canal one way, a freight train could make multiple trips between the two destinations. The revolution in transportation and communications lowered costs and increased speed in distributing goods. Firms now had an important incentive to increase the scale of production and to more efficiently organize the production process.

Railroads and finance

Building up a railway network required capital, and the nation's financial institutions often played a dominant role in the spread of the rail network. Over time, these same financial institutions were fundamental in the growth of the modern industrial firm. During the preindustrial era, an entrepreneur, a single family, or a group of partners could, in fact, gather the capital necessary to start a plantation, a textile factory, or even a fleet of ships. The amount of capital required for the construction of a railway, however, was significantly greater, and other sources had to be found for the financing of these new activities. The channels for this kind of financing were honed during the second half of the 1800s. In Germany, as was mentioned earlier, railways favored the creation of the universal banks that played a significant role in the growth of the biggest firms in the country. In the 10-year period starting in 1850, the enormous amount of money necessary to build the railroads in the United States led to the creation of specialized investment banks. Large institutions, such as J.P. Morgan, invested heavily in the railroads prior to 1900, frequently with European capital that served to finance the American system of transportation and communications. These same institutions, including J.P. Morgan, also played a formidable role in financing American industrial mergers between the end of the nineteenth century and the beginning of the twentieth century. In the initial stages of the merger movement, the banks encouraged the technical–organizational rationalization of manufacturing and services.

The pressing financial needs of the big railway companies in the United States brought about a concentration of financial markets in the second half of the nineteenth century. The majority of the Wall Street firms and their financial instruments were focused on the railways and related companies such as Western Union, Pullman Palace Car Company, and some coal manufacturers that fostered the growth of the railroads. These leading financial institutions made it easier for the railroads and associated enterprises to expand through mergers and acquisitions. Some of the classic speculative techniques of the stock market (e.g., short sales, marginal sales, puts and calls) were fine-tuned during the 1850s, when the financial world invented modern methods for selling and buying stocks and bonds.

Railways and management

The growth of the railroads necessitated a new distribution of ownership assets among the firms involved and, more importantly, brought about new forms of corporate management. Unlike the small firms that had preceded them, for the first time the railway companies found themselves in the situation of having to manage enormous investments, to hire very large numbers of workers, and to coordinate their activities so as to provide for safe, efficient travel. The quantity and the variety of responsibilities faced by management gave birth to a fragmentation of corporate property and a systematic division of roles. On the one side were the large numbers of shareholders who owned the company and on the other were the salaried managers with their specific skills and abilities who were entrusted with running the company full-time. Starting in the mid-nineteenth century, the need to deal with the specific financial and administrative issues arising in railroad operations effectively rendered these managers pioneers in creating and diffusing new forms of management. Subsequently, when firms that manufactured or distributed goods and services began to transform themselves into multiunit giants scattered across ever larger territories, the experiences of the railway companies in developing efficient organizations became models worthy of imitation.

As they grew, most of the world's telegraph and railroad companies needed to hire increasing numbers of full-time managers to coordinate, control, and evaluate their many operating units. They developed new American models for creating and controlling their workforces and finances. Over time, the United States became a trailblazer in business management innovation.

The fact that most of the United States was covered by single rail tracks made it imperative that each railroad company have a managerial hierarchy responsible for programming and coordinating precisely the circulation of trains. An efficient coordination guaranteed speed, regularity, and reliability in a system that moved a wide variety of goods between hundreds of cities and towns. The bigger the firm, the more often that the operating decisions were entrusted to a manager who usually had few (if any) shares in the company. Thus, ownership and direction of the firm began to pull apart into separate roles.

With the increasing size and complexity of the enterprise's activities, managers started to delegate more and more tasks to other managers and lower-level employees. Intermediate level managers were appointed to oversee and supervise the various functional tasks (such as determining train schedules, organizing track maintenance, and accounting for the thousands of daily transactions) within each division. The distinction between *line* and *staff*, a distinction probably copied from military organizations, was adopted early on by the roads. This role structure, which was functional and flexible, made it easier for executives to run these complex organizations. Line managers controlled the movements of people and trains, following a hierarchy that went from president to managing director at the top down to superintendent general and then divisional superintendent. Staff was made up of men who were responsible for standards and advising the managers of the functional departments.

Over the course of just a few decades, the railroad organizations showed themselves to be highly qualified to deal with new problems of running very large, complex enterprises. Managers working for the railway companies established standards for tracks and equipment such as switches, air-powered brakes, and signals. This allowed them to move trains carrying goods between hundreds of sites on uninterrupted tracks and without problems when passing from the tracks of one company to the tracks of another. Working for the railway companies, managers had taken on the task of perfecting tools such as the bill of lading, agreements between firms, and accounting rules for train cars belonging to other companies. Semiprofessional associations such as the Society of Railroad Accounting Officers and the American Society of Railroad Superintendents established standards that made it possible to transfer a fully loaded railway car 3,000 miles from one coast to the other in the United States without having to shift the goods at any point.

Around 1850, before the expansion of railroads, moving merchandise from Philadelphia to Chicago required the use of both covered wagons and barges, with a shipment taking as much as 3 weeks and crossing through nine points of loading and unloading. By the end of the nineteenth century, thanks to the railways and their efficient and coordinated shipping process, the same trip took only 2 days and the merchandise loaded at its point of origin and then only unloaded at its final destination. As this suggests, the professional managers at the railways had been vigorously searching for ways to improve operations and enjoying considerable success. The network's complexity and size had forced the companies to adopt organizations based on independent territorial divisions that were run by general managers. They controlled the activities of their various functional departments and answered to an internal central management unit responsible for making the strategic decisions. Working together, the general managers coordinated the flow of traffic in this enormous national system.

Trains, industrial relations, and regulation

The railways also played a pioneering role in the delicate arena of relations between management and workers. They were also the first sector of the American economy in which competition was regulated by the federal government.

As railway companies grew, they had to face on a large scale some classic issues of industrial relationships. Recruitment, training, and managing workers were some of the problems, but there were new dilemmas related to organizing the efforts of workers who were scattered over vast geographical areas. Large railroad companies were the first to introduce ongoing worker recruitment, establish fixed salaries, and define a clear internal hierarchy with established career paths. They were also the first to introduce rudimentary systems of insurance and pensions for their employees. In the area of industrial relations, strikes were just as common in the United States as they were in Europe. Still, management held the only legitimate source of authority in a system where workers were not permitted to express their opinions or to intervene legally in operations. At least until World War I, unions were not officially recognized, and collective bargaining was virtually unheard of. Among the few exceptions were the workshops that built freight and passenger cars and were owned by the railway companies. Here, the workers had a greater say in how things operated, and often their unions were accepted by management.

The railway sector in the United States and elsewhere developed various cartels and price-fixing agreements in an effort to control competition. This was the rail companies' answer to a sector that was highly oligopolistic and intensely competitive. In the 1870s, as a response to the system of informal alliances that had grown up between competitors and between firms traveling the same rail routes, a formalized federation was created; activities, control procedures, and sanctions were now prescribed in detail. Still, incentives to rebel were many, and the stability of the accords was low. At the beginning of the 1880s, almost all railroad owners and managers were in agreement that even the best-planned cartels were incapable of keeping competition under control if good faith and truthfulness between competitors were lacking.

Some of the industry's leaders favored a turn to government stabilization as an alternative to so-called "cut-throat competition." A legislative approach seemed indispensable since the legislature could give substance to the agreements and enforce them. Political support for this position was weak, however, and, when the US Congress decided to adopt regulatory legislation with the Interstate Commerce Act of 1887, it refused to recognize the railroad cartels and even outlawed them. Regulation played a decisive role in aligning the strategies of companies in the railroad sector long before the Sherman Antitrust Act did something similar for the industrial system of the United States.

The strategic and organizational know-how that had been acquired in the railways was rapidly transferred to other industrial sectors, thanks to the important contribution of managers and entrepreneurs who had started their careers in the railroad companies before embarking into manufacturing. For example, Andrew Carnegie, strengthened by his experiences while working for the Pennsylvania Railroad, was the first to take full advantage of the economies of scale now possible for the steel industry. His decision to adopt systematic cost-control methods (until then virtually unknown in industry) came out of his experience in railroads. The same can be said for the choice to expand the scale of his company's activities, even though growth called for an enormous initial investment—a strategy that Carnegie understood would eventually lower production costs. Just as it was most economical to load big trains with the greatest quantity of goods possible, Carnegie perceived that, by producing steel in significantly larger quantities, his company could realize enormous economies of scale. The Carnegie strategy, as we will see in the next chapter, became a very popular strategy among large US manufacturing firms.

The revolution in distribution and production processes that occurred in the years between the nineteenth and twentieth centuries was thus built on the material, financial, organizational, and institutional foundations developed by the new US transportation and communication infrastructures.

Notes

1 Karl Marx and Frederick Engels, *Manifesto of the Communist Party*, 1848. For a recent edition, see that of Cosimo Classics, New York, 2006.
2 S. Pollard, *The Genesis of Modern Management: A Study of the Industrial Revolution in Great Britain*, E. Arnold, London, 1965, p. 271.
3 F. Braudel, *Civilization and Capitalism, 15th–18th Century*, Harper & Row, New York, 1981, p. 429.

Further reading

A.D. Chandler, Jr., *The Visible Hand: The Managerial Revolution in American Business*, Belknap Press, Cambridge, MA, 1977.
A.D. Chandler, Jr., *Scale and Scope: The Dynamics of Industrial Capitalism*, Harvard University Press, Cambridge, MA, 1990.
A.D. Chandler, Jr. and J.W. Cortada (eds.), *A Nation Transformed by Information: How Information Has Shaped the United States from Colonial Times to the Present*, Oxford University Press, Oxford, 2000.
T. Gourvish, *Railways and the British Economy, 1830–1914*, Macmillan, London, 1981.
H. Livesay, *Andrew Carnegie and the Rise of Big Business*, Longman Publishers, New York, 2006.
S.W. Usselmann, *Regulating Railroad Innovation: Business, Technology, and Politics in America, 1840–1920*, Cambridge University Press, Cambridge, 2002.

Appendix

Table 7.1 Global transport cost changes and commodity price convergence indicators

A. Transport declines		
American export routes, deflated freight cost	1869/1871–1908/1910	From 100 to 55%
American east coast routes, deflated freight cost	1869/1871–1911/1913	From 100 to 55%
British tramp, deflated freight cost	1869/1871–1911/1913	From 100 to 78%

(Continued)

Table 7.2 (Continued)

B. Commodity price convergence		
Liverpool vs. Chicago, wheat price gap	1870–1912	From 58 to 16%
London vs. Cincinnati, bacon price gap	1870–1913	From 93 to 18%
Philadelphia vs. London, pig iron price gap	1870–1914	From 85 to 19%
London vs. Boston, wool price gap	1870–1915	From 59 to 28%
London vs. Buenos Aires, hides price gap	1870–1916	From 28 to 9%

Source: Own elaboration on Kevin H. O'Rourke and Jeffrey G. Williamson, *Globalization and History: The Evolution of a Nineteenth-Century Atlantic Economy*, MIT Press, Cambridge, MA, 1999.

Table 7.2 Kilometers of railroad track in service, 1870 and 1913

	1870	*1913*
Belgium	2,897	4,676
France	15,544	40,770
Germany	18,876	63,378
Italy	6,429	18,873
United Kingdom	21,500	32,623
Spain	5,295	15,088
Austria–Hungary	6,112	44,800
Russia	10,731	70,156
United States	85,170	400,197
Japan	0	10,570

Source: Own elaboration on B.R. Mitchell, *European Historical Statistics*, Macmillan, London, 1992; B.R. Mitchell, *International Historical Statistics: Africa and Asia*, Macmillan, London, 1982; B.R. Mitchell, *Historical Statistics: The Americas and Australasia*, Macmillan, London, 1993.

8 Technology and organization

Technologies of the Second Industrial Revolution

New transportation and communication systems rapidly set off the transformation of entire sectors of the economy toward the end of the 1800s. First, they were a success in commercial distribution. In fact, in the last decades of the nineteenth century new sales vendors took the place of traditional traders. Department stores started to appear in the second half of the century and quickly gained popularity thanks to innovations like free admittance, fixed prices, a vast assortment of goods, special sales, and low margins which made it possible for quick turnover of inventory. These new emporiums first became popular in the United States (Wanamaker, Macy, Bloomingdales, Marshall Fields) and then in France (Bon Marché, Le Louvre, Le Printemps, La Samaritaine). By the 1870s they also began to appear in other European nations.

The United States was also the pioneer in two related sectors: mail order sales, as well as retailing chains. The mail order concept was popular in markets far from urban areas; the sector leaders were Montgomery Ward and Sears. They offered a larger range of products than was sold in stores and were able to meet almost all the needs of a rural family. The store chains, which often got their start with foodstuffs, grew quickly starting at the beginning of the twentieth century. These mass retailers grabbed important shares of the market from traditional shops thanks to their economies of scale and diversification. In a short period of time they brought on management teams that focused on purchasing and coordinating distribution among various sales points.

The area where the transportation and communication infrastructure made its biggest impact was in manufacturing. In this era, the birth of large manufacturing firms, over the course of a short period of time, gave a significant push to economic growth in the three most important industrialized nations—the United States, Germany, and Great Britain. At the end of the nineteenth century these three accounted for two-thirds of world industrial production.

The impact that these new networks had on the transformation of the industrial world was even more significant than what occurred in the area of trade. This is due in part to the fact that a large variety of manufacturing processes in sectors like machinery, chemicals, electricity, and electro-chemicals in the 1870s were invented or refined in such a way as to be easily put to use by manufacturing firms. This in turn offered a chance for growth unlike anything previously available for these enterprises. For example, the invention of automatic packaging machinery transformed the food industry and had a similar impact on consumer goods produced by chemical companies. Other new processes became more widely available. For example, distillation was now used by firms that operated in sectors as varied as oil, sugar, vegetable oils, and alcoholic beverages. Important changes took place in firms that produced and assembled interchangeable parts used in manufacturing various types of machinery and even automobiles. The availability of a new and more flexible energy source like electricity made possible interactions between chemicals and metallurgy; this impacted products made on a vast scale such as chlorine and aluminum.

This complex interconnection of innovations, currently defined as the "Second Industrial Revolution," differentiated itself from the previous phase of industrial change by the fact that volumes were significantly increased and the rate of change was much faster. By combining these new technologies to the regularity, greater volume, and increased speed of shipping goods that was made possible by new transportation systems, big manufacturing plants were able to develop new processes, fine-tuning them to produce goods at much lower per unit costs than their small factory competitors. Their competitive advantage was made possible by the pursuit of important economies of scale—due to the reduction of manufacturing or distribution costs thanks to the greater volume—and the associated economies of scope that came about by using a single operating unit that was capable of producing or distributing several different products.

Sectorial dichotomy and the conditions for success

The impact of the technologies of the Second Industrial Revolution differed across industries. It created a deep dichotomy between sectors that was destined to last for all of the twentieth century and it marked a distinction between those areas where the large corporation predominated and the other sectors. Already at the beginning of the twentieth century the biggest firms operating in the United States, Germany, and Great Britain were concentrated in the same sectors where they would remain predominant into the 1970s—food, chemicals, oil, metallurgy, machinery, and transportation vehicles.

In other industries where the mechanization process was simpler and machinery was used to help workers rather than replace them (sectors like clothing, woodworking, textiles, leather goods tanning, saddle making, furniture, construction panels, and printing), neither the quantities produced nor the speed at which they were produced would significantly change. These were, in fact, sectors that were characterized by a high level of manpower and where technology meant the ability to refine or fine-tune the machinery used. But these innovations did not lead to building bigger plants that would allow for the continuous, rapid manufacturing that would lead to large economies of scale. Increasing production in these sectors meant adding more workers and machinery dedicated to the process. In short, it would be necessary to add operators and operating units while reassessing the minimum efficient scale of the machinery. During the twentieth century, industry sectors traditionally characterized by technologies of this type continued to be highly labor intensive and conducted in small- to medium-size plants.

In contrast, in sectors where manufacturers were able to take advantage of the new technologies of the Second Industrial Revolution, very large firms dominated as the introduction of modern manufacturing techniques rapidly spread. This happened especially in industries where a large quantity produced in a single plant was not only possible but, more importantly, necessary. For this type of firm, multiplying its manufacturing capacity yielded lower unit costs obtained through economies of scale. Factories, therefore, started to grow and be structured specifically so as to take advantage of the full potential of the new technologies. Fossil fuels were increasingly used, machinery was improved, and operations were moved into bigger plants with layouts adequate for the new processes.

This transformation was especially notable in the oil industry. In the United States the process of restructuring the industry and constructing refineries that could obtain bigger economies of scale was decisive. An intensive use of energy was involved in introducing distillation through heated steam and high-temperature cracking which then led to the creation of larger size distillers. This, combined with better factory design, enabled petroleum producers to increase both speed and volume of production. In the decade between 1860 and 1870, the fixed costs for constructing a refinery grew from 30–40,000 dollars to almost 60,000 dollars. But the increased costs could still be recovered; in the same period, a refinery went from producing 900 barrels per *week* to 500 barrels per *day*. At the same time, the cost of a barrel dropped from 6 to 3 cents. Similar trends were seen in related industries, including sugar, whiskey, alcohol for industrial use, cottonseed and linseed oils, sulfuric acid, and other chemical products. Each of these industries used distillation and refining processes.

An entrepreneur eager to take advantage of the lower costs made possible by the new mass-production technologies was most likely to make investments in three correlated activities: building new plants at the minimum efficient scale, integrating production and mass distribution, and growing and fine-tuning the management hierarchy operative in its central offices and functional departments.

Necessary investments: production

The first objective that these large corporations sought to achieve was to reach a high level of manufacturing and keep it stable so as to fully exploit economies of scale and diversification. The initial capital investment in these sectors during the Second Industrial Revolution and the fixed costs for operating and maintaining their factories were much higher than in their labor-intensive counterparts. The only way to benefit from these investments was by a full use of the plants. Two considerations were decisive in determining costs and profits. The first was the nature of the manufacturing capacity that was installed and the second was throughput, the quantity of raw materials put into the manufacturing operations in a given amount of time. The only way to take full advantage of the potential cost reduction was by a constant and elevated flow of materials in the plant.

The following two examples demonstrate the importance of pursuing economies of scale and scope, and the impact they could have on unitary costs once investments had been made in reorganizing the production system.

The first concerns the rise of Standard Oil, one of the first modern firms to appear in America, and the transformation that took place in the US oil industry in the last decades of the 1800s. At the beginning of the 1880s, there were 40 firms operating in the oil sector. They worked together in an alliance that gave them the ability to control production. Even though these companies were independent and each was a separate legal and administrative entity, every one of the 40 firms had ties with John D. Rockefeller's Standard Oil Company via exchanges of shares and other financial stratagems. Even though this cartel system allowed these companies to have a monopoly on oil production, in 1882 they decided to formally come together as the Standard Oil Trust. The main advantage of this new organization was that the formation of a trust granted the legal tools necessary for the creation of a centralized office that could focus on rationalizing the sector and taking full advantage of economies of scale. The central office's first task was to decide on a reorganization plan for manufacturing processes based on closing or restructuring some refineries and building new ones. The second job was to coordinate the flow of materials not only within the many refineries but also to determine flows from oil wells to the refineries and then from the latter to the end clients. In a short period of time, the reorganization realized by the trust had practically cut in half the average cost for producing a gallon of kerosene.

While Standard Oil invested in large refineries to take advantage of economies of scale, German dye manufacturers made even bigger investments to take advantage of economies of scope, as well as scale. Bayer, Hoechst, and BASF were the first chemical firms to make the investment necessary to get these cost advantages. By significantly expanding their plants, they were able to use the same system and the same raw materials, together with intermediate chemicals, to manufacture not only hundreds of different dyes but also pharmaceuticals. The pursuit of economies of scale and diversification gave these firms lower unit costs and, as a consequence, allowed them to set lower prices for their products. A new synthetic dye, red alizarin, dropped in price from 270 marks per kilo in 1869 to just 9 marks for the same quantity 17 years later. Similar price reductions were achieved with other dyes.

As shown in these examples, over the course of the 1880s and 1890s, the new technologies of the Second Industrial Revolution in the area of mass production allowed for a net reduction in costs once the size of a plant reached the minimum efficient size. In many industrial branches the volumes produced by a single fast and continuous cycle plant were sufficient and permitted a small number of these plants to satisfy national—or even global—demand. Sectors with these kinds of characteristics quickly became oligopolies, with just a few big firms in competition between themselves on a global basis.

Even if access to these technologies had been available decades earlier, it would have been impossible for these same firms to realize economies of scale and scope in capital-intensive industries. This was due primarily to the fact that only the completion of a modern network of transportation and communication, together with the organizational and technological innovations required for managing an integrated system—all of which appear in the 1870s—allowed for the creation and maintenance of fast, continuous production cycles in some sectors. Clearly, it would not have been possible to achieve a similar outcome if procurement and distribution had continued to operate under the conditions of uncertainty that existed with the unreliable transportation systems before the arrival of the railways.

One important consequence of the magnitude of these investments was their impact on labor organization at the workshop level. No longer could control be delegated to a foreman and remain an unknown for management. At the end of the nineteenth century Frederick W. Taylor's gospel of the "scientific organization" of work was diffused. On the basis of a careful study of the reality of factory manufacturing, Taylor argued that work should be divided into essential tasks. All the organizational know-how was to be collected by management, which could then impose a new and more efficient order on the workers; in this way operational autonomy on the shop floor was eliminated. To make up for dehumanizing the labor process, the worker was to be compensated with the higher salary rendered possible by the additional earnings produced by "scientific organization." As is well known, Taylor's philosophy became a reality with the arrival of the assembly line for automobile production in Henry Ford's factory. The assembly of Ford's Model-T brought higher salaries for workers, but there was also no interference in plant operations by the foremen, the workers, or unions.

Necessary investments: distribution

The investments made in machinery and plants of ample size for large-scale production were not sufficient to guarantee good economic results to big firms. As the history of the first modern large corporations demonstrates, to achieve profitable economies of scale and scope firms could not put off for long adopting a higher level of vertical integration (upstream or downstream) in order to maintain a constant throughput within the manufacturing process. Thus they could avoid obstacles or delays in supplies or distribution that would affect regularity. When the distribution channels that already existed started to become less convenient and showed signs that they were insufficient for selling and distributing large quantities of merchandise made by modern industrial processes, it became necessary to make a significant investment in distribution activities, integrating them vertically.

Before the technologies of the Second Industrial Revolution reigned supreme, the typical intermediary was concerned with commercializing products of many manufacturers. By gathering the merchandise of numerous firms, sellers could count on a greater volume than what a single firm could generate. This allowed distributors, as well, to realize economies of scale and lower per unit costs by handling more than what the single manufacturer could offer. The greater variety of products distributed also allowed intermediaries to foot the cost of marketing and gave them lower distribution costs than those of the manufacturers. Distributors could achieve their own economies of scope by large-scale distribution both on a wholesale as well as a retail basis.

The intermediaries' advantages of scale and scope quickly disappeared as the technologies of the Second Industrial Revolution took hold. On one side, the greater volume produced by firms gave them the same advantages of scale as the retailers. On the other side, some new products required that new structures and special competencies for their marketing and distribution be developed. It was easier for a manufacturer to do this in-house than for retailers to develop a set of similar skills. The ability of intermediaries to distribute a large variety of related products for different entrepreneurs quickly became less important as each firm started to differentiate its products from its competitors. Product characteristics were more personalized and this called for special skills related to how they were sold and installed. In some cases, they also needed special structures for transportation or storage or even, at times, special credit plans for their purchase.

In the beginning, trade intermediaries were forced to cover the high costs of building these structures necessary for the distribution of products and they hired employees with the applicable technical skills. However, the new structures and skills could only be used for a single line of products and this made the traders more dependent on the manufacturers for whom they were distributors. In short, the advantage once held by distributors moved from retailers back to the manufacturing entrepreneurs who could count on their improved know-how of the techniques, tools, and services needed for marketing and distributing their products. Marketing and distributing these new products called for greater investments and ended up discouraging intermediaries while, at the same time, giving incentives to manufacturers to take over the expenditures themselves.

The case of machinery firms illustrates well what happened in many capital-intensive sectors. The machinery that was produced in the last decades of the 1800s was in fact new and relatively complex compared with its predecessors; for the first time specialized services of marketing were necessary. Their complexity and innovative features necessitated that the sales process start with a demonstration. After the product was sold, it had to be installed, was subject to periodic maintenance, and, in the event of a problem, would need to be repaired by a specialized technician. Given the high prices of these machines, the purchaser often needed financing. While manufacturers had the resources and skills to offer all these services for selling their own products, wholesalers were seldom in a similar situation to take upon themselves the costs of demonstrating, maintaining, repairing, and even offering credit to purchase this specialized machinery.

In the United States, sewing machine manufacturers were among the first to integrate into the distribution system. At the beginning they had relied on independent agents who were in charge of marketing in a specific area, working full time, and being paid a small salary supplemented by commissions. This system had two main limitations. First, the vendors usually had limited skills in operating the sewing machines; often they were neither able to explain how the machine worked to a potential buyer nor, when necessary, were they able to service and repair the machines. The second limitation was that vendors could not offer special payment terms to potential buyers of a relatively expensive machine; many potential clients were interested in buying some type of an installment plan. As an alternative plan, the majority of manufacturers began to open their own wholly owned and managed sales points to give clients all the services they sought. By the 1850s, Singer had opened its own showrooms. At each sales point there was a female employee who would demonstrate how the machine worked, a technician who took care of repairing and servicing sewing machines, a vendor responsible for the actual sales work, and a commercial director who negotiated payment conditions with customers and oversaw the other store employees. Manufacturers of typewriters, photo cameras, and cash registers quickly followed the example of Singer and its industry colleagues, choosing to concentrate their stores in highly populated areas.

The decision to incorporate distribution internally had another advantage for these companies: a constant flow of information regarding customers' likes, preferences, and needs. By investing in distribution functions, the structures of these firms underwent a transformation. In a short period of time they needed to hire employees to take orders from customers, oversee advertising, organize product deliveries, coordinate installation, maintenance, and repairs of the products, and plan financing programs for customers.

The effects of integrating distribution's activities could be seen in corporate strategies as regarded vertical integration upstream or improvements in organizing the procurement process. When a large corporation decided to create a national— or even global—distribution network, it also needed to organize an equally extensive supply system. Maintaining a high volume of manufacturing required a stable and constant supply of raw materials and the ability to coordinate production flows within the various plants. Large corporations created centralized offices with specialized personnel responsible for procurements. These buyers would find sources for raw materials and negotiate requirements, prices, and delivery dates with suppliers. They also worked closely with other employees who oversaw the logistics and were responsible for shipping goods to various plants. Specializing supply activities by single product lines was as important and complex as the distribution function. There were complex steps necessary in working with raw materials in corporations that transformed them into final products like cigarettes, distilled beverages, canned vegetables and meats, cheeses, and chocolate confections. As soon as the raw materials for these perishables were received, they required adequate warehousing facilities where they could be stored in appropriate conditions until the firm made sure that they flowed toward the plants where they would be transformed into a finished product. If the system was successful, the company that purchased large quantities of semifinished goods could lower costs significantly.

In this way the upstream integration toward suppliers and the downstream integration toward distribution allowed businesses to eliminate the middlemen and to assure that the production process would not be interrupted. They could thus avoid the substantial economic losses they might have experienced in their supply and distribution functions.

Necessary investments: managerial hierarchy

By investing in production systems that were large enough to generate cost advantages and, at the same time, setting up networks for marketing, distribution, and purchasing for single product lines, big businesses became significantly and increasingly complex in a relatively short period of time. How could the new large corporations effectively oversee production and distribution activities, coordinate incoming and outgoing flows of goods, and adequately allocate resources for future production and distribution? It was necessary to make a third decisive investment by hiring and training mid-level managers who had professional capabilities in these fields. Unlike economies of scale that were strictly a technology-related phenomenon, the need to maintain a high and constant flow of production in a big corporation required a buildup of managerial capabilities. Know-how and teamwork were some of the fundamental components in creating a group of employees inside the organization who could best take advantage of the potential associated with the Second Industrial Revolution's technological innovations.

While the success of the entrepreneur of the first wave of industrialization came from his ability to control the workforce in the factory and to coordinate activities with a technical expert or two as well as a couple of talented vendors, the critical component in the Second Industrial Revolution was the entrepreneur's ability to create and control an extensive managerial hierarchy. Here managers, within a framework defined by the entrepreneur, enjoyed decision-making autonomy in a good-size segment of the firm's activities: we can group these activities under the acronym POSDCORB, *planning, organizing, staffing, directing, coordinating, reporting, budgeting*. Already in the years between the 1800s and the 1900s, some managers introduced innovations in their fields. Albert Fink, for example, a manager in the railroad industry in the 1870s, perfected a system for separating fixed costs from variable ones. A few decades later in 1914, a young manager at DuPont, F. Donaldson Brown, invented a concept ("return on investment") that would play a vital role in the strategic decision-making process in corporations for decades to come.

In the beginning, managerial hierarchies were organized on the basis of departments that were responsible for specific functions. In charge of the departments was an intermediate level of managers responsible for coordinating and controlling the actions of the lower level managers, creating incentives for the latter to attain better results. These lower level managers oversaw the various operating units of the firm—plants, sales and purchasing offices, research laboratories—by supervising the workers who operated in the various units. Functional departments were organized as *line and staff* activities as described earlier when we examined the large railroad corporations. Line managers had executive powers and were busy with the activities related to manufacturing goods. Staff managers, instead, worked behind the scenes and performed functions such as bookkeeping and accounting, quality control, warehouse coordination, and personnel management.

For the first time, specific departments dedicated to production and sales were created, as were departments for procurement and supplies. These were followed by the formation of other, smaller departments responsible for various functions. One of the most important departments was dedicated to financial control. It coordinated the distribution of financial resources among various units while also assuring that information flowed smoothly within the company. It was the flow of information that gave management the tools necessary for monitoring the units' results and made it possible to shift resources between units as needed. In order to do their job better, employees in the office of financial control invented and adopted innovative accounting and verification procedures. They took over responsibility for financial reports to be provided to the outside world. Obtaining new capital and paying interest or dividends on shares were some of their tasks. The research and development department also took on an important role, especially in companies that operated in technologically advanced sectors where laboratories were put in place to guarantee an accurate control of manufacturing processes and to assure constant product quality. Some of the other departments created in this period included those dedicated to traffic, legal issues, real estate, and eventually personnel and public relations.

A classic example of this type of organizational form was the American chemical company, DuPont, which had a Central Office that worked together with staff in focusing on corporate strategy and supervision. The single functions (finance, sales, production, purchasing, R&D, traffic) were overseen by the departments under which the operating units were gathered. Top management supervised the entire ensemble, the middle managers oversaw the various departments, and the lower level managers were responsible for the operating units. The variations on this kind of a structure were many. Unlike the first American firms based on functions, Germany's Thyssen, for example, expected managers of the various departments that were organized on product lines to do most of the marketing tasks as well as those related to production. Managers in this firm enjoyed a great deal of independence. The guiding principle of founder August Thyssen was that, by decentralizing authority, the firm could delegate to managers as much control as possible while keeping overall supervision centralized.

In some integrated industrial corporations, the decision-making nucleus was made up of the heads of the principal departments, the president, and, at times, a full-time head of the board of directors. In the United States, the combination was known as the Executive Committee of the Board, while in Germany it was called the *Vorstand*. In Great Britain this core group became known as the Managing or Executive Directors. Even before the onset of World War I, major industrial corporations in the United States and Europe were thus putting into place managerial hierarchies that would allow them to keep daily activities of production and distribution under control. The central, decision-making organization determined the allocation of funds for future ventures.

This was not an easy passage as it required a high degree of power sharing inside the corporation and hence within the nation's capitalistic system. As a result, the firm became a new kind of political entity as well. On one side there were strong financial demands that called for an extensive group of shareholders who were interested in dividends. On the other hand, at the highest levels of top management, there was the need to use the firm's profits to fund expansion. Systems that were relatively autocratic came to know (often with much resistance) a gradual and painful process of sharing power.

The new dynamics of competition

The modern industrial corporation of our era has its origins in the years bridging the nineteenth and twentieth centuries. It appeared in firms where the entrepreneurs decided to invest in manufacturing plants that were big enough to achieve economies of scale and scope, in distribution systems and specialized workers for single product lines, and in a managerial organization that was able to coordinate all these activities. The pioneers of these expensive and risky investments frequently acquired significant competitive advantages, often referred to as the advantages of the "first movers." In order to compete with a first mover, potential rivals were obliged in the next decades to build plants of similar dimensions, to make investments in distribution and research, and to hire and form a managerial hierarchy. Still, by constructing factories of the size that would achieve economies of scale and scope, these companies found themselves with excess production; they had soon to embark on a plan of stealing clients from the first movers.

The dynamics of competition were thus ever bitterer in the period between the end of the 1800s and the first decades of the twentieth century. There was a progressive saturation of national markets that stimulated corporations to pursue various new strategies of growth. This tension continued for much of the twentieth century as firms added new units according to the plans used in the past or even inventing new models of industrial organization. In some cases these choices were driven by defensive reasons, for example when a company decided to integrate horizontally so as to protect investments already made; the firm could acquire or merge with other firms that in large part utilized the same manufacturing processes to produce the same goods that were destined for the same markets. Other firms opted for vertical integration, bringing together units involved in the activity either upstream or downstream in the manufacturing process and competing on the basis of their superior technology, organization, and products. Still other firms sought to utilize their own resources and, above all, their specific organizational abilities to enter new markets, undertake new activities, or push into new geographical areas.

Further reading

A.D. Chandler, Jr., *Strategy and Structure: Chapters in the History of the American Industrial Enterprise*, MIT Press, Cambridge, MA, 1962.
A.D. Chandler, Jr., *The Visible Hand: The Managerial Revolution in American Business*, Belknap Press, Cambridge, MA, 1977.

A.D. Chandler, Jr., *Scale and Scope: The Dynamics of Industrial Capitalism*, Harvard University Press, Cambridge, MA, 1990.

J.P. Hull, "From Rostow to Chandler to You: How Revolutionary Was the Second Industrial Revolution?," *Journal of European Economic History*, Spring 1996, pp. 191–208.

D. Landes, *The Unbound Prometheus: Technological Change and Industrial Development in Western Europe from 1750 to the Present*, Cambridge University Press, Cambridge, 1969.

P. Scranton, *Endless Novelty: Specialty Production and American Industrialization, 1865–1925*, Princeton University Press, Princeton, NJ, 1997.

Appendix

Table 8.1 Industrial distribution of the 200 largest industrial firms in the United States, Great Britain, Germany, France, and Japan: World War I

Group	Industry	USA (1917)	UK (1919)	Germany (1913)	France (1912)	Japan (1918)
20	Food	30	63	26	20	31
21	Tobacco	6	3	1	1	1
22	Textiles	5	26	15	8	54
23	Apparel	3	1	1	3	2
24	Lumber	3	0	1	1	3
25	Furniture	0	0	0	0	0
26	Paper	5	4	4	3	12
27	Printing and publishing	2	5	0	7	1
28	Chemicals	20	11	30	28	23
29	Petroleum	22	3	5	2	6
30	Rubber	5	3	4	3	0
31	Leather	4	0	2	3	4
32	Stone, clay, and glass	5	2	7	8	16
33	Primary metals	29	35	49	36	21
34	Fabricated metals	8	2	5	4	4
35	Nonelectrical machinery	20	8	25	9	4
36	Electrical machinery	5	11	7	14	7
37	Transportation equipment	26	20	16	39	9
38	Instruments	1	0	2	9	1
39	Miscellaneous	1	3	0	2	1
	Total	200	200	200	200	200

Source: Adapted from Alfred D. Chandler, Jr. and Takashi Hikino, "The Large Industrial Enterprise and the Dynamics of Modern Economic Growth," in Alfred D. Chandler, Jr., Franco Amatori, and Takashi Hikino (eds.), *Big Business and the Wealth of Nations*, Cambridge University Press, Cambridge, 1997, p. 32.

Table 8.2 Founding dates of some 1994 Fortune 500 companies, 1880s–1920s

Founded in the 1880s	Founded in the 1890s	Founded in the 1900s	Founded in the 1910s	Founded in the 1920s
Eastman Kodak	General Electric	Weyerhaeuser	Black & Decker	Chrysler
Chiquita Brands Int.	Knight Ridder	USX	IBM	Time-Warner
Johnson & Johnson	Ralston Purina	Ford Motor	Merrill Lynch	Marriott Corp.
Coca-Cola	Reebok Int.	Gillette	Safeway	Walt Disney
Westinghouse Electric	Harris Corporation	3M	Boeing	Delta Airlines
Sears Roebuck	Pepsi Co.	United Parcel Service	Cummins Engine	Ace Hardware
Avon Products	Goodyear	General Motors	Reynolds Metals	Fruit of the Loom
Hershey Foods		McGraw Hill		Northwest Air

Source: Selected from Harris Corporation, "Founding Dates of the 1994 Fortune 500 US Companies," *Business History Review*, 70 (Spring 1996), pp. 69–90.

9 National patterns

National variations

By the beginning of the twentieth century, new technologies operating at high capital intensity and producing large volumes transformed the economies of several countries. Some existing sectors were completely revolutionized and, in other cases, entirely new industries were developed.

The United States and Western Europe were the first to experience the revolution that in the following few decades would extend around the world. The large corporations appeared with significant differences and timing among nations. The United States, well endowed with raw materials and a population that continued to grow, became the leader in taking advantage of the new opportunities brought about by new technologies. Before World War I broke out, the large corporation was common in North America, as was rapid economic growth. At Queen Victoria's Great Exhibition in London in 1851, the United States did not even fill the space it was assigned. However, by 1913, the United States was providing 36 percent of global industrial production while Germany supplied 16 percent and England only 14 percent. The European nations were significantly smaller than the United States, their resources were less abundant, their markets much narrower. This often meant that the development of new corporate organizations was much slower and was taking place in a smaller number of industries. There were exceptions. In some of the most advanced European nations, such as Germany, firms in many sectors were not far behind the United States. Indeed, in some cases they even surpassed the US situation.

The large corporation in advanced nations

In order to thoroughly understand the differences with which the three most advanced nations—the United States, the United Kingdom, and Germany—took advantage of the new opportunities brought about by the Second Industrial Revolution, there are several intertwined factors that seem especially pertinent to a comparison of entrepreneurial actions. The principal ones include market characteristics, governmental regulation of economic competition, social attitudes toward big business, and the cultural resources available to corporations.

The United States

On the eve of World War I, large corporations in the United States had developed in all sectors—from consumer goods to industrial products—where technological development made it possible. In most cases, the characteristics of these firms were very different from those of previous forms of enterprise. First of all, they were based on stock shares and not partnerships as was common in the past. Second, these companies tended to integrate a growing number of activities inside the firm, pursuing horizontal expansion as well as upstream and downstream integration. Many became multinationals. The management of these new large corporations was different. For the first time, it was possible to note a distinct separation between ownership and control in the largest companies. In this period, the panorama was not uniform: families did neither disappear as participants in the governance of US corporations, nor was there a complete divorce of ownership from control. But a progressive shift from a "personal capitalism" to "managerial capitalism" (where ownership was beginning to separate from control in the largest enterprises) was clearly emerging.

Boards of directors enlisted members from both within as well as outside the firm. The outsiders represented ownership and they were present on the board in larger numbers but they did not have the time, the information, or the skills necessary for managing the company on a daily basis. Instead, they relied on the inside directors who were salaried managers present in the firm on a full-time basis. These managers often made not only strategic decisions but also decisions regarding their own succession in the company.

In parallel with these developments was an incredible transformation of the size of firms in America. In the mid-nineteenth century, it was rare that a US firm had more than a million dollars of capitalization or more than 500 employees. In 1901, United States Steel Corporation became the first "billion dollar" company with its 1.4 billion dollars of capitalization and more than 100,000 employees. It accounted for 7 percent of Gross National Product (GNP). Some of the giants to emerge by the early 1900s included Standard Oil, Remington (office machinery), American Tobacco, DuPont (chemicals), Singer (sewing machines), and the food manufacturers, Heinz and Campbell.

The market in the United States was as large as that in Continental Europe and was extremely dynamic due to the exponential population growth and the increased power of the American consumer. The other determining factors for the growth and consolidation of large corporations were public opinion and the choices adopted by legislators in the United States. The country was about to become the first nation of mass consumption, and Americans favorably viewed the improvements in material comforts and living standards brought on by the growth of big business. At the same time, however, they also showed signs of mistrust (or even, at times, true hostility) as big business shook up traditional ways of manufacturing and distribution. The large corporation also threatened some of the country's fundamental values such as faith in free competition and the conviction that in the race for wealth and power all started from the same position of strength.

In the 1880s, new interest groups became vociferous in their opposition to giant combines. The impact that new technologies had on manufacturing processes had brought about an imbalance between supply and demand. In most cases, this situation was exacerbated by an overall drop in prices that in turn pushed big corporations to agree on ways of controlling the market. The most vocal in the so-called "antitrust" battle were small entrepreneurs. Their most combatant group was made up of merchants as they often played an important role in the small cities and towns that made up the America of the Progressive Era. For these traders, both the growth of mass retailing and the marketing advances made by large industrial firms were serious threats. Without a doubt these lobbies achieved a certain level of success. In 1911, for the first time the courts chose to break up large corporations such as Standard Oil and American Tobacco.

After a decade in which the control of big business had been at the center of political discussion, this topic became the key issue in the Presidential election of 1912. Two years later, the winner—Woodrow Wilson—convinced Congress to pass the Clayton Antitrust Act and to create the Federal Trade Commission. These were two important tools for reinforcing earlier legislation that banned intercompany agreements.

However, it is impossible to ignore a true "American paradox" when we talk about regulating competition between firms. On the one hand, the political forces and the courts in the United States were intent on limiting the growth of large corporations, but the reality is that antitrust legislation produced the opposite result. The legal prohibition of firms pursuing loose combinations (i.e., price-fixing and cartel agreements) brought about a wave of mergers (i.e., tight combinations). This process of industrial concentration had its start in the 1880s but reached its boom years the following decade. Every year between 1895 and 1903 an average of 300 firms were absorbed by other companies.

During this period, new and giant corporate entities were formed that were different—often superior—in productive and organizational terms. One of the effects was that they were able to put into the market products with lower unit costs and lower prices. As we can now see, the large corporation is essentially a bureaucratic organization inside which a personal or family domain is obliged to coexist or even to cede control to a structure governed by universalistic criteria. In the period between the end of the nineteenth and the beginning of the twentieth centuries, the sociocultural environment in the United States appeared to be particularly favorable to this development. The transformation involved a passage from groups of small dimensions, with local perspectives, and capable of regulating themselves in informal ways, to complex organizations of national dimensions with a formally defined structure. The emergence of an authority based on precise responsibilities and decisional powers grounded in objective criteria is a common feature in the evolution of many different institutions, including trade unions, political parties, lobbies, and professional associations.

All of these modern institutions, like big business, arose in the four decades between 1880 and 1920. They can be seen as the successful attempts made by America's urban middle class and working class to establish a new order based on efficiency, continuity, and systematic controls. The effects spilled over into all of American society, resulting in a reorientation in this direction, a process that could not be changed even by a dramatic political election.

If big businesses were able to grow and establish deep roots in the United States, it was due also to the educational and training system in place. Higher education in America was quick to adapt to the needs of industry. Prior to 1880, colleges were still primarily focused on training middle- and upper-class Americans for citizenship. Only a few focused on preparing the technicians necessary for constructing railroads. Beginning in the late nineteenth century, however, schools such as the Massachusetts Institute of Technology (MIT), Purdue, and Cornell instituted new courses to prepare mechanical, electrical, and chemical engineers. MIT played an especially important role given its close ties with DuPont, Standard Oil, General Electric, and General Motors. In addition to these centers of high-level technical training, business schools became important players. Here, students became familiar with the strategies and the management practices of big integrated business groups. The first of these business schools was the Wharton School of Finance and Commerce, established in 1881 at the University of Pennsylvania. Twenty-seven years later, Harvard University launched its Business School, and by 1914 there were 30 business schools in the United States, turning out about 10,000 graduates each year.

The antitrust legislation reflected America's faith in competition and mistrust of concentrating power, but the rise of big business represented the even stronger desire for economic growth. At the eve of World War I, in the United States, the structure of new sectors—with few exceptions—was oligopolistic, that is, dominated by three to five very large companies. Monopoly was rare, as was so-called "pure competition" in industry. Within the oligopolies, new firms of national dimensions continued to compete on functional and strategic levels for a share of the market and the resulting profits. The emergence of large corporations naturally altered the impact that the smaller firms, in terms of output, could make on the country's wealth. But small firms did not become obsolete in the United States; a number of them were able to find a place in these newly concentrated markets, successfully coexisting with the biggest corporations. In an economy that was driven by big business, opportunities in some industrial fields still existed for companies of much smaller dimensions. The principal advantage of the latter was their flexibility, which allowed them to manufacture goods with excellent characteristics of differentiation and to restructure their production lines more quickly so as to respond immediately to shifting market and consumer needs. Small firms were also able to stay in the forefront of many of the commercial and service sectors. In the United States of that period, the growth of big business went hand in hand with an increase in the number of small firms.

Germany

Prior to 1914, large corporations in Germany showed characteristics fairly similar to their American counterparts. But there were also some clear differences. Among these, owners in Germany continued to exercise a greater say in management decisions and continued to make the investments required for expansion. German owners were also attentive to making an extensive and well-designed management hierarchy into a reality. In Germany, as in the United States, public opinion was favorable toward large corporations. Furthermore, thanks to the long tradition of an efficient bureaucracy that served the State, it was easier for German entrepreneurs to coexist with management. The expansion of firms, the tendency to organize on the basis of cartels and trade associations, and the close ties between industry and the banks (which brought about the inclusion of more nonfounder members in the boards of directors) created some unique complexities for the heads of the big corporations. Management methods based on family traditions or passed on from person to person were no longer adequate for expanding firms and, because of the greater need for coordination and efficiency, could actually become counterproductive. The systematic development of management on a vast scale was a timely response to the new economic and technological climate that these firms faced.

But, unlike what occurred in the United States, in Germany the large corporation did not take on a leadership role in all sectors in which the Second Industrial Revolution made it possible. As had happened in America, the first large corporations were in the railroad sector and then the phenomenon extended to other industries such as electromechanics, metallurgy, chemicals, and heavy machinery. In the area of consumer goods, however, large corporations were virtually nonexistent, given the lower per capita income (when compared with the United States or the United Kingdom) as well as the fact that British and American firms quickly occupied the field.

By contrast, beginning in the 1880s, German electromechanic manufacturers Siemens and Allgemeine Elektricitäts-Gesellschaft (AEG) joined together with General Electric and Westinghouse in America to dominate the sector at a worldwide level for more than 60 years. At the start of the twentieth century, the two German firms controlled 70 percent of their own national market. The situation was similar for the chemical industry where, by 1913, three firms (BASF, Bayer, and Hoechst) not only dominated the national market but also manufactured between 75 and 80 percent of world demand for synthetic dyes. Germany was predominant in the heavy machinery industry, which called for a high level of capitalization and frequently experienced a problematical cash-flow management, characteristics that help explain the significant role of the many "universal banks." Indeed, these banks owned shares in a number of the companies capable of exploiting the new technologies.

In Germany, early on the relationship between firms and the universal banks was very different than the situation in the United States or Great Britain. German banks played a determining role in national economic growth. On the basis of their assessments, money would flow into investments in specific companies or specific industry sectors. As a shareholder, the bank, which could usually count on a well-informed staff in the sectors where it had invested, exercised a bigger role in the management of firms. In fact, representatives of the German *Grossbanken* (big banks) took a much greater part than their American and British counterparts in decision-making at the highest levels of the new industrial firms. This can be attributed to two fundamental differences. First, as universal banks, German financial institutions were much larger (both in capital and in number of employees) than American institutions. Just as important, because of the bigger role they played in financing firms, German banks were able to acquire more opportunities to participate in decision-making at the highest levels. Eventually, the German and Anglo-American relationships converged. By the early part of the twentieth century, the leading German firms in industries like metallurgy, machinery, and chemicals had grown to the point where they could finance on their own future growth. At the same time, the increasing complexity of managing problems related to production, marketing, and new product development reduced the role that bankers could play in these firms.

The dimensions and the characteristics of both internal and foreign markets, the attitudes of political authorities toward big business, and the resources that were available were some of the determining elements in the creation of Germany's system of big business. Unlike the United States, where the internal market was so large and dynamic that it was the principal target of firms, German manufactures understood that foreign markets played a critical role in their success. One of the principal motors of the growth of German firms was exports, especially of chemicals and machinery. They found new markets in the countries of southern and central Eastern Europe. There, starting around 1870, some areas (even though urban population levels and per capita income were not high) embarked on a process of industrialization that involved factories for the manufacture of textiles or metal mechanics. There were also increased needs for networks of electricity, railways, and telegraphs. In 1913, Germany was the largest exporter in industries such as chemicals (28.5 percent of world exports), electromechanics (35 percent), and industrial machinery (29 percent). The combination of an internal market and growing markets abroad offered sufficient stimulus to German entrepreneurs to make heavy investments in innovating and growing to more significant dimensions.

In Germany, there was no pressure from the government or from the courts on how big business operated. The situation was so different from America that, over a period of three decades starting in 1875, the number of German cartels regulating markets grew from 4 to 106 (1890), then almost doubled to 205 in 1896, finally reaching a hefty 385 in 1905. In fact, there was no specific legislation against monopolies or monopolistic policies in Germany. In 1897, practically in the same period that the US supreme court confirmed that the Sherman Act (which made agreements between firms illegal) was constitutional, Germany's High Court (*Reichsgericht*) produced a sentence confirming that contractual agreements on prices, production, and market shares could be sanctioned by the courts. They were, the court said, advantageous not only for those who had reached the agreements but also for the common good. This full legal recognition of agreements limited the influence of mergers and acquisitions in Germany. The process of combination was certainly more limited than what occurred in the merger movement of the United States. Cartels characterized the most dynamic sectors of the German economy. They did not eliminate competition between firms; instead, they simply changed the rules of the game. In Germany, the participation of its largest corporations in cartels did not mean they sacrificed efficiency. Companies that took part in an agreement on prices, for example, had strong incentives to pursue economies of scale and diversification, to search out better, more efficient operations, and to integrate vertically in order to reduce those unit costs that would allow them to increase the distance between the prices established by the cartel and their own manufacturing costs. Some studies have also shown how cartels brought a positive outcome in the area of innovation, by stabilizing volatile markets and thus allowing firms to invest heavily in research and development.

In the case of Germany, it is important to recognize the significance of the growth of excellent institutions of higher education. They represented an important component of business success in several industries. Starting at the end of the nineteenth century, Germany was home to some of the best science departments in the world and German universities became important research centers in science and technology, much more so than their American and British counterparts. The State played a determining role in this phenomenon since early on German leaders understood the importance of investing resources in the links between science and industry. Also important for the country's rapid and solid corporate growth was the age-old existence of a highly trained class of artisans who made it possible to shift toward a relatively flexible factory production with limited costs for training and supervising the workers. In addition, the presence of some sectors of entrepreneurial associations allowed for the development of long-term growth plans and strategies coordinated with public policies as well as negotiated with other industry sectors. These associations also played an important role in coordinating policies among different regions of the country. For example, local chambers of commerce were important not only for their worker-training programs but also for the contribution they made in the formulation and implementation of basic standards that could be extended to cover all regions of the country. Thanks to its ability to bring together the interests of industry, the universities, and the professional associations in a context that was open to new technologies and their practical applications, Germany placed itself at the forefront in promoting a new middle class made up of engineers, technician-bureaucrats, and researchers. This new middle class successfully guided Germany's process of industrialization and economic modernization.

As was the case in the United States, the affirmation of the large corporation as a critical protagonist of the German economy changed, but did not destroy, the small firms, which continued to play an important role in the economy. Many small- and medium-size German firms continued to be extremely dynamic and, thanks to significant artisan skills and the support of local associations, they quickly identified highly promising manufacturing niches. In most cases, these local firms were family owned and diverse in their activities.

Great Britain

The advent of new technologies of mass production and the challenge of increasing international competition had a strong impact on the birthplace of the First Industrial Revolution, Great Britain. In the years immediately preceding World War I, firms such as Dunlop (rubber), Courtaulds (synthetic fibers), and Pilkington (glass) had successfully integrated manufacturing with a good marketing network and thus were already competing on an international level. More than a century of industrialization had made the United Kingdom a nation that was very different from the others. The constraints as well as the opportunities that British entrepreneurs faced were different from those of their peers in Germany and the United States. For this reason, large corporations in England took on some characteristics different from what has been described so far; they were, for instance, especially concentrated in consumer good sectors where, in some cases, they decided not to make investments in mass production, mass distribution, and management. In the years bridging the nineteenth and twentieth centuries, big business in the United Kingdom differentiated itself by limited vertical integration and, in the majority of cases, by the persistence of a good number of family businesses where there was little room to build up an extensive managerial hierarchy.

Although the high number of family businesses among the biggest firms in Great Britain is a fact, not all business historians agree that its capitalism should any more be defined as "personal" or "family" than the German or American versions of the same era. Furthermore, it is not easy to demonstrate that family-owned businesses had lower levels of efficiency than those with professional managers at the helm. If the persistence of the families is often considered synonymous with industry's backwardness when facing the imperatives of new technologies, it should also be remembered that the context that characterized Great Britain at the end of the century made it more rational for entrepreneurs to adopt the US paradigm of the triple investment. The path that Britain's large corporations usually followed was, in some ways, less efficient. It did not allow them to take full advantage of the economic potentials offered by the new technologies. Nevertheless, it was probably the best choice for many British entrepreneurs who needed to combine the new economic context with the material and immaterial structures they had inherited from the First Industrial Revolution. The obstacles and the opportunities that British entrepreneurs faced included the characteristics of their markets, the attitudes of the public, and the positions taken by their legislators as regards large corporations and the education system.

Overall, English firms seemed to enjoy the advantage of vast internal and international markets. In 1870, Great Britain had one of the world's highest per capita incomes as well as the highest level of urbanization. The ten million inhabitants of the "golden quadrilateral" (London, Cardiff, Glasgow, and Edinburgh) made up the first "consumer society." At the same time, between 1870 and the outbreak of World War I, British exports were almost 30 percent of GNP. However, looking at this data more closely, we discover that for British firms, unlike their American and German counterparts, neither internal market demand nor that coming from clients abroad stimulated them to take advantage of the new opportunities presented by the Second Industrial Revolution. The internal market, for example, was less dynamic because, after a century of unparalleled growth, increases in per capita income in Great Britain had begun to slow down, especially when contrasted to that of the United States or Germany in the same era. Equally significant was the fact that Britain continued to export products typical of the *First* Industrial Revolution. In the early 1900s, textiles made up 38 percent of exports, 14 percent was iron and steel, machinery represented merely 7 percent, and coal corresponded to 10 percent. When compared to the United States or Germany, Britain's socioeconomic structure also failed to pursue the large corporation based on the American model either economically interesting or even rational. Back in 1870, England had completed its transformation into an urban-industrial society. While significant parts of the American population moved further and further from urban areas, forcing US corporations to create their own marketing networks, in the mid-nineteenth century, the majority of Britain's inhabitants already resided in urban centers that were supported by infrastructures, which had been developed at the same time as industry. This made the choice to internalize distribution within the company an impractical option. Furthermore, English cities were not in need of expansion or being rebuilt as was the case with urban centers in Germany, where a rush to grow made its cities desperate for metal structures and electrical plants and therefore among the best clients for modern industries. It seems likely that given these conditions, had British entrepreneurs chosen to follow the path pursued by American or German corporations in the same sectors, they would have seen their costs *increase* rather than decrease in the short term.

The reasons why large British corporations were different were not limited to those mentioned. Another difference had to do with regulation. In Great Britain, agreements controlling competition among firms were entirely effective. The law could neither sanction them nor place obstacles in their way. This attitude of "benign neglect" was prevalent because the large corporation was not excessively disruptive for either traditional commerce or for small firms, thanks to the agreements that actually assured that even the *least* efficient manufacturer could survive—and thrive. Without a constituency that believed its rights to be under attack, there was little reason to adopt antitrust policies. The same wave of mergers that arose in the United States also appeared in England, but the number of firms, as well as the amount of capital involved, was far less. At its peak in 1899, in the United States, there were 979 firms that merged with combined capital (in pounds sterling) of 400 million while 255 English firms merged for a total of 22 million pounds. The most significant difference, however, was the kind of organization that emerged from the mergers. In the United States, most mergers brought about a centrally organized managerial hierarchy and the development of new organizational abilities. In the United Kingdom, the companies that resulted from a merger remained federations of firms, smaller than their American counterparts. They were able to establish new forms of cooperation (e.g., in purchasing or advertising) but openly declared their objective was to assure each member firm would keep its market share and absolute managerial independence. English mergers did not need the skyscrapers that housed the extensive management structures of some of the reorganized American corporations; they were happy with a much smaller headquarters where the leaders of the associated companies could meet a few times a year so as to establish prices, subdivide production quantities, and verify that the agreement was respected by all partners.

The relationship between large corporations and the educational system was also quite different in Great Britain, where institutions of higher education were much slower to respond to the needs of the country's new industrial firms. In 1910, there were slightly more than 1,100 students enrolled in engineering programs in England, whereas the same specialization in Germany had more than 16,000 first-year students. Though some steps were taken to create universities that could respond to the technical necessities of British business, little or nothing was done regarding managerial training. Some have attributed this and other aspects of the British situation to a profound revolt against industrialized society on the part of the intellectual elite as well as many segments of general public opinion. However, the empirical evidence today is not strong enough to support such a theory. Certainly, in British family businesses, the owners were reluctant to share or cede corporate control and, as a consequence, the investments they made in their companies were substantially smaller than what occurred in similar firms in America or Germany. Third-generation English entrepreneurs also had a form of cultural resistance to the technological and organizational needs of the new industrial revolution. Combined, these different factors perhaps get us close to explaining why big business was managed differently than the large corporations in America and Germany.

If we compare the success obtained by big business in the United States and Germany, the situation in Britain after 1880 can be described as in part a story of missed opportunities or delays that eventually, with much suffering, were overcome. Emblematic of this interpretation is the synthetic dyes sector. In 1870, England seemed to possess all the prerequisites for large-scale development and domination of the industry on an international basis. It was an Englishman, William Perkin, who invented the first artificial colorings in 1856; the country was blessed with large supplies of coal (the first raw material for producing dyes), had an enormous textile industry that offered the best potential market, and had no bottlenecks for securing capital or technical skills. Yet it was the large German corporations who took on the role as first movers in the last decades of the 1800s, completely updating their plants and investing in an extensive marketing network. Over time, the British experienced similar defeats in industries such as metallurgy, heavy machinery, and the manufacture of mass-produced light machinery. The consequences were fierce and unsettling for the nation's economy.

Although Britain thus fell behind the United States and Germany, the British remained strong in a number of sectors, including international finance that would become very important to its economy late in the twentieth century. The British were also far superior in many cases to levels of performance in other European nations or even around the world. Great Britain's GNP remained slightly greater than Germany's or France's GNP up to almost the 1950s. Although falling behind in heavy industry, Britain was the first (and the fastest) nation to support the birth of large corporations in service industries such as international and retail trade. It was also one of the major promoters of the multinational enterprise, a field in which the British showed themselves to be capable of developing the right set of organizational skills for managing complex and diversified activities. In addition, in Britain the system of big business (with its successes and failures) operated side by side with a lively mixture of small- and medium-size firms that in some fields, such as textiles, gave birth to extensive and profitable industrial districts.

The latecomers

Because of the technological levels achieved by the most advanced nations, those who decided to embark upon the path to industrialization in the last two decades of the 1800s were obliged to weave through a mixture of strong competitors from the "First" and the "Second" Industrial Revolutions. This inevitably brought about a close association between business and the State. The impact of capital-intensive sectors, inadequate accumulation, and scarcity of the sociocultural resources necessary for modernizing of the economy ended up making the government's role much more than simply regulating competition. The State supported big business with protectionism, subsidies, commissions, and rescues. In some cases, over time the State itself was transformed into the role of entrepreneur; as a result, a significant change in corporate strategy came about. While with the experiences in England and Germany, and especially in the paradigmatic American case, the reasons for growth were almost exclusively economical (the objective was to lower unit costs), for large corporations in the latecomer nations there are numerous examples of "strategic growth" guided by political objectives or pursued by a company so as to reach a stronger bargaining position with the State.

France

With the Second Industrial Revolution as our reference point, the French case falls midway between what happened in countries such as the United States, England, and Germany on one side and Russia, Japan, and Italy on the other side.

France has usually been classified as an industrial latecomer. Several scholars have claimed that it was because of the French Revolution and its political and economic inheritance that the national path to industrialization was rendered longer and more difficult. At the eve of World War I, effective French large corporations were quite rare when compared with the United States. The existing ones were concentrated above all in non-manufacturing sectors, such as mining, transportation, electricity, and banking, and in some manufacturing industries, such as primary metals and chemicals. Moreover, French big businesses were consistently smaller than their American and German counterparts. It is possible that financing represented a serious problem, even though the relationship between banks and industry is still a topic of scholarly debate. What is certain is that almost all the largest companies in the country were still owned and controlled by families, an element that probably slowed investments in mass production and mass distribution.

Nonetheless, at the beginning of the 1900s, France, too, saw the arrival of big businesses in sectors that came of age with the Second Industrial Revolution. While a large number of companies in almost every sector in France remained small and family owned, some enterprises began to increasingly resemble the modern corporations that had begun to spread across the United States, Germany, and Great Britain. Just like the most advanced corporations in the world, in most cases the French firms grew by investing in new technologies, professionalizing their management structures, and developing organizational competencies that allowed them to secure and maintain a long-term role of leadership within their sectors. In this sense, France can be considered close to the norm in a comparison with the so-called first-mover nations. The iron and steel industry, though smaller than its German counterpart due to fewer raw materials and a smaller domestic market, was very dynamic and witnessed the emergence of the first examples of managerial capitalism and mass production in this country. Le Creusot represents one of the most famous cases of creating managerial hier-archies in France. Relevant success stories are also to be found in other sectors such as textiles, glass, cement, publishing, transportation equipment, and instru-ments, where the major French companies were as big as those in Germany. On the eve of World War I, large corporations in France were concentrated both in some of the mature sectors transformed by the technologies of the Second Industrial Revolution as well as in some of the new branches such as petroleum, rubber and tires, automobiles, electricity, and aluminum. Though it moved at a slower rate, France, too, proceeded in the same direction as the more advanced nations. GNP in France at the end of the 1920s was only three-fourths of Germany's or Great Britain's and just one-seventh of American GNP. But between the end of the 1800s and the first three decades of the next century, France laid the groundwork for the future expansion of successful large corpora-tions and managerial capitalism.

Russia

The history of the Russian large corporation has its start prior to the October Revolution of 1917 and, while it appeared in a version with characteristics similar to that of other latecomer nations, it also had some distinct characteris-tics that we will discuss in Chapter 15. Intervention by the government in

Russia had a critical role in promoting and subsidizing local initiatives, using tariffs to protect businesses that served the national market, and attracting foreign investments after ascertaining that local interest was scarce. The State also intervened directly in promoting infrastructures fundamental for the process of industrialization and modernization of such a large nation. The growth of the railways (which—as had happened in other nations—represented the first big business and provided stimulus to other important sectors such as metallurgy and machinery) owed much to the initiative and financial support of the government. The State subsidized entire lines and took over other lines between 1892 and 1903 by repaying the private companies that owned them. By the beginning of the twentieth century, the State managed 70 percent of Russia's existing rail system.

The first large industrial corporations created either by local or foreign initiative were primarily in capital-intensive sectors such as metallurgy, machinery, petroleum, rubber, transportation, and naval shipyards. These markets were for the most part oligopolistic, just as was the case in the same industries in most of the other industrialized nations. In Russia, as in Germany and Britain, large corporations often formed cartels, which the State did not block in any way. In 1892, the "Oil Syndicate" was approved by the government. Three years later it was the government that transformed an informal agreement between sugar refiners into an official cartel. In some branches, Russia's success was significant. For example, Russian industry succeeded in importing very advanced technologies for steel production. By the beginning of the twentieth century, the area around the Don River boasted some of the largest metalworking factories in the world. Still, the progress made in the industrial world did not extend to the rest of the nation's economy, which remained primarily rooted in peasant agriculture and small-time commerce.

Japan

As we will discover in Chapter 16, Japan was the first non-Western nation to reach a front-row position in the international economy. Starting at the time of the Meiji Restoration in 1868, the government actively encouraged industrialization and took upon itself the task of creating and managing companies in fields such as mining, cotton mills, cement mills, glassworks, and shipyards. Often the government brought in foreign experts and guaranteed subsidies. Still, the State was not the only protagonist of Japanese industrial growth. Private initiative took on an important role in Japan when the government came to understand that it was not capable of managing some of the large corporations it had created and thus turned them over to private firms. Thus began the central institution of Japanese industrialization, the *zaibatsu*—a diversified industrial group owned and controlled by a wealthy family such as Mitsui, Iwasaki (Mitsubishi), or Sumitomo. The typical zaibatsu was diversified in various related sectors; many were concentrated in finance, shipping, and international trade, especially in the importation of machinery. The economic progress made by Japan in the years bridging the two centuries was significant and opened the way toward the country's phenomenal growth in the second half of the twentieth century. But the limitations of the national market and the inability to develop adequate technological competencies kept Japanese firms in this first stage of industrial development from reaching a level of efficiency comparable to that of the leading nations.

Italy

In the two decades prior to the outbreak of World War I, Italy underwent a hefty process of industrialization. The country lived through an experience that mixed aspects of the First Industrial Revolution with others from the Second; a predominance of small firms in traditional sectors coexisted with a precocious set of oligopolies in fields such as metallurgy, various types of machinery, and the electrical industry. Given Italy's combination of resources and the international technological frontier at the time, it was almost inevitable that there would be close ties between big business and the State. The State intervened with well-known tools such as protectionism, state orders, special favors, and subsidies. To this mixture, Italy added "industrial rescues," a relatively original instrument (especially for the number of times—four—that it was utilized in the 50 years starting with the 1880s). There were important large private firms in Italy: Fiat (automobiles), Pirelli (rubber), Falck (steel). But the limits of internal demand hindered them from growing into firms that could be considered comparable to the large corporations of the most advanced industrial nations. At best, they made Italy the only nation in Southern Europe where industrialization was a relatively extensive and consolidated phenomenon.

In the final analysis, we see that national patterns of business development during the Second Industrial Revolution were more alike than unalike. The role of the State was different from nation to nation—as was (in many cases) the size and nature of the market. Some economies reacted quickly to the new opportunities, while others lagged behind. There were cases where the social/cultural environment favored change and growth, while in others it imposed constraints.

But increases in the *size* of business were almost universal, as was the trend toward management with technical capabilities. This was true even in firms in which family control remained strong.

Further reading

A.D. Chandler, Jr., *Scale and Scope: The Dynamics of Industrial Capitalism*, Harvard University Press, Cambridge, MA, 1990.

A.D. Chandler, Jr., F. Amatori, and T. Hikino (eds.), *Big Business and the Wealth of Nations*, Cambridge University Press, Cambridge, 1997.

T. McCraw (ed.), *Creating Modern Capitalism: How Entrepreneurs, Companies and Countries Triumphed in Three Industrial Revolutions*, Harvard University Press, Cambridge, MA, 1997.

M.S. Smith, *The Emergence of Modern Business Enterprise in France, 1800–1930*, Harvard University Press, Cambridge, MA, 2006.

K. Yamamura, "Entrepreneurship, Ownership and Management in Japan," in P. Mathias and M.M. Postan (eds.), *The Cambridge Economic History of Europe, Vol. 7: The Industrial Economies. Capital, Labour and Enterprise*, Cambridge University Press, Cambridge, 1978.

Appendix

Table 9.1 Per capita income—levels

	UK = 100		
	1820	*1870*	*1913*
Austria[a]	74	57	69
Belgium	74	81	82
France	69	57	69
Germany[b]	63	59	76
Italy	62	45	50
United Kingdom	100	100	100
Spain	61	42	45
Russia[c]	43	31	30
United States	73	75	105
Japan	40	23	27

Source: Adapted from A. Maddison, *Monitoring the World Economy*, OECD, Paris, 1995, tab. 3.1.

Notes
a   Current borders.
b   Federal Republic of Germany borders.
c   USSR borders.

Table 9.2 Relative shares of world manufacturing output, 1830–1990 (%)

	1830	*1860*	*1880*	*1900*
Europe as a whole	34.2	53.2	61.3	62.0
United Kingdom	9.5	19.9	22.9	18.5
Habsburg Empire	3.2	4.2	4.4	4.7
France	5.2	7.9	7.8	6.8
Germany before unification/Germany	3.5	4.9	8.5	13.2
Italy before unification/Italy	2.3	2.5	2.5	2.5
Russia	5.6	7	7.6	8.8
United States	2.4	7.2	14.7	23.6
Japan	2.8	2.6	2.4	2.4
Third World	60.5	36.6	20.9	11.0
China	29.8	19.7	12.5	6.2
India/Pakistan	17.6	8.6	2.8	1.7

Source: Adapted from Christopher Freeman and Francisco Louçã, *As Time Goes By: From the Industrial Revolution to the Information Revolution*, Oxford University Press, Oxford, 2001, p. 183.

Table 9.3 Population (millions) and per capita GDP (in 1990 dollars) of the United States, the United Kingdom, and Germany, 1870–1913

	United States	*United Kingdom*	*Germany*
Population			
1870	40.2	31.4	39.2
1898	73.8	40.3	52.8
1913	97.6	45.6	65.0
Per capita GDP			
1870	2,445	3,190	1,839
1898	3,780	4,428	2,848
1913	5,301	4,921	3,648

Source: Adapted from Angus Maddison, *Statistics on World Population, GDP and Per Capita GDP, 1–2006 AD*, http://www.ggdc.net/maddison/. Last accessed October 6, 2010.

Part IV

State and market in the period between the two world wars

10 The multidivisional corporation and managerial capitalism

Organizational change in large American firms: from the U-form to the M-form

At the end of World War I, large firms in the United States, the world's leading industrial country, were partly a product of internal growth and partly a result of mergers. In the second case, the outcome was often something far superior to the combined sum of the initial parts. In the process of merging, inefficient plants were closed and others were built according to state-of-the-art technology in order to take advantage of economies of scale and scope. These state-of-the-art plants continued to manufacture the same products as the old plants but they also were part of a new organizational design. One sure sign of a merger's success was a drop in the cost per unit and subsequent growth in market share.

The key management characteristic of the large American firm was, in general, the unitary-form (U-form) whereby the organization was based on functions such as production, marketing, logistics, human resources, finance, and legal services. Often these functions were overseen on a day-to-day basis by members of the board of directors; management and the board were one and the same. Authority was highly centralized. The difficulty of implementing this type of functional organization was not to be underestimated because the firms were multiunit entities with plants, distribution centers, warehouses, laboratories, and offices spread across a nation or several nations. The task of blending all these elements was complicated and challenging.

In the United States, these problems were ironed out over the four decades preceding World War I. The pioneers acquired technical and managerial know-how while they improved organizational design and established clear lines of authority and communication. Important organizational changes continued to take place in the 1920s as the role of professional management took increasing importance. Out of these changes arose the modern multidivisional corporation.

The appearance of this new form of corporate structure was due to factors within as well as outside the firm. In the 1920s, GNP and aggregate demand started to stabilize only to experience a dramatic drop in the 1930s. Firms were no longer able to count exclusively on external factors—such as population growth, the construction of railways, and booming cities—for expansion. Avoiding a drop in demand became essential. At the same time the process of internal growth and mergers in many firms created a surplus of internal resources—people, instruments, and, especially, know-how and competences—due to earlier investments in functions not directly related to production. Managers had to get rid of these resources or make better use of them.

In certain sectors such as electromechanics and chemicals, the growth in research and development (R&D) opened the possibility of developing new products based on the original technologies. In situations like this, a firm's growth was based not on external developments (such as changes in prices, in preferences, or in other factors of demand) but rather on developments within the company itself. For a company's management, underutilized resources thus constituted a continuous stimulus for growth; sometimes it was management itself that was the most precious of these resources.

Thus was born a process of diversification that could not be managed within the old organizational framework. In fact, if corporate diversification seems to elude the limits of growth via the "law of decreasing returns," the only limit that was still in place was the ability of a firm's management to reorganize and reposition itself given its increasing responsibilities. The process of diversification placed many firms squarely in the forefront of a new and important organizational breakthrough.

Expanding product lines that were difficult to handle inside the typical pyramidal structure of the centralized U-form created tensions within the firm. Top management was especially disoriented because now managers were expected to track an increased number of product lines and were left with insufficient time to focus on strategic decisions.

The pioneers in solving those problems included DuPont and General Motors. The leaders of these corporations understood that the problem was multifaceted and called for a focus on strategy as well as the ability to allow managers a certain amount of freedom when dealing with their markets. Independent divisions based on product lines or geographic areas were established. The new divisions had all the line and staff functions that were necessary to operate effectively but now there was one important difference: top management was no longer occupied in the day-to-day operations. Instead, it concentrated on supervising, coordinating, assessing, and allocating resources for the entire entity. To pursue this strategic role, headquarters had to have a sufficient staff to monitor all of the divisions. This kind of system assured that there would not be breakdowns among the overall decision makers and between those decision makers and operations.

The newly created divisions were normally built on a common technological or geographical base. From nitrocellulose, DuPont moved into artificial leathers, varnishes, synthetic fibers, and plastic materials while at General Motors they manufactured diesel locomotives, tractors, and airplanes. With this kind of a common base, the multidivisional enterprise kept a high degree of cohesion while still achieving flexibility. Top management was able to oversee the diversification process and to transfer financial, technical, and managerial resources from one division to another. The ties between management and the divisions meant that the multidivisional firm (also known as the M-form) did not represent discontinuity vis-à-vis the integrated company that took hold in the years before World War I. Rather, it was a product of natural evolution. The basic limitation on firm size changed. Technology was the basis of the integrated company in the Second Industrial Revolution. Now, in the case of the multidivisional firm, the limitation was the proximity of new businesses to the firm's core sciences and technologies. In this way, the process of growth could continue but it was effectively controlled.

The multidivisional model required a greater diffusion of decision-making powers in the firm. If the top managers were viewed as the commanders-in-chief, the division heads acted as their field generals. This was accepted, but often with initial resistance. The model had to demonstrate its success using the same indicators that had signaled the success of the integrated firm: how much market share is controlled and how much can per unit costs be cut? The multidivisional structure adopted by a few pioneers in the United States in the period between the two wars proved itself and spread through the US business system in the 1940s. Then it became the organizational model adopted by many large firms in the other nations that competed head-on with the United States in the international forum.

In the early 1940s, the pessimism of one of the most renowned economists, Joseph Schumpeter, does not seem justified. Schumpeter had written that industrial capitalism was based on big business and expressed concern that the latter would end up suffocating the sparks of entrepreneurship that he associated with a bourgeoisie hegemony. The great thinker—who in the end acknowledged the existence of corporate entrepreneurship—did not realize that the multidivisional firm was a concrete example of the ability of the American model of capitalism to assure that an entrepreneurial spirit could be diffused throughout an entire, bureaucratic organization. The ideas of Oliver Williamson, too, seem slightly off-center if we are trying to grasp the phenomenon of the multidivisional firm's long-term pattern of growth. Williamson provided us with brilliant insights on the nature of vertically integrated big business. He established that the effort to limit transaction costs was a key element in the growth of large firms. He also explored to good effect the limited rationality of top management, the necessity for certain specific investments, and the opportunistic behavior of those from whom goods and services were purchased.

But Alfred Chandler's perspective, with its vision of the company as a pool of technical and managerial resources, appears to be much more all encompassing. His way of looking at companies—which was very close to the intellectual framework of the economist Edith Penrose—enabled him to deal with both horizontal and vertical integration and to thus establish a sound foundation for our understanding of the modern firm. His work was crowned with the publication of *Strategy and Structure*, the volume that provides the basis of this chapter's narrative.

General Motors: a case both of successes and internal conflicts in a large multidivisional firm

At this point it would be wise to emphasize that the multidivisional solution is anything but a simple or universally successful outcome. Henry Ford, probably the greatest entrepreneur of his time and a man with an aversion to organizational charts and corporate bureaucracy, was unable to make this passage. This American "hero" with his adamant determination to pursue standardization, vertical integration, and his great innovation—the assembly line—brought about incredible transformations. The process of assembling an automobile decreased from 12 hours and 8 minutes in 1913 to just 90 minutes the next year. The cost of the same dropped from 850 to 290 dollars in the period between 1908 and 1925, even as Ford introduced the concept of a minimum wage, doubling a worker's pay to 5 dollars for an 8-hour workday. The investments made by Ford in manufacturing, notably the factory of Highland Park near Detroit, became the symbols of modern serial production and of the economies of scale. By 1921, Ford was by far the number one manufacturer of automobiles in the world, covering 55.7 percent of the US market. General Motors was a distant second with its 12.3 percent share.

Created in 1908 by an enthusiastic empire builder—William C. Durant— General Motors (GM) was the result of a merger of many pioneers of the automotive industry in the United States: Buick, Oldsmobile, Cadillac, Pontiac, and some small producers of autos, trucks, and components. For Durant, the objective of the mergers was not to reduce costs by rationalizing production capacity but, rather, to restructure the plants with the aim of further increasing production. Unfortunately, Durant's overly optimistic demand forecasts, his inability to integrate the various companies in a rational manner by creating a central office, and his failure to develop a capable managerial hierarchy left GM with increasing financial difficulties in the 1910s. By 1920, the major shareholder of GM was the chemical giant, DuPont, which decided to appoint Pierre S. DuPont to take over Durant's role and to entrust an executive of the company, Alfred Sloan, with its operational management. Sloan was an MIT-trained engineer. He had joined GM after selling his own company, Hyatt Roller Bearing, a GM supplier, to Durant. In a short period in the early 1920s, Sloan and DuPont transformed the eclectic mixture of operating units put in place by Durant into a coordinated multidivisional firm. GM was now composed of independent divisions that manufactured automobiles, trucks, and other commercial vehicles, as well as auto parts and accessories. Each division had its own organization for both production and distribution.

Restructured, GM soon raced ahead of Ford. Ford's motto was "any color as long as it's black" whereas Sloan adopted a different philosophy with his "a car for every purse and purpose." Automobile manufacturing at GM was subdivided into five divisions, each of which focused on a different level of consumer income. Production was precisely programmed on the basis of important indicators such as monthly registration reports that supplied information not only about GM's market share but, more importantly, that of the competition. Sloan understood that automotive marketing had changed: no longer was the aim to sell a customer his first car. Instead, GM wanted drivers to start thinking about the purchase of a replacement automobile. The company focused on improving the styling, comfort, and performance of its various models in varied colors.

As Ford started to lose hold of some of the company's vantage points as first mover, he reacted by firing some key managers. Sloan quickly hired them for his organization with the aim of further improving his top-rated management team. Starting in 1921, Ford himself once again took on the role of day-to-day manager of his empire, but the results were still dismal: his company was only able to produce the same automobile and with the same methods, most of which were no longer "cutting edge." In 1925, Ford's share of automobile sales dropped to 40 percent whereas GM's increased to 20 percent. By the end of the decade (1929) the market inversion was complete: Ford's share had dropped to 31.3 percent whereas GM's had grown to 32.3 percent, and a third major player—Chrysler— controlled another 8.2 percent.

In the years between 1927 and 1937 Ford booked a loss of 15.9 million dollars. In the same period GM's net profits reached slightly below 2 billion dollars. The year 1940 marked the fatal fall: Ford's share of the auto market dropped to 18.9 percent, less than Chrysler's 23.7 percent, whereas GM had almost half of the market with its 47.5 percent. When Sloan's company overtook Ford as the number one automobile manufacturer in the United States, the meaning was clear: strong professional management and a well-designed administrative structure were key components in maintaining a large firm's competitiveness. Only after Henry Ford's death (1947) was the company able to reconquer some of the terrain it had lost. It copied GM's form of organization and hired a number of strong managers. The multidivisional solution was successful because it responded to the crucial problem of allocating decision-making powers in a complex, very large, modern firm. If power was vested only at the highest levels, the organization suffered because of a lack of timely information and motivation to innovate. Anarchy was the outcome if power was distributed only among the lower ranks.[1] Sloan's structure was not perfectly delineated, but it was a highly successful advance over the U-form.

The most common explanation for what occurred is that Sloan was able to translate from theory to practice in a few months a project which he had fostered for a while: he introduced a structure that separated headquarters from the divisions and strategy from day-to-day routine management. To do this he relied on the detailed work of Donaldson Brown, former treasurer at DuPont, who had created an elaborate system of financial control that consistently monitored incoming data so as to provide top management with the information needed for decision-making.

The practice of corporate reorganization was of course more complicated and personalized than the theory of the M-form suggests. Feuds and compromises abounded and influenced the power structure at GM as they had at Ford. The owners (primarily the DuPont family) pushed for a strict application of the theoretical model of the multidivisional firm and, most especially, wanted to exclude the divisional heads from headquarters and concentrate power in an Executive Committee made up of top management and a few representatives of the stockholders. Their objective was to control the enterprise while, at the same time, protecting GM from the tendency of uncontrolled growth which had characterized the firm before Sloan's arrival in 1921. For the most part, they were successful. GM delegated responsibility to top management, at the same time preserving the overriding rights of the big stockholders as they maintained the right to veto managers' decisions by not financing them. This prerogative was the purview of the Finance Committee which was controlled by the owners.

Some members of top management—especially Alfred Sloan—were, however, wary of the idea of completely separating strategic planning from day-to-day operations. In the perspective of these managers, the most important thing was to create consensus within the divisions and to stimulate an entrepreneurial spirit within the ranks of middle management. To do so, GM's top executives were expected to involve division managers in strategic planning as well as in decisions regarding the allocation of resources. This preference was based on a profound sense of practicality. Top managers understood that the divisions would undoubtedly oppose any kind of initiative imposed from "above." They also understood the high price the company would pay if such a tactic was pursued and they were ready to compromise by bartering a say in decision-making in exchange for consensus and support.

The issue of who should be included in the planning process was not the only pressing question on which owners and management differed. Top managers vigorously fought ownership's right to veto new investments, arguing that the key decisions regarding the strategic future direction of a firm could not be made by a group that tended to look exclusively at the bottom line. This battle between owners and managers as to who should guide the company's organizational transformation was influenced by institutional and technical constraints. In particular there were two factors that over time impeded owners from realizing their version of the theoretical M-form they longed for. The first was the government's antitrust policy; in the late 1940s, the Department of Justice launched a legal battle (ultimately successful) against DuPont, the stockholder. The other factor was GM's success itself. The enormous profits accumulated by GM in the decades immediately before and after World War II effectively cancelled ownership's pressure and allowed the managers of GM, paraphrasing Sloan, to "have the money necessary to do whatever they wished." As long as the capital necessary for new investments had been scarce and state interventions were minimal, GM's owners had not hesitated to insist on a theoretical M-form that was characterized both by a distinct separation between strategy and operations as well as by ownership's control via an allocation of financial resources. This system had impeded the top executives from getting the heads of divisional units in headquarters involved, forcing them instead to use informal means for developing consensus within the organization. Thus, divisional managers were admitted to meetings at headquarters though it was not possible to formally grant voting rights to them. This period in GM's history was rather short, thanks to the incredible profits that produced fresh capital for new investments. The top managers in this way greatly weakened ownership's ability to command via financial leverage. This allowed division managers the opportunity to participate directly in the planning process and decisions regarding the allocation of resources.

GM's owners were only able to take back control of the firm when the company's performance started to slide in the years between 1956 and 1958, at which point the "pure" M-form was finally adopted. The new structure created in 1958 reestablished the power of the shareholders' financial veto and imposed a rigid separation between the divisions in headquarters. The new top management (by now Sloan had retired) made no attempt to involve middle management in creating strategy and even less in convincing middle managers to accept their decisions. The outcome was a growing sense of mistrust and dissent. On one side there was growing animosity among operational managers who became increasingly uncooperative in effecting the policies proposed by headquarters, with no regard as to whether or not the new policies were more effective than the old. On the other side, top management became ever more invasive and tried to get around middle management's opposition by getting involved in operational details. Instead of increasing efficiency and improving governance at GM, adopting the M-form in its theoretical version ended up causing the destruction of consensus and led to the long, slow decline of the company. Global competition in the 1960s brought these limitations to the surface.

The ascent of managerial capitalism in the debate between contemporaries: the problem in the separation between ownership and control and the role of managers

Regardless of the outcome of the GM case, there's little doubt that the arrival of the multidivisional firm was a strong factor in affirming the importance of the managerial firm with its separation of ownership from control. In the early 1930s, law professor Adolf Berle and economist Gardiner Means officially acknowledged this transformation and its impact on the concept of ownership. They focused on the accompanying divorce between those who govern and those who own a system. Berle and Means' 1932 volume, *The Modern Corporation and Private Property*, offered a groundbreaking series of reflections on corporate America. These were based on extensive research conducted through a survey of large firms in the United States. The two authors highlighted the fact that the publicly traded company had become the dominant economic form of the modern world. By making it easy to transfer ownership of shares, it became possible to concentrate the wealth of numerous individuals into enormous aggregates. But this also profoundly changed relations between a corporation and its owners, transforming the "old" members of the firm into investors and separating ownership of shares from control of the company. One significant consequence of this separation was the possibility that there would be a divergence between the interests of the controlling group (identified as the top management of the firm) and the interests of the majority of the shareholders.

Berle and Means' opinion on managers was pessimistic: the authors were not only convinced that the upper echelons of the corporation were completely independent from the owners and were capable of perpetuating their position to the point where they no longer had to justify their choices to anyone. For the authors, managers were capable of shifting profit flows to their advantage, arranging things so that they could choose how to invest these profits, possibly in the pursuit of objectives that would bring them prestige, power, and personal satisfaction rather than focusing on the interests of the majority of the shareholders. One example given was that management could opt to reinvest profits so as to increase their power rather than distribute more generous dividends to the shareholders. For Berle and Means, management expropriated the owners' prerogatives and tied the survival of a firm to those who oversaw its day-to-day management. Controlling power handed over to management was not a simple effect of the progressive fractioning of ownership but, rather, a consequence of the organizational revolution that followed the growth of the large corporation since the phenomenon also appeared in corporations where there was not a fractioning of ownership.

Far from being complementary or related parts of the same system, for Berle and Means control and ownership were positioned on opposite axes, to the point where one worked against the other. The fundamental question, therefore, was how to establish to whom the members of a group were to be held responsible. For the authors, there were three possible answers to this question and they were directly tied to three possible forms of modern corporate governance. The first was based on the belief that the interest and the responsibility of managers should refer exclusively to the shareholders, essentially going back to the traditional concept of the rights of the owners. By doing so, however, the final result would be an anachronism, transforming management into a sort of steward that would operate exclusively for the benefit of the shareholders, even if the latter had effectively surrendered their power. The second solution, too, did not appear entirely reasonable: give official recognition to the situation that had emerged, that of executives managing the firm for their own interests. Fortunately, wrote Berle and Means, "a third alternative existed"—recognition of the principle that the modern listed company was to be at the service not only of its owners (or the individuals who managed it) but, rather, of the entire community. It was this third option, they said, that opened the path to developing the modern firm along more socially acceptable lines. Faced with complexity in the structure and in the interests that it organizes, the modern public company should exist to serve not only the shareholders or its management group but the entire society. The answer to the problem of corporate control (stockholders vs. management) would then move to a different level with a focus on stakeholders: employees, suppliers, distributors, and the end clients, eventually extending to the community in its widest sense.

This stance matched well with the climate created by Roosevelt's New Deal and with the mood of the country during the worst economic depression in American history. In an effort to cope with that crisis, the New Deal turned first to the National Recovery Act (NRA, 1933), which tried to design a more cooperative kind of capitalism and a new form of regulating business. The NRA failed, however, and was gone by 1935. What was left was a strong sense that something important had changed and might not be altered by the government's traditional policies of regulation or antitrust. This later prompted James Burnham to write *The Managerial Revolution*,[2] which acknowledged the new position of power reached by managers.

Burnham even envisioned over time the advent of a planned economy that would converge the United States with Nazi Germany and the Soviet Union.

Years earlier, and in an entirely different context (post-World War I Germany), Walter Rathenau, an esteemed manager as well as political figure, had arrived at similar conclusions, declaring that the firm and the State should integrate themselves into society in the same way that the various groups that make up a company should integrate themselves to be of service to the community. Like Berle and Means, Rathenau focused on the phenomenon of a gradual withdrawal of the shareholder from the daily management of the firm. Rathenau observed two types of shareholders: those who have made a permanent investment of their capital and those who acquire shares purely for speculative reasons. Although he was convinced that the objectives of the first group were in line with those of management, for the latter group he believed that there were continuous risks of a conflict of interests because these shareholders were interested in short-term gains whereas firms wanted to accumulate and reinvest earnings in the company. Rathenau sided with legislation that limited the rights of shareholders to be kept abreast of how the company was performing (so as not to inadvertently share valuable information with competitors) and to assure management of the possibility of internal financing for future growth. For Rathenau, it was not conceivable that the firm should sacrifice itself for the private interests of shareholders who no longer had close ties with the company. The large firm was no longer an organization with interests regulated by private law but, rather, a fundamental component of the national economy and, as such, a "part" of the community. For Rathenau the power that was generated within a firm and concentrated in its management group implicitly brought upon the latter a social responsibility that was to be handled as if they were entrusted with that responsibility by the various groups making up the firm and the community, too.

Rathenau, like Berle and Means, concluded that the interests of a firm could essentially be integrated within the organization and be aligned with those of the community, too. The American authors moved from this premise to draw the power of the managers into the tradition of checks and balances of organized Anglo-Saxon pluralism. Rathenau, however, looked at the situation differently. For him, the objective was to make sure that managers not only respected the old rights of property but also that they adhered to regulations and public constraints. His reference point was his home country, Germany, with its concept of the special relationship between individuals and a society, a tradition that favored the needs of the latter over the rights of the former. These ideas were deeply embedded in German culture. As a result, weakening ownership and its depersonalization were for Rathenau not only a natural development of the big firm but also a precise objective of public policy and one of the elements in designing a "new economy" in which the firm would place itself at the service of collective interests and assume the role of a pillar of the conservation and defender of the nation State.

Like Rathenau, Berle and Means were struggling with two fundamental problems that are still with us today in the midst of the Great Recession: first, they wanted to establish society's role in control of the great corporations emerging from the Second Industrial Revolution; second, and more specifically, they sought to implement a stakeholder concept of corporate governance, another issue of great contemporary importance. As the fact that these issues are still with us indicates, neither problem was solved in the 1930s by the New Deal, nor by the National Socialism that was the German variation on industrial reform. What did emerge after World War II was a greatly strengthened and enlarged version of the M-form corporation, now a multinational actor as well as a dominant national institution in the United States and the other developed nations.

Notes

1 See T.K. McCraw, *American Business, 1920–2000: How It Worked*, Harlan Davidson, Wheeling, 2000, pp. 22–23.
2 J. Burnham, *The Managerial Revolution*, John Day Company, New York, 1941.

Further reading

A. Berle and G. Means, *The Modern Corporation and Private Property*, Macmillan Press, New York, 1932.
A.D. Chandler, Jr., *Strategy and Structure: Chapters in the History of the American Industrial Enterprise*, MIT Press, Cambridge, MA, 1962.
P.F. Drucker, *Concept of the Corporation*, John Day Company, New York, 1946.
R.F. Freeland, *The Struggle for Control of the Modern Corporation: Organizational Change at General Motors, 1924–1970*, Cambridge University Press, Cambridge, 2001.
W. Rathenau, *New Society*, Williams & Norgate, London, 1921.
O. Williamson, *The Economic Institutions of Capitalism: Firms, Markets, Relational Contracting*, Collier Macmillan, London, 1985.

Appendix

Table 10.1 The adoption of the M-form by the 100 largest companies of the five most industrialized countries (%)

	1932	*1950*	*1960*	*1970*	*1980–1983*	*1990*
United States	8	17	43	71	81	n.d.
Japan	0	8	29	55	58	n.d.
Germany	n.a.	5	15	50	60	70
France	3	6	21	54	66	76
United Kingdom	5	13	30	72	89	89

Source: Adapted from L. Hannah, "Marshall Trees and the Global 'Forest': Were 'Giant Redwoods' Different?," in N. Lamoreaux, D. Raff, and P. Temin (eds.), *Learning by Doing in Markets, Firms and Countries*, University of Chicago Press, Chicago, IL, 1999.

Table 10.2 Estimated number of shareholders of American corporations (1900–1928)

Year	Total capital stock of all corporations in the United States ($)	Average no. of $100 par value shares per stockholder	Estimated no. of stockholders in the United States	Annual rate of increase (compounded annually)
1900	61,831,955,370	140.1	4,400,000	
1910	64,053,763,141	86.3	7,400,000	5.2%
1913	65,038,309,611	87	7,500,000	0.5%
1917	66,584,420,424	77.3	8,600,000	3.5%
1920	69,205,967,666	57.3	12,000,000	12.0%
1923	71,479,464,925	49.7	14,400,000	6.2%
1928	91,881,243,985	51	18,000,000	4.5%

Source: Adapted from A.A. Berle and G.C. Means, *The Modern Corporation and Private Property*, tenth printing 2009, Transaction Publishers, New Brunswick, p. 56.

11 Europe between the two wars

Convergence and divergence with the United States

On December 25, 1925 several German chemical firms, among the largest of the country (Agfa, Hoechst, Bayer, and BASF), set up a formal agreement that took the form of a federation called IG Farben ("IG" stood for Interessen-Gemeinschaft or "community of interest"). IG Farben was the largest European chemical concern and one of the largest in the world. Technically, IG Farben was not a pure cartel, but a merger with impressive headquarters in Frankfurt. It employed about one hundred thousand people. One of the main purposes behind the creation of IG Farben (also known as IG Farbenfabriken) was to restore German leadership in the world's chemical industry that had been lost after the war. The international relevance of IG Farben is witnessed by the fact that, before the outbreak of World War II, it had devised several international and secret agreements and cartels, for instance with the US leaders Standard Oil and DuPont. Another consequence of the creation of the German chemical concern was felt at the European level: immediately after, both in Britain and France, similar consolidation strategies were implemented; they brought into business, respectively, Imperial Chemical Industries (ICI) in 1926 and Rhône-Poulenc in 1928.

This process of consolidation by mergers and federations had many determinants, both of an economic and political nature. In the chemical industry, which was of central importance in the Second Industrial Revolution, consolidations took place in part to stabilize profits and in part to reduce unit costs by benefiting from economies of scale and scope. One constant was the unification of R&D activities, knowledge, and patents. At the same time, however, politics played a relevant role. The case of the formation of ICI is telling in this respect. Immediately after its organization, IG Farben started an aggressive strategy of foreign acquisitions in order to penetrate promising markets. Understandably, the first target was the British market where the potential demand for superior-quality German dyestuffs was considerable. IG Farben made a bid in 1925 to take over a Manchester-based firm, the British Dyestuffs Corporation (BDC), which in its turn was the result of a government-driven merger of smaller producers that took place during World War I. The German move was considered unacceptable by the British government, which managed indirectly to promote an "all-British" merger that materialized on the first day of 1927, when BDC merged with four other British chemical companies creating ICI.

An imperfect convergence

The ICI case was, as said, not isolated in interwar Europe. But it is particularly telling in many respects. First of all, behind the whole story lies the unescapable logic of the Second Industrial Revolution. World War I was a crucial divide in the economic development of the West, and particularly in Europe. Beyond the considerable material damages incurred throughout the continent, the loss of human life, and the major changes in the political and institutional makeup of most European countries, the war made it clear that a profound modernization was taking place in the leading sectors of the modern European economies. Those which dominated in the First Industrial Revolution (textiles, iron, and metalworking) were progressively giving way to the capital-intensive ones of the Second Industrial Revolution: chemicals, electricity, and metallurgy. Most of the countries involved in the conflict had tested the advantages brought by high volumes of production and scale intensity, since the war had proved the effectiveness of domestic production systems and industries at all levels. This was the case of the mechanical industry, and also of chemicals, steel, and electricity. Almost everywhere the war effort necessitated the creation of large organizations, some so large that later they could hardly adapt to peacetime conditions.

Even in peripheral European countries, ones that had only very recently been involved in the process of industrial modernization, the technological imperatives of the Second Industrial Revolution were compelling. The success of the new capital-intensive industries was convincing to the leaders of European firms, and the effect could be seen especially on their strategies and their organizational structures (even if on average the United States remained unchallenged). On the eve of World War II, of the top 50 industrial groups ranked by market capitalization worldwide, 32 were located in the United States, 11 in Britain, and 4 in Germany (Schmitz 1993: tab. 2). All of the available comparative surveys emphasize the fact that, in the interwar period, the largest European companies were, on average, still far smaller than their American counterparts. In the technological- and capital-intensive electrical machinery sector, in 1930 the assets of the top four US firms totaled nearly 1.3 billion dollars, against the 358 million of their German competitors and 135 million of the French.

Second, the ICI case clearly indicates the characteristics of the economic, cultural, and political environments of the "European Corporation" during the interwar period. The policies were protectionist, "corporatist," and increasingly interventionist whether the governments were authoritarian or democratic. Agreements and cartels were condoned at a national and international level; this context shaped the nature of European large firms, bringing at their extreme consequences the features already highlighted in Chapter 9.

At the origin of the "European model": small markets

Generally speaking, the dynamics of the diffusion of the Second Industrial Revolution in Europe present some puzzling issues for the historian. Like their

US counterparts and despite some differences among countries, the imperatives of the new technological wave necessitated that the European business systems' entrepreneurs and governments look to new organizational, financial, and competitive practices. European entrepreneurs in capital- and technology-intensive industries had to put into practice policies of growth and integration, obtaining appropriate supplies of capital and raw materials, organizing a disciplined labor force, and opening up new channels of distribution for the goods they were producing on a larger scale than in the past. Many of them indeed succeeded in these efforts, building internationally competitive corporations characterized by strong and enduring capabilities.

However, the framework in which all these efforts took place was different from that in which American entrepreneurs and managers were operating. World War I had brought the first global economy to an abrupt end, depriving European entrepreneurs of the kind of continental-scale market that remained available to US companies. Additionally, European history shaped a cultural environment with less favorable attitudes toward business and business–government relations than American firms enjoyed. This culture influenced entrepreneurial opportunities and decisions. In sum, the European response to the challenges of the Second Industrial Revolution was different from the response by American companies. The diffusion of the model of the managerial corporation in Europe was slowed by these several factors, by market structures, and by the industrial policies adopted by each country.

It is not difficult to find explanations for the relatively slow European transition to managerial capitalism. During the first half of the twentieth century Europe was embroiled in crisis and chaos: two world wars, a huge economic crisis, dictatorships, and the economic nationalism of the 1930s all had an impact. A leading element that shaped the nature of the European firms was also the small size and limited dynamism of internal markets. In 1870, the index of per capita income in the United States was 100; for the United Kingdom it was 130, for Germany 75, in France 76, with Italy at 59. On the eve of World War I, this gap had widened: Britain had dropped to 92, Germany 68, France 65, and Italy 48. From the second half of the nineteenth century until World War I, the United States more than quadrupled its population, while in Germany and Britain, the increase was less pronounced or, as was the case in France and Italy, almost zero.

As mentioned in Chapter 9, Britain maintained her leadership position in the industries characteristic of the First Industrial Revolution. Britain still concentrated a significant portion of international investments in textiles, for instance. As shown by the ICI case, in capital-intensive industries like the new ones of the Second Industrial Revolution, Britain was lagging far behind the United States and Germany, and it was only during the war that consolidations took place, frequently under the government's auspices.

Continental peripheries (such as Southern Italy and, to some extent, the most rural provinces of France) were still characterized by a diffuse social and economic "backwardness," and by an overall predominance of agriculture. This meant that not only did these countries suffer from low levels of demand, but consumption styles were in some ways antithetical to those of mass-consumption societies. This was evident in the food and beverage industry, as well as in clothing, footwear, and furniture, in which medium and small scales of production prevailed.

When considering an industry that was fully representative of the achievements of the new era—the automobile industry—the differences between Europe and the United States emerge even more clearly. In the mid-1920s the United States boasted over 160 cars for every thousand inhabitants; but in Britain this number was only 15, in France it was 13, and in Germany and Italy only 3.

Increases in exporting activity could have boosted relatively stagnant national systems, as could have foreign direct investments. This had happened before the war and would have helped European countries fully exploit their competitive advantages. However, in the interwar period, characterized by the end of the "first globalization" and by the autarkic economic regimes which arose in the Great Depression, it was not easy to establish large, competitive, international companies. Strategies for internationalizing production through direct investment continued to be adopted primarily by those companies located in nations with very small domestic markets. This was also pursued when the end of the war left the European market fragmented into nationally protected economies in which a limited penetration of foreign investments and products was allowed. The internationalization of companies belonging to small continental economies had started even before World War I in some cases, when it was clear that domestic economies would not be able to sustain the growth of large-scale, integrated businesses. Many Dutch and Swiss companies were able to become multinationals well before World War I. Such was the case of Nestlé, founded in the late 1860s, which immediately internationalized its operations, selling its main product (the dried powder "formula" substitute for breast milk) in France and Germany.

In general, however, foreign investment was greatly affected by World War I and the end of the "first globalization." Companies in countries involved in the conflict were especially impacted. In addition to the requisitions and nationalizations during the war, the war's end brought an extensive expropriation of the losing countries' international assets. The extensive network of European subsidiaries that German companies had built during the pre-World War I years was thus dismantled by the victorious Allied Powers.

Britain provided a partial exception to this framework. In the interwar years, British companies continued to rely on a degree of internationalization higher than average in Europe. British multinational activity through foreign direct investment was concentrated in specific industries, such as mining and oil. All too often, however, even the British companies that adopted policies of vertical integration focused on exports that were the typical products of the First Industrial Revolution in Britain, including textiles. Meanwhile, high barriers to capital mobility, which culminated in the autarkic policies of the early 1930s, kept Europe fragmented into small national markets, each with growth rates significantly lower than that on the other side of the Atlantic. While the US GNP per capita grew in the period from 1914 to 1950 (2.8 percent per year on average), in

Europe only the Netherlands and Sweden were able to exceed a 2 percent annual growth, while the rest lagged far behind, around 1–1.2 percent on average.

The origin of the European model: the role of institutions

One consequence of the structural "backwardness" of Continental Europe was the adoption of public policies aimed at accelerating access to the technological frontier. State institutions in Europe played a role in shaping competition policies and entrepreneurial choices with effects that varied widely from country to country.

Cartels

First of all, legal institutions played an important role in regulating markets and competition. Europeans were much more tolerant of collusive behavior than Americans, who had introduced federal antitrust legislation in 1890. By contrast, as we have seen, cartels became a norm in Germany during the process of diffusion of the Second Industrial Revolution, and the State considered agreements among firms as a relevant instrument of industrial policy. During the interwar period, cartelization spread all over Europe, becoming an essential component of economic policies undertaken and planned by dictatorial regimes as well as by democracies. Cartels allowed their participants to benefit from relative stability in prices and demand. The control over prices and quotas was a serious limitation to the incentives to pursue strategies of integration and growth. It is also true, on the other hand, that stable agreements on prices encouraged companies to pursue internal efficiency in order to push operating costs as low as possible below the agreed price.

From a social point of view in the European culture, cartels were a good alternative to the huge "US-style" industrial concentrations. This was especially true in countries like Germany, where large corporations and *Finanzkapital* were socially, politically, and ideologically unpopular. Stability of market quotas allowed companies to carefully plan their investments while maintaining a relatively stable level of employment, something which in interwar Europe was highly desirable. This was especially true after the outbreak of the financial crisis at the beginning of the early 1930s.

The number of cartels in interwar Europe was thus considerable. According to some estimates, during the 1920s—and so even before the crisis—European cartels and agreements numbered in the thousands. They were present both in small countries (around 50 in Austria, 100 in Switzerland) and in the large economies. France had about 80, Britain over 400, and Germany more than 2,000.

During the turbulent interwar years, the cartels quickly spread even on an international scale. This was clearly one of the "logical" outcomes of the stagnation and instability in the global market. Companies had strong incentives to look for a higher degree of coordination in order to reduce uncertainty. Examples of international cartels and "associations" could thus be found in many industries, from chemicals and pharmaceuticals to artificial fibers, incandescent lamps, electromechanics, and mining. At the end of the 1930s, almost all the main European leaders were members of an international cartel. In France there were 69, in Germany 57, in Britain 40, in Switzerland 25, in Italy 16, and over 40 in the Low Countries.

Entrepreneurial and interventionist states

In the Continental European experience, governments played—with many *nuances*—a relevant role in the creation, support, and ownership of a number of investments in capital-intensive industries.

In several cases the government was the main customer for large concerns. This was especially true in areas directly related to national security; in other cases, through orders, protection, tariffs, and even financial aid, state support aimed at creating a modern and efficient industrial base in countries characterized by relatively weak internal demand. This was evident in countries like Italy, where the interventionist attitude of the State had colored the industrialization process since its inception. In Italy, the State became the direct owner of some of the most important production facilities in the country. Since the mid-1920s, the Italian State had *de facto* become an influential shareholder in a number of companies in manufacturing (and especially in capital-intensive industries) through various "rescues" undertaken to help Italian companies avoid bankruptcies and failures. This policy continued into the early 1930s when, with the establishment of IRI (Institute for Industrial Reconstruction, a public agency that took over the shares owned by Italy's major banks), the Italian State became by far the most important the investor in the country. By 1937, the government in Italy controlled more than 80 percent of the share capital of shipbuilding, around 25 percent of the mechanical industry, and 50 percent of the steel industry. In some cases this paved the way for the rationalization and modernization of entire branches of manufacturing, with significant effects on the adoption of the most advanced technology.

The Italian experience can be considered an almost unique case, and one seldom imitated by other European countries. The ICI case, for instance, exemplifies another, less invasive and direct, form of intervention, closer to the informal pressure which later on characterized Japan's Ministry of International Trade and Industry approach to industrial policy. Different kinds of public support for enterprise could be found across Europe, and each had a direct impact on the forms that capitalist structures took in their different national contexts.

Capital markets, corporate finance, ownership, and control

A second important factor in determining the particular forms that large European companies took in the years between the wars were the structures of financial markets and their impact on corporate financial strategies. In Britain, while local and regional banks financed most small businesses which operated in the fields characteristic of the First Industrial Revolution, a dynamic stock market played an important role in supporting entrepreneurial initiatives in manufacturing and commerce. At the eve of World War II, about 1,700 companies were listed on the London Stock

Exchange. This active market channeled the resources necessary to foster growth to a number of important mergers and acquisitions (M&A) in the capital-intensive sectors. From 1920 to 1940, around 3,200 companies were involved in consolidation processes. In some cases, the consolidation process resulted in the creation of large corporations characterized by relatively modern, decentralized organizational structures, and accounting methods. This was, for instance, the case with Dunlop which, starting from the 1920s, introduced a divisional structure to cope with its strategies of progressive acquisition and related diversification. In other cases, however, and even in technologically advanced industries such as electricity, the growth process was managed through the perpetuation of the traditional approach of a federation under a holding company. In this organizational structure, a financial company directly controlled a large number of subsidiaries. These were often combined in pyramidal structures that employed dense networks of interlocking directorates.

Even if listed on the Stock Exchange, many British industrial firms remained largely "personal," with representatives from the founding families occupying large numbers of seats on the board of directors (sometimes even disproportionate to the rights conferred by the actual shares they held). Several scholars have pointed out the fact that, notwithstanding some organizational innovations, there was "a reluctance in the business class as a whole to pursue anything other than defensive strategies which were based on the aim of preserving family control and ownership, whatever the costs" (Wilson 1995: 177).

These social patterns influenced the large companies that emerged from the process of merger and acquisition. This type of British holding—which allowed the families to preserve their role in business—was not the integrated and decentralized M-form. This practice brought about the federative system based upon associations and partnerships that had characterized English industrial capitalism in the last decades of the nineteenth century. Many of these mergers were nothing more than cartels within which a collusive division of the market took place.

In Germany, the growth of large companies was supported by the stock market, along with a consistent self-financing and an efficient banking system with many large institutions. As we noted before, "universal" banks shaped the structure of the German financial market, supporting a process of concentration in which the relevant owners were either families, individuals, or other companies. These structures were often backed by the main banks which invested in industrial securities and also exerted influence through proxy voting. From this period onward, banks became a key component of German capitalism. Banks were important creditors and influential shareholders. In many cases they effectively influenced the company, selecting and closely monitoring the top management. The involvement of the main banks shaped the German financial market, progressively weakening the role of the Stock Exchange as a way to channel financial resources toward the industrial system. A partial attenuation of this system took place immediately after the war, when the weakness of the main banks led German firms to seek additional financial resources in the stock market, in Wall Street above all. This situation did not last, however, and banks' power and influence was restored shortly after the conflict.

In the rest of Continental Europe, capital markets took a different, somewhat intermediate, form. In France and especially in Italy, entrepreneurial families in capital-intensive industries were able to maintain tight control of their companies. They held the top managerial positions and made relatively limited recourse to the stock market, depending instead on the credit provided by the main banks.

Industrial relations

A further area of divergence between Europe and the United States concerned the relations between capital and labor, both from the perspective of workers' participation as well as managerial practices. In the European business culture (even under the most authoritarian, dictatorial regimes), blue and white collars remained among the most relevant stakeholders in the company's constituency. Worker participation in governance was characteristic of the European experience after World War I. A relatively favorable cultural climate in Weimar Germany encouraged the direct participation of workers in the management of the enterprise, a practice that gradually acquired a more and more defined shape until the Nazi years. In this case, as to some extent in the French one of the *Front Populaire* (Popular Front, a leftist coalition briefly in power in the late 1930s), work councils were the bodies through which employees could get information about major managerial decisions and gain a sense of which direction the company was heading. These participation practices re-emerged after World War II and deeply affected the climate of European industrial relations during the years of growth following postwar reconstruction.

In other European countries, such as Italy and Spain, workers' participation took different forms. Under authoritarian regimes that limited workers' freedom and unionization, formal employee involvement with management was sometimes established in order to keep class conflict under control. This was the case of Fascist Italy, where the 1930s saw the introduction of "*Corporazioni,*" institutionalized legal bodies aimed at managing the relationship between capital and labor on an industry basis. These bodies also served to regulate, under the control of the Fascist Party, potential conflicts, and at least formally to treat labor and capital as equals.

Purely formal attempts at workers' involvement notwithstanding, the European workforce maintained a prominent position in the corporate framework. Labor was in fact generally characterized by a strong political identity and by a degree of unionization higher than that characterizing the US system of industrial relations before the New Deal. On average, the well-paid American worker was less often unionized and less interested in direct involvement in corporate life than his European colleagues. This difference was related to the fact that in almost all of the large European corporations the workforce maintained some degree of control over the production process on the shop floor, a process carried on by skilled blue-collar workers who enjoyed a high degree of autonomy.

When modern, bureaucratic techniques of job management were introduced in Europe, they were filtered through this unique system of labor-management relations. When not totally rejected, they were heavily adapted to the local European environment. This was true of the scientific management practices so popular in the United States. Some successful attempts at introducing scientific methods of work organization took place, as in the case of the Bedaux system, which aimed at increasing workers' productivity through tight controls over the job's rhythm and timing. In the 1920s, most of the European car manufacturers (particularly the French) moved to adopt the Taylorist management techniques which were used overseas. But even with these techniques ostensibly in place, levels of efficiency on the European lines remained lower on average than those in the US automotive industry. There was, in sum, a deeply grounded social resistance to the introduction in Europe of the US-centric system.

There were also sharp differences between Europe and the United States in the composition of the managerial class. In America, managerial careers offered a way to achieve upward social mobility and were therefore very attractive to young members of the middle and upper segments of the working class; managerial disciplines were part of specialized training courses offered by *ad hoc* institutions and by business schools. In Europe there was very little specific training for management. Training was generally on-the-job, and internal company career paths often brought clerks, blue-collar workers, and salesmen to positions of leadership. A partial exception was the engineer, the only high-level employee with specific training who could develop a managerial career. The polytechnic universities were the main sources of professionals for French, German, and Italian entrepreneurs. This specific training resulted in a prevalent managerial practice that was more oriented toward technical aspects of production than toward the requirements of the market.

Strategies and structures of European companies in the interwar years

As a result of these developments in the interwar economy, European companies were on average smaller than their American counterparts. They were less likely to foster a separation between ownership and control. They were less diversified. As a consequence, "mono-business" strategies, coupled with elementary organizational structures, persisted everywhere. This allowed the major stakeholders—individuals, families, the banks, or even the government—to maintain control over business and avoid some of the problems they associated with the US style of corporate enterprise. Power was thus less concentrated. Organizations were—with some significant exceptions—less likely to employ professional managers and formal systems of decentralization of power and responsibility.

Instead, Europe followed a different path, including a progressive diffusion of the holding company (H-form), which turned out to be flexible and adaptable in different situations. In the British case, as mentioned above, it was the instrument that enabled the consolidation process to take place smoothly, and it kept British federative attitudes alive. On the European continent, particularly in countries characterized by underdeveloped capital markets and family-run businesses, the same H-form made possible both horizontal and vertical integration. Owners could raise funds for integration while also preserving their power over the firm and its subsidiaries.

Further reading

F. Carnevali, *Europe's Advantage: Banks and Small Firms in Britain, France, Germany, and Italy since 1918*, Oxford University Press, Oxford, 2005.

Y. Cassis, *Big Business: The European Experience in the Twentieth Century*, Oxford University Press, Oxford, 1997.

C. Fohlin, *Finance Capitalism and Germany's Rise to Industrial Power*, Cambridge University Press, Cambridge, 2007.

L. Hannah, *The Rise of the Corporate Economy*, Methuen, London, 1976.

C. Schmitz, *The Growth of Big Business in the United States and Europe, 1850–1939*, Cambridge University Press, Cambridge, 1993.

J.F. Wilson, *British Business History, 1720–1994*, University of Manchester Press, Manchester, 1995.

Appendix

Table 11.1 Number of domestic cartels in Europe, 1865–1930

Year	Germany	Austria	Hungary	Switzerland	France	Britain	Japan
1865	4						
1887	70						
1890/1	117		8				
1900/2	300	50					
1905/6	385	100	50			40	
1911/12	550–660	120					
1921						446	8
1929/30	2,100	40–50, 70–80		More than 90	80+		30+

Source: Adapted from Jeffrey Fear, "Cartels," in Geoffrey Jones and Jonathan Zeitlin, *The Oxford Handbook of Business History*, Oxford University Press, Oxford, 2008, p. 275.

Table 11.2 Relative shares of world manufacturing output, 1880–1938 (%)

	1880	*1900*	*1913*	*1928*	*1938*
Britain	22.9	18.5	13.6	9.9	10.7
United States	14.7	23.6	32	39.3	31.4
Germany	8.5	13.2	14.8	11.6	12.7
France	7.8	6.8	6.1	6	4.4
Russia	7.6	8.8	8.2	5.3	9
Austria–Hungary	4.4	4.7	4.4	—	—
Italy	2.5	2.4	2.4	2.7	2.8

Source: Adapted from Christopher Freeman and Francisco Louçã, *As Time Goes By: From the Industrial Revolution to the Information Revolution*, Oxford University Press, Oxford, 2001, p. 249.

Table 11.3 Average levels of nominal protection, 1877–1926

	1877	1889	1897	1913	1926
United States	29.91[a]	30.1[a]	21[a]	18.9[a]	13.5[a]
	42.58[b]	45.4[b]	41.6[b]	40.5[b]	38.6[b]
	68.4[c]	66.2[c]	51.2[c]	46.5[c]	34.9[c]
Germany	—	8.8	9.6	6.9	5.2
Russia	14.6	34.5	33.8	30.3	—
United Kingdom	5.3	4.9	4.7	4.5	8.6
France	5.2[d]	8.3[d]	11.6[d]	9[d]	5.7[d]
	6.6[e]	8.6[e]	10.6[e]	8.8[e]	—
Austria–Hungary	0.9	6.6	7.7	7	7.7
Italy	8.45[d]	16.8[d]	16.2[d]	7.5[d]	3.1[d]
	7.3[f]	17.6[f]	18.5[f]	9.6[f]	11.9[f]
Japan	4[a]	2.5[a]	2.5[a]	10[a]	6.5[a]
	4.5[b]	3[b]	3.5[b]	19.5[b]	16[b]
Europe (average)	9.2	12	11.9	9.3	8.3

Source: Adapted from Vera Zamagni, *Dalla rivoluzione industriale all'integrazione europea. Breve storia economica dell'Europa contemporanea*, Il Mulino, Bologna, 1999, p. 119.

Notes
a   Total trade.
b   Only products subject to protection.
c   Products subject to protection as % of the total trade.
d   Data Brian R. Mitchell, *European Historical Statistics 1750–1975*, London: Macmillan 1981.
e   Estimates Maurice Levy-Leboyer and François Bourguignon, *L'Économie française au XIX siècle,* Economica, Paris 1985, tab. VI.
f   Data Giovanni Federico and Antonio Teña, "Was Italy a Protectionist Country?", *European Review of Economic History,* vol. 2, issue 1, pp. 73–97, 1998.

12 At the origins of the Japanese miracle

Entrepreneurship, the State, and business groups

We have seen in recent years that capitalism has taken many different forms as the system evolved in different nations and regions around the world. The differences and similarities need to be kept in mind as we look at Japanese business and the Japanese economy in the modern era.

Between 1820 and 1870, Japanese gross domestic product (GDP) grew at an average annual rate of nearly 0.2 percent compared with Europe's 1 percent per annum. During the following 40 years (until the outbreak of World War I), Japan's economy developed at an average rate of 1.5 percent per year, while the rate of economic growth in Europe remained unchanged. Behind these figures lies the fascinating story of one country's extremely rapid economic development; this growth is even more intriguing when one considers the general isolation that characterized Japan until the last quarter of the nineteenth century. Japan's development was made possible by a unique national model of industrialization that embraced entrepreneurship, new forms of business organization, and planning buttressed by a nationalistic culture.

From feudalism to modernization

The year 1868 signals the start of the so-called "Meiji Revolution" (frequently referred to as the "Meiji Restoration"), when a group of oligarchs, aristocrats, and samurai took control of the country. This followed two and a half centuries during which the Emperor (*tenno*) in the Tokugawa dynasty had been confined to a symbolic role, while a political and military leader, the *shogun*, effectively ruled the country. This revolution is conventionally considered the birthdate of modern Japan. During the centuries preceding this radical political and economic transformation, Japan had developed a number of distinctive economic features, some of which ultimately influenced its process of modernization. Tokugawa Japan had been a country impervious to external influences. From the early seventeenth century, the hostility of the ruling class toward foreigners succeeded in keeping the Western presence out of Japan and thereby interrupted the flows of trade, human capital, and technology that characterized Europe's economy at the time. There were some exceptions made for Dutch and Chinese merchants but, for the most part, Japan remained isolated from the West and its capitalist economy.

This isolation was accompanied by a high degree of social rigidity. Premodern Japanese society was divided into castes, which were characterized by very little social mobility. Peasants made up the majority of the active labor force, which was mainly devoted to rice cultivation. The entire national economy, including the taxation system, was based on rice production. Although numerically much less significant, artisans and merchants constituted the second and third castes. The aristocracy and a military élite, the samurai, belonged to the upper class. Despite its rigidity, premodern Japan had a high level of urbanization that would become a foundation for the future establishment of groups of merchants and entrepreneurs.

Some merchant families, such as the Mitsui and Sumitomo, began to occupy increasingly significant roles in the economy. These mercantile dynasties established close relationships with powerful politicians, providing banking and other financial services such as tax collection. Their crucial role and relationships provided these "political merchants" privileges in foreign trade, which were at the origin of their future investments in manufacturing.

Japan also had an efficient system of education based on thousands of primary schools scattered throughout the country. A strong central government was also an advantage because the population was accustomed to pervasive economic policies, exemplified by a strict control on currency. Although almost a monoculture based on rice, the primary sector in premodern Japan was characterized by high levels of technical skill. The country also had an efficient network of roads and irrigation systems. After the radical political changes of the Meiji Revolution, the new government's main objective was economic modernization, which it believed was necessary to maintain Japan's status as an independent nation. Strong and widespread nationalism encouraged aggressive interventionist public policies, implemented by an efficient bureaucracy. Japan's explicit goal was to "catch up," and the new Meiji leadership exerted considerable pressure on the entire society to abandon tradition to achieve this new objective.

The catching-up strategy was introduced in several areas: modernization of infrastructures, acquisition and dissemination of recent technologies, development of an industrial policy that was based on the direct intervention of the State, and the creation of new monetary and fiscal policies. The process of institutional modernization was carried out through the imitation of Western models. The Japanese Navy and the communications and postal services were modeled after the British example, while France offered benchmarks for the reorganization of the judicial system and also that of primary school education. The Japanese Army imitated the Germans, and Japan's new banking system was "imported," virtually intact, from the United States.

Japan set out to create high-quality human capital through education. The results were remarkable: in 1875, less than 30 percent of Japanese children had access to primary education; 20 years later, this percentage had risen to over 60 percent, reaching almost 100 percent just before World War I. At the end of the 1870s, a modern university system was set up in Tokyo, including one of the largest polytechnics in the world. The Japanese government systematically funded graduate students' educational travels in the United States and Europe. Moreover, the Japanese government tapped knowledge from overseas by hiring many foreign professors, technicians, and other experts. Between 1870 and 1880, the government made the acquisition of foreign knowledge and technology a priority by establishing state-owned enterprises (SOEs) in industries typical of the First Industrial Revolution: mining, shipbuilding, engineering, textiles, cement, and glass.

Notwithstanding their relevance as importers of new technologies and knowledge, the operational success of these enterprises was limited. These "pilot plants" were relatively inefficient, poorly managed, and underutilized. Their real function was to promote the gradual dissemination of up-to-date technology, because there was initially a lack of private initiatives in these fields. Given that goal, the efforts undertaken by the Meiji government were an almost immediate success. They uncovered the latent entrepreneurial talent in the population. Private enterprise quickly took hold. During the last two decades of the nineteenth century, when Japanese GDP increased annually by 4.3 percent, Japan's total public expenditure grew on a yearly average basis of over 4 percent per year. This resulted in an increase of capital stock around 5 percent annually. The output of the mining sector grew at a rate of over 10 percent per year, while manufacturing grew at more than 6 percent. In the mechanical and textile industries, growth approached and exceeded 10 percent, which was the same size as the trade balance.

As the Japanese industrial base grew stronger, it began to serve the military ambitions of this small but nationalistic country. Japan was triumphant in the 1894 conflict with China, and almost 10 years later in the war against Russia for the control of Korea. Allied with Britain, Japan entered World War I fighting successfully against Germany in Asia. These military efforts helped to boost the endogenous growth of the industrial basis and the overall growth of the country, witnessed by the trend in GDP per capita at constant prices: the index jumped from 100 in 1870 to 152 in 1895, 194 in 1915, and 230 in 1920. At the same time, as in most of the Western countries involved in the conflict, the structure of the manufacturing sector was changing. While textiles continued to remain the leading industry in terms of manufacturing and exports, such "modern" industries as chemicals, steel, and machinery became increasingly important.

Due to military procurement and the encouragement of cartels, the interwar years saw a further increase in the strength of Japan's capital-intensive industries. Their contribution to the total output of the manufacturing sector grew from 34 percent in the early 1930s to more than 55 percent in 1937. Between 1915 and 1940, the yearly growth rate of Japan's stock of fixed assets was around 7–8 percent; the chemical, mechanical, and steel industries experienced double-digit increases each year.

From merchants to entrepreneurs: the birth of the zaibatsu

As stated previously, Japan's amazing performance was based on a centrally driven intensive policy of modernization, accompanied by the important contributions of private entrepreneurs. Education fostered private entrepreneurship, as did the opportunity to build enterprises in a relatively stable political and financial setting.

So successful was the private sector that the government could begin to back out of the economy in some regards. By the end of the 1880s, the Japanese government had decided to end its direct involvement in the process of industrial modernization and started to sell its "pilot plants" at affordable prices to private entrepreneurs. Some of the businessmen who purchased these enterprises had been active in the Tokugawa era, and they used their wealth to acquire these former state undertakings. This allowed them to achieve more diversification of their own business activities. A good example of this practice can be found in the Mitsubishi group, which, on the basis of older maritime trading activities, began to diversify into the mining sector in order to secure the coal supplies that were needed for their ships. Later they moved into shipbuilding, buying another plant that had previously been owned by the state. Their next investment in the steel industry was made with the idea that it would let them provide basic materials for their shipyards, and the same strategy was used when they moved into the insurance field.

Businesses like Mitsubishi were known as "zaibatsu," or "financial groups." During the years between World War I and World War II, the zaibatsu expanded in capital- and labor-intensive industries, financial services, banking, and insurance. Their increasing strength was exemplified by the fact that, on the eve of World War II, the five major zaibatsu—Mitsui, Mitsubishi, Sumitomo, Yasuda, and, later, Nissan—accounted for one-third of the entire output of the Japanese manufacturing sector and for more than 10 percent of the total capital invested in the country as a whole.

The zaibatsu were different from the American M-form corporations and the European H-form businesses. They had less central control than the former and more than the latter. Their particular ownership and organizational structures gave them the ability to develop a diversified set of businesses, some of which shared technologies and all of which shared common sources of funding. The zaibatsu were extremely efficient and their strategies were suitable to Japan's rapidly expanding industrial economy.

During the interwar years, these large Japanese business groups were characterized by a "multi-subsidiary" structure based on holding companies. These holding companies were fully controlled by each zaibatsu's founding family. The holding companies were active in many different sectors, including banking and insurance, and were themselves often at the top of other pyramidal chains of shareholding control. A particularly important part of this complicated structure was the *Shosha*, the group's trading company, which provided trading services and ensured financial liquidity for the zaibatsu as a whole. Family control of each zaibatsu was secured and strengthened by the use of leverage equity, which was combined with other mechanisms of control, such as cross-shareholdings and directorates.

During the early 1930s, the four largest zaibatsu owned around 10 top tier subsidiaries; their businesses included everything from textiles, such as cotton and silk spinning and weaving, to electrical engineering with electromechanics and electrochemical plants and even holdings in mines, railways, and steel mills.

The Mitsui group, the largest zaibatsu, had more than 100 subsidiaries and companies under its control.

The "house bank" of each zaibatsu acted as both creditor and shareholder. These banking agencies even played the role of "house cleaners," when they were used to allocate resources to the zaibatsu's members. Evidence of their mounting relevance and power, which went well beyond their purely economic value, was revealed when, on the eve of World War II, three-fourths of all Japanese loans came from the four main zaibatsu banks.

From an organizational point of view, the zaibatsu relied on decentralized production structures to successfully manage hundreds of companies and thousands of employees. Unlike the major US corporations of the first half of the twentieth century, these Japanese businesses normally expanded by creating new subsidiaries. Sometimes, these were in entirely new fields, so the zaibatsu could grow through internal expansion, vertical integration, and diversification—with or without a common technology.

Communities of companies

The zaibatsu were crucial to Japan's economic growth, but the contribution of other entrepreneurial initiatives should not be underestimated. Small- and medium-sized enterprises were scattered everywhere throughout the country. The small "entrepreneurial" enterprise often specialized in craft-oriented industries, such as machine-tool manufacturing and light engineering. An example is the geographic area of "Ota Ward" (south of Tokyo), where small mechanical businesses clustered. During the 1930s, the area contained more than 2,000 companies, each of which employed less than 50 people. Before World War II, Japanese firms with fewer than 100 employees accounted for 95 percent of all production units in the country, employing around half of the active manufacturing labor force and generating over 40 percent of Japan's industrial output. The availability of a cheap labor force and the diffusion of the small electric engine were important factors in the persistence of the small Japanese business. The Japanese production system was thus characterized by a sort of "dualism." There were a few giant, large-enterprise groups, surrounded by a plethora of small and microbusinesses.

Often these small and medium enterprises were not fully independent. Small businesses were frequently linked to the main companies of the zaibatsu by means of long chains of subcontracting relationships. Entrepreneurial initiatives could emerge from this lively seedbed, and they were led mainly by skilled technicians and blue-collar workers.

"Families reigning but not governing": management, labor organization, and industrial relations in the zaibatsu

Large Japanese diversified groups set up managerial hierarchies quickly because they needed suitable organizational structures in order to manage their increasingly complex and decentralized business activities. These hierarchies shared some characteristics with European and US businesses, but they functioned in different ways. Authority did not have to be specified as formally as it did in US organizations. Cooperation and competition were balanced in unique ways shaped by Japanese culture and social relations. The expansion of the hierarchies was incessant during the interwar years, particularly in the zaibatsu just before World War II. Large cohorts of managers filled the top levels of both the holding and the controlled companies.

Until World War II, the separation between ownership and decision-making in the zaibatsu had been achieved through the appointment of a "Bantô." The bantô was a kind of general manager, a person who did not technically belong to the zaibatsu family, but who, through many years of employment, was bound by close ties of loyalty to them. Thus, owners slowly became detached from the operational functions of their companies. By the end of World War I, the majority of zaibatsu families "reigned" over rather than "ruled" their corporations.

The process of diversification and expansion, which characterized the major Japanese companies during the 1920s and 1930s, was driven by salaried managers who held long-standing positions at the top of each zaibatsu company. These top managers, who occasionally came from the ranks of the public administration, were young university graduates, technicians, and engineers. During the mid-1920s, two out of every three top Japanese executives had a university degree.

Many of these young, highly motivated executives had international experience. These men were instilled with a nationalist spirit, which prompted them to pursue Japan's success through business. When these managers were able to formulate and implement sound strategies for industrial growth, they could depend on the zaibatsu owners to fund their proposals. The promotion of professional managers enabled the zaibatsu to push into high-tech, capital-intensive industries.

At the same time, the rise of an "industrial proletariat," a group of workers who came largely from the countryside, forced companies to confront the issue of motivating, regulating, and managing a vast workforce. The traditional, paternalistic models, which had regulated preindustrial Japanese society, emphasized principles of seniority, discipline, and respect for authority, but in Japan, as elsewhere, the process of industrialization eroded some of the paternalistic culture, encouraging workers to look elsewhere for authority. Industrialization brought sometimes harsh social conflicts, both before and immediately after World War I, when factory discipline deteriorated, in part in response to difficult living conditions. Social pressure together with the need for management to retain former peasants trained inside the factory encouraged corporate owners and managers to figure out a different model of industrial relations.

When dealing with their workforce, zaibatsu managers promoted employment stability through welfare programs, insurance, and education, which they also extended to workers' families. For most zaibatsu employees (even though not for everybody), specific training programs and a wage structure based on a system of performance and profit bonuses allowed many of the managers to motivate their workforce and link their allegiance to the firm.

Nationalism, militarism, and industrial growth in the interwar years: the role of the State

The zaibatsu were crucial to Japan's unique style of industrial modernization. During the 1930s, the growth of Japanese nationalism drew the Army and the large industrial groups closer, for the zaibatsu were the major beneficiaries of public military procurement. Between 1930 and 1935, the resources allocated to military spending grew from less than one-third to about one-half of all public expenditures; this had a positive effect on capital-intensive industries. Japan's military spending passed from one-third of the country's total manufacturing output in 1931 to over 55 percent in 1937. One year later, the Army assumed full control of the strategic industries.

In the meantime, top zaibatsu managers were vigorously seeking technological advancement by acquiring knowledge from abroad. Emphasis was placed on "reverse engineering," that is, the imitation of Western technology for improving quality and efficiency. Japan's agreements with the major European and US industrial groups were important to this process. In the case of electromechanics, for example, Toshiba developed a close relationship with General Electric, whereas the Mitsubishi group fostered ties with Westinghouse. Fuji Electric was born out of a joint initiative between Siemens and a Japanese mining group.

At the same time, the Japanese government was channeling the findings of its public research laboratories into the industrial system. In the electrical industry, two research centers—one under state control and the other under the auspices of the Japanese Army and Navy—made important discoveries in the fields of radio communications and radar. Similar operational relationships existed in shipbuilding, aircraft manufacturing, and, of course, steel. The preparation for and management of war were, as far as the manufacturing industries were considered, the Japanese government's top priority. Coordination of production and allocation of raw materials—modeled after actions being taken in Nazi Germany—were achieved by creating partnerships between companies. This was undertaken by the Ministry of Trade and Industry, called "MCI" and later "MITI," founded in 1925 as a Ministry of Commerce and Industry. At this time, it began to exercise pervasive influence over the country's industrial system, backed by strong legislation.

In the 80 years that passed between the end of Japan's centuries-old isolation and the outbreak of World War II, Japan achieved modernization and transitioned quite successfully from the First to the Second Industrial Revolution. Although initially a peripheral country, Japan was able to achieve status as one of the world's leading economies during the second half of the twentieth century, at least partially, because of the distinctive business techniques and organizations it adopted during this time.

The role played by the Japanese State was substantial. Although it abandoned direct involvement through SOEs in the industrial modernization of the country, it nonetheless maintained a strong influence over the economic system as a whole. It ultimately determined the shape of industrial development in many "strategic" industries. During the interwar period, an effective system of industrial relations (characterized by a high level of "consensus" and a disciplined, committed workforce) was established in many Japanese business organizations. The organizational and ownership structure of the zaibatsu was distinctive; these large, diversified groups were responsible for a substantial share of Japan's entire manufacturing system and were characterized by a technically advanced ruling class of professional managers. These men planned and put into action the long-term business strategies, which would enable Japan to push ahead at a rapid pace. Japan's large firms were a significant part, in quantitative terms, of a very broad entrepreneurial landscape. The Japanese entrepreneurial community in the years of the country's industrial revolution was an extremely variegated group, which included former samurai, merchants, technicians, nobles, and even peasants. It was also comprised of people coming from the low ranks of Japanese society. The presence of a varied entrepreneurial seedbed provided to the largest groups further opportunities of expansion. One telling example is offered by the early history of one of the most famous Japanese companies, Toyota. Established by Sakichi Toyoda, the son of a carpenter, in 1867 (just one year before the Meiji Restoration), it initially produced mechanical (and afterward, automatic) looms, which enhanced textile productivity. The commercial and industrial success of the initiative—which just before World War II turned to the production of cars and changed its name to Toyota—was due to the agreement that Toyoda set up with a zaibatsu, Mitsui, which commercialized on a large scale the company's products. Companies belonging to the Mitsui group have been since then and for a long time stable shareholders of Toyota. While the diverse world of small Japanese enterprises remained largely complementary to that of the big groups, entrepreneurial organizations such as Toyoda were significant contributors to the country's progress.

These achievements were a solid basis on which Japan was able to build the first part of its solid foundation for success in the industries of the Second Industrial Revolution. Japanese capitalism was different than the Western variety, but it was growing rapidly and its businessmen were developing business institutions suited to Japanese culture and normal social practices. Meanwhile, they were drawing upon Western technology to boost the production and efficiency of their leading industries.

Further reading

A. Gordon, *The Evolution of Labor Relations in Japan: Heavy Industry, 1853–1955*, Harvard University Press, Cambridge, MA, 1985.

A. Goto and H. Odagiri, *Innovation in Japan*, Clarendon Press, Oxford, 1997.

J. Hirschmeier and T. Yui, *The Development of Japanese Business, 1600–1980*, George Allen & Unwin, London, 1975.

T. Ito, *The Japanese Economy*, MIT Press, Cambridge, MA, 1992.

H. Morikawa, *Zaibatsu: The Rise and Fall of Family Enterprise Groups in Japan*, University of Tokyo Press, Tokyo, 1992.

H. Morikawa (ed.), *A History of Top Management in Japan: Managerial Enterprises and Family Enterprises*, Oxford University Press, Oxford, 2001.

D.H. Whittaker, *Small Firms in the Japanese Economy*, Cambridge University Press, Cambridge, 1999.

Appendix

Table 12.1 Composition of national income in Japan, 1888–1987

Year	Primary	Secondary	Tertiary
1888	0.415	0.122	0.463
1910	0.315	0.257	0.428
1920	0.247	0.321	0.432
1930	0.209	0.435	0.356
1955	0.167	0.293	0.54
1970	0.059	0.475	0.466
1987	0.028	0.46	0.512

Source: Adapted from Ryoshin Minami, *The Economic Development of Japan*, St. Martin's Press, New York, 1992, p. 92.

Table 12.2 Composition of labor force in Japan, 1888–1987

Year	Primary	Secondary	Tertiary
1888	0.699		0.301
1910	0.602		0.35
1920	0.534	0.239	0.2273
1930	0.495	0.244	0.261
1955	0.371	0.297	0.333
1970	0.172	0.418	0.41
1987	0.082	0.402	0.516

Source: Adapted from Ryoshin Minami, *The Economic Development of Japan*, St. Martin's Press, New York, 1992, p. 212.

Part V

From the postwar years to the fall of the Wall

The age of "shrinking space"

13 From World War II to the Third Industrial Revolution

At the outbreak of World War II, many of the world's most industrialized countries were in a contradictory situation. While they were struggling to survive the aftermath of the Great Depression, they were also trying to encourage their entrepreneurs to take full advantage of the economic opportunities generated by the technologies of the Second Industrial Revolution. By that time, capital-intensive industries had spread around the world and contributed to increasing levels of gross national product (GNP) for many countries. There were important national differences in the proliferation and impact of these industries. There was variation in the strategies and organizational structures adopted by each corporation. On the whole, however, "big business" was one of the major products of this technological revolution, and it now played a crucial role in the process of economic growth. Three features of the large corporation stood out: the existence of complex organizational structures; the presence of often conflicting actors, including entrepreneurs, managers, shareholders, employees, local communities, and the State; and the increasingly strategic role played by research and development (R&D). From the 1920s on, R&D departments supported the diversification strategies that were so popular in large corporations. As we saw in a previous chapter, they did this by identifying new technologies and developing new products and processes.

In large corporations, the process of innovation became institutionalized and linked to national and international scientific and engineering networks. The people who worked in corporate R&D maintained relationships with the professors and teachers who had trained them, which meant that cooperation between corporate laboratories and the departments of major research universities became common. This process of the institutionalization of innovation was particularly well developed in "leader economies" such as the United States and Germany.

One result was an overall increase in the number of research laboratories, scientists, and researchers. In the United States, the number of employees in the R&D departments of big corporations increased from less than 3,000 in 1920, to 10,000 in 1933, and finally to nearly 30,000 on the eve of World War II. Researchers and scientists were concentrated in fields such as chemicals, oil, glass, telecommunications, and rubber.

From an organizational point of view, all of this increased R&D activity led to a systematic process of innovation. The practice that prevailed in an earlier period had been characterized by a strong emphasis on individual creative effort, but now innovation became a collective process. This was comparable with what was happening in the factory with the assembly line and was characterized by a business system with bureaucratic rules, defined roles, and a relatively complex and rigid hierarchy. In an article published in the mid-1920s by a Bell Laboratory scientist named E.B. Craft, the author argued that "the outstanding characteristic of this organization . . . is its conduct of research and development by a group method of attack." Craft, who worked in part of the "research core" of American Telephone & Telegraph, explained how his laboratory functioned:

> When a problem is put up to the Labs for solution, it is divided into its elements and each element is assigned to that group of specialists who know the most about that particular field but they all cooperate and make their contribution to the solution of the problem as a whole.
>
> (Craft cited in David Noble, *America by Design: Science, Technology and the Rise of Corporate Capitalism,* Knopf, New York, 1979, p. 119)

R&D thus became a strategic asset, particularly in industries with a high degree of technological sophistication. Possession of better scientific knowledge and superior technology was crucial for companies that wanted to achieve domestic and international success. Because they were so cutting edge, the company's products often had to be protected by patents; corporations depended on this protection for their viability. There was initially a strong interest in pursuing vertical integration strategies and keeping all research activities within an organization. Corporations hoped this would enable them to maintain control over some "highly sensitive" assets, which generally could not be outsourced; they also recognized the interdependence between R&D and other important departments within the organization, such as production and marketing.

The high costs of R&D had a significant impact on many companies' investment budgets. This could be a difficulty when the creation of a new technology depended on a large amount of basic research—the sort of research that involved a high degree of uncertainty and long delays in getting payouts. The main companies created a system of incentives for their R&D workers, and they frequently pursued technological advancement on a large scale with the support of public policy. Where they were successful, the resulting innovative capabilities were crucial to the competitiveness of companies, industries, and even nations as a whole.

In the countries leading the Second Industrial Revolution, R&D departments operated alongside a network of other institutions that were also committed to technological advancement. These included private universities and polytechnics (in the United States, private companies often gave them financial support to develop basic research) as well as state laboratories funded through regular departments, *ad hoc* agencies, or by the military. The flow of inventions and innovations generated by all of these groups created a series of "spill-over effects," which benefited the manufacturing sector as a whole. These benefits were quite substantial due to the high and growing costs of basic research.

Some of the countries involved in the R&D transformation built complex "national systems of innovation," in which many institutions, at every level, were cooperating in making the innovative process smoother and more productive. In Germany, technical skills and engineering were cultivated, and the country was able to reach, in the 1930s, the most advanced technological level in Europe. Still, the most sophisticated and efficient "national system of innovation" was undoubtedly found in the United States. In the interwar years, the American national system of R&D laboratories relied primarily on large enterprises whose main activity consisted of the practical application of pure research. This type of work was also carried out within universities such as the Massachusetts Institute of Technology (MIT) in Boston. The corporations themselves either directly funded this research or provided generous scholarships to the scientists who worked in the university labs.

Besides the research universities and R&D departments, there were also a number of private research laboratories. These independent laboratories often were founded by former academics performing commissioned research; they had every reason to maintain close ties to the national and international academic communities.

On occasion, the federal government undertook research projects, but this was done on a very limited basis before World War II. These projects took place on three levels: first, the provision of funds for research institutes and university laboratories; second, through targeted procurement policies, especially in the military, which pushed contractors to develop specific technologies; and third, through federal agencies that played a role in basic and applied research. The National Research Council (NRC), a public institution with close links with the business community, was set up at the end of 1916, shortly before America's intervention in World War I. Its purpose was to promote and organize cooperation among various research institutions, whether public or private. Between World War I and World War II, the NRC directed its efforts toward the development of new, advanced technologies in strategic fields, including telecommunications and oil refining.

Industry shaped by technology: the role of World War II

The "national systems of innovation" that had taken shape during the first half of the twentieth century were seriously tested during World War II. The war imposed intense demands on manufacturing industries in all the countries involved.

The war quickly removed most of the budget constraints that had hampered research in both the public and private sectors during peacetime. In the United States, federal expenditures for research between 1940 and 1945 grew from 80 million dollars to more than 1.3 billion dollars. The government established an Office of Scientific Research and Development (OSRD), headed by Vannevar Bush, a distinguished engineer who became the leading "science advisor" to the federal government. The OSRD supplied public funds to research institutions and ensured that private companies were actively contributing to American competency in research- and technology-intensive industries.

During World War II, both the United States and Germany were able to make significant technological advances in many areas of applied military research, including chemicals, pharmaceuticals, air transport, electronics, and "new materials" (e.g., synthetic fibers and plastics). These were crucial innovations and were the basis for radical changes in the structures of markets, in industries, and, especially, in the companies involved.

Similar radical innovations emerged independently in a number of countries. They generated a wide range of technological alternatives, many of which would have significant effects after the war. A good example was radar technology, which was developed experimentally during the interwar period. It was applied, improved, and then became indispensable in World War II. The technology, based on the use of electromagnetic waves, was developed simultaneously in the United Kingdom, Germany, and the United States. The jet engine was developed both in Germany and the United Kingdom during the early 1930s and was used in efficient prototypes in the early 1940s. The United States lagged in creating planes with jet engines but was able to mitigate this problem through the help of the United Kingdom and the National Advisory Committee for Aviation (NACA). The NACA promoted cooperation between the Navy and large private corporations such as Westinghouse and General Electric.

The war also indirectly stimulated the selection and application of many new technologies. Raw material shortages made it necessary to identify efficient substitutes. Synthetic rubber was developed in this way in the United States after the Japanese invasion of southeast Asia created shortages of natural rubber supplies. Similarly, fibers and synthetic polymers (developed well before the conflict by DuPont in the United States and IG Farben in Germany) were widely used during the war. They provided substitutes for increasingly scarce materials such as silk. German experiments in the field of jet engines and in the air transportation of soldiers, bombs, and materials proved to be fundamental to the development of modern aviation.

At the end of the war, research efforts intensified in those areas characterized by "big science," where innovative activity was based on large-scale projects, both in terms of budget and in the degree of human and physical resources involved. This process was particularly intense in the case of the United States, which committed itself to being at the frontiers of research in many of the leading sciences. During the 1950s and 1960s, the Cold War drove US military spending up until it accounted for about 10 percent of America's gross domestic product (GDP). Total federal spending for R&D rose from 30 billion dollars in 1955 to over 80 billion dollars in 1965. The peak was more than 90 billion dollars in 1969.

"Big science" encouraged a convergence between those research programs that were linked to the military and those that had been undertaken by private companies for purely commercial purposes. Private companies were encouraged by this favorable environment and invested heavily in R&D. In the United States, scientists and engineers employed in R&D laboratories rose from 50,000 in 1946 to more than 300,000 in 1960, reaching nearly half a million by 1980 and 700,000 by 1990. Similar, though less dramatic, changes were taking place in Britain, Germany, and Japan.

New industries for a new industrial revolution

One very large part of the wave of innovations in products and processes that characterized the Second Industrial Revolution was "chemical" in nature; these innovations took place in the chemical, pharmaceutical, refining, food and beverage, and steel industries. This stands in contrast to the new technologies and industries of today—microelectronics, the Internet, jet engines, mass air transport, and nuclear energy—in which the major science base of innovation is found in physics and in the effort to go beyond the limits of space, of time, and of existing materials. This "Third Industrial Revolution" is marked by the creation of totally new industries, with new market opportunities and radical changes in at least three broad clusters of businesses.

The first cluster was in communications, in which changes were characterized by the diffusion of both the Internet and modern telecommunications systems. Massive communications networks were made possible both by the dissemination of personal computers on a global scale and by technological advancements in fixed telephony and, later, in cellular systems.

The second area was in transportation, which changed as a result of the technological advancements associated with the emergencies of World War II. Bigger and faster aircraft were built out of more sophisticated or even totally new materials, such as plexiglas. These machines were powered by jet engines, and they ran on special fuels. This affected civil aviation as well, which benefited from the resulting reduction in transport costs. An era of mass air transport was launched.

The last area in which Third Industrial Revolution innovations clustered was in physical materials. The seemingly endless possibilities of applied physics had been realized in the "Manhattan Project" and the creation of the atomic bomb. Research programs using atomic energy for peaceful purposes were initiated immediately following the war, and commercial programs soon spread rapidly through the developed nations. Nuclear experimentation was particularly important to those industrialized countries that faced both shortages and price increases in traditional sources of energy, oil, and coal. While this was happening, an entirely new field of "biotechnology" emerged as a result of research advances in the 1950s and 1960s in molecular biology, biochemistry, and genetics. Now, for the first time, cells could be used as tiny factories to produce new and natural substances.

As was the case during the previous industrial revolutions, a key factor in all sectors of the Third Industrial Revolution was the availability of General Purpose Technologies (GPTs). GPTs could be applied to a wide range of industries. The semiconductor—and its successor, the integrated circuit (or microchip and microprocessor)—played the same role in the Third Industrial Revolution that steam power had played during the First Industrial Revolution and that electricity and chemistry had played during the Second Industrial Revolution. The semiconductor was crucial to many of the products and processes typical of the Third Industrial Revolution: telecommunications, household appliances, medical devices, machine tools, and weapons. Semiconductors, integrated circuits, and microchips were essential to the transportation and communications industries because they enabled innovative firms to develop the personal computer and its subsequent application, the Internet.

The first transistor was developed at the end of 1947 by a group of scientists including William Shockley, a researcher at Bell Labs, the R&D laboratories of American Telephone & Telegraph (AT&T). Shockley was an expert in solid-state physics. AT&T was particularly interested in developing an efficient alternative to the vacuum tubes and electromechanical devices that were used as switches in telephone communication systems. Anticipating substantial growth in data and voice communications, the Bell System recognized that its existing systems were reaching their upper limits in terms of the traffic they could carry in the United States. The transistor provided an ideal solution to that problem.

Shockley and his team won the Nobel Prize in physics in 1956 for their practical application of Bell Labs' research. Semiconductor technology—immediately made available to the public by AT&T itself—replaced vacuum tubes and electromechanical switches, removing a major bottleneck in the telephone system by the end of the 1950s. This occurred precisely when it became necessary to increase the efficiency and performance of America's giant telecommunications network. But the most important application of Shockley's invention was discovered later. The discovery was made almost simultaneously by two firms, the first, Texas Instruments, a consolidated firm, and the second, a business start-up led by scientists, Fairchild Semiconductor. Texas Instruments and Fairchild Semiconductor almost simultaneously invented the integrated circuit. The first microchips, which were made of germanium and silicon crystals, materials characterized by semiconducting properties, were developed in the early 1950s. This innovation was followed a decade later by the microprocessor, designed and manufactured by Intel, a start-up founded by some of Fairchild's former employees.

Given their wide range of applications, semiconductors immediately captured the interest of the defense industry, and especially of the military and industrial leaders involved with the missile and space programs. By 1955, about 40 percent of transistor production was for military purposes, a figure that climbed to 50 percent by 1960. Private consumption eventually grew to surpass public procurement. By 1960, the US government's percentage had dropped to just over one-third, which was still a significant level, particularly given the fact that the federal government funded the basic research in the field. This funding was acquired through resources provided by the National Aeronautics Space Agency (NASA), among others.

By the late 1970s, when the US semiconductor industry had become less competitive with the Japanese and southeast Asian producers, the US government once again encouraged R&D in the semiconductor field with the creation of Sematech. Sematech was a consortium of key companies, whose goal was the sharing of information and the coordination of production. The creation of microchips, microprocessors, and memory capacities able to process huge amounts of information, quickly and at a rapidly decreasing cost per unit, was essential to the development of personal computers that became ubiquitous from the early 1970s onward.

Global trends

By the mid-1950s, it was apparent that the technologies of the Third Industrial Revolution were generating formidable new economic opportunities, first in the leading nations and then around the entire globe. The impact of these new technologies was summarized by Raymond Vernon, who claimed that they created "shrinking of space," that is, a reduction of physical distances, and an elimination of barriers to the movement of people and goods, of capital and resources, and particularly of knowledge and data. Combined with a series of political, social, and cultural alterations around the globe, this shrinking space rapidly transformed business both at the macro- and the microeconomic levels. In less than 25 years, entrepreneurs and innovative organizations took advantage of the new opportunities to create new types of businesses suited to the transformations taking place in their technological and economic settings.

The last quarter of the twentieth century witnessed a new period of globalization, which was marked primarily by an increase in the volume and intensity of world trade. Worldwide, the index of imports and exports in the year 2000 was 100; this had been achieved by rapid growth, for in 1980 the sum of imports and exports was 30, by 1990 it was 54, and it was 85 in 1995. By 2005, the index had grown to more than 160. Much of this trade took place—and still takes place—among developed countries. In economically advanced areas, globalization is rapid and easily attainable. For wealthy nations, globalization results in an impressive increase in the flow of foreign investments, many of which are made by major companies worldwide. Globalization also entails a significant cost saving for companies because the new technologies allow cheaper monitoring and information collection.

Worldwide, foreign investment in GDP rose from 4.8 percent in 1980 to 8 percent in 1990 and reached 24 percent in 2005, together with an enormous increase in the trade among advanced countries as well as between advanced countries and the developing economies. There was a parallel increase in the number and volume of crossborder mergers and acquisitions, which, on a global scale, increased from about 2,500 in 1990 to 7,000 in 2000.

The financial markets were another area where a combination of institutional innovation and new technology had the effect of exponentially increasing the flow of financial resources available worldwide for loans and investments. There was a concomitant emergence of new actors in the field of financial intermediation. This made more and more resources available to the largest multinational corporations. According to the Organisation for Economic Co-operation and

Development (OECD), between 1990 and 2000 the assets available to active OECD institutional investors (mutual funds, pension funds, insurance companies, etc.) almost tripled in volume, exceeding 35 trillion dollars. This was more than ten times the level it had reached only 15 years before.

Globalization also profoundly affected the flow and value of human capital. Looking again to the data provided by the OECD, the 2000-based index (2000 = 100) of immigration flow to the most industrialized countries was about 60 in 1985. It exceeded 120 in 2004. This growth changed significantly the labor markets of the world's most developed countries, including the markets for professionals and for skilled and unskilled workers.

Intense globalization skyrocketed after the negative economic cycle of the 1970s, fostering a radical change in business competition. Enterprises and entrepreneurs were subjected to increasing pressure about their strategies, structures, and organizational performances.

Enterprise and entrepreneurs in the age of "shrinking space"

The new technologies of the Third Industrial Revolution generated a range of different entrepreneurial reactions, as companies adjusted to their competition and new market opportunities.

Consolidated companies had to renew their strategies and reaffirm their positions as first movers. A number of openings were created for new entrepreneurial ventures and niche producers. This was particularly evident in the computer industry, where two areas were most affected: the production of mainframes and minicomputers, and the semiconductor industry. Like the businesses of the Second Industrial Revolution, those in the computer industry were rewarded for being first movers and for having a bundle of capabilities in manufacturing, technology, and marketing.

In the production of the first mainframe computers, and later of personal computers, the market was theoretically global, although in practice it was controlled almost totally by US companies. Among the top ten firms were the leaders of the electric machinery industry, companies such as General Electric, AT&T, and Philco (a manufacturer of consumer electronics). Three office machine companies were represented: National Cash Register (NCR), Burroughs, and IBM. IBM's incentive to diversify into computers was driven both by the antitrust suit the company faced and by the obvious link between their data-processing business and the new technology. An industry leader by the beginning of the 1960s, Control Data Corporation (CDC), had been founded after World War II by an electrical engineer named William Norris. Norris' CDC gained a strong market position in scientific data processing, and it simultaneously developed an aggressive strategy of vertical integration through the acquisition of smaller firms. This strategy allowed CDC to control the production of all of its necessary components, but it also enabled it to become an important supplier to other companies. IBM was one of the computer industry's first movers, due to strategic investments it had made in the early 1950s in human capital and R&D.

IBM's investments allowed its engineers to improve the design of computers and also let them implement a language needed for their operation: software. In just a few years, the number of IBM engineers and technicians grew from 500 to over 5,000. Some indirect support for the company and its CEO, James Watson, came from the US government, which, besides being the company's largest customer, also played a crucial role in financing its R&D activity, in testing new products. In effect, the government gave the firm an entry barrier in a new and promising market. By the end of the 1950s, IBM dominated the market (its sales were ten times higher than its closest competitor, Remington Rand) and IBM covered virtually all of the segments of the industry.

Despite its dominance, IBM faced challenges in the development of personal computers, where some specialized producers operated—including CDC and the Digital Equipment Corporation (DEC). IBM also had serious problems with the lack of compatibility between IBM computers and software that had been designed by different producers; it was particularly hard to manage the company's different market segments that included both mainframes and personal computers. This situation limited IBM's ability to take advantage of economies of scale and pushed the company to develop a "family" of computers, all of which were equipped with standard interfaces and a common language. This strategy enabled IBM to cover an increasingly broad range of market segments.

In 1963, IBM launched System 360, which was equipped with a new microprocessor technology. This innovation had required a huge investment; in 4 years, IBM had hired 60,000 new employees (1,000 of whom were dedicated full-time to software development), constructed five new plants, and made a total investment of about 7 billion dollars. As a consequence, IBM suffered heavy losses until the end of the 1960s, when System 360 emerged as the worldwide standard in mainframe computers. With the introduction of System 360, IBM finally realized growing revenue in the computer division: 1.2 billion dollars in 1963, and almost 9 billion dollars 10 years later. Economies of scale in software design, hardware production, marketing, sales, and maintenance led to extremely high entry barriers. IBM held about 70 percent of the world market, whereas its competitors held only marginal positions in small niches. Large incumbent producers in household goods, General Electric and Westinghouse, initially persevered with older technologies like vacuum tubes.

The early semiconductor industry was dominated by relatively small companies; Fairchild was founded as a small entrepreneurial enterprise in 1957. These companies often were active in related industries. Motorola had been an established producer of car appliances when it began working with semiconductors. Texas Instruments had been active in the production of detection equipment for the oil industry, but during the war, it began working in high-technology industries in order to manufacture radar and sonar equipment. Quickly, Motorola and Texas Instruments (which was one of IBM's main suppliers) were able to beat their competitors and dominate the market until the mid-1980s.

Texas Instruments introduced the integrated circuit at the end of the 1950s (see above) after a lengthy investment in production and marketing. This started a process of international expansion that quickly made Texas Instruments the largest semiconductor producer in the world. The firm held between 11 and 12 percent of the market, followed by Motorola, which had adopted similar strategies. Fairchild, which tried to imitate the two leaders, failed. Fairchild was a purely entrepreneurial "business" led by strong and charismatic leaders, but they faced a difficult transition as they tried to convert the company into an integrated, bureaucratic organization.

In the international markets for semiconductors and memory storage, newcomers willing to invest at the right scale were able to acquire leadership positions. The technologies that made this success possible emerged from the trials and errors of hundreds of small ventures, which were clustered in technological districts such as Silicon Valley in California. Then, however, the nature of the semiconductor game changed drastically with the maturation of the technology of microchips and microprocessors; this was especially true for small entrepreneurial firms, whose growth had been supported by innovative methods of financing, such as venture capital investment (see Chapter 20). Semiconductor production facilities became larger and increasingly more expensive; higher economies of scale created a drop in the average unit cost of manufacture, which in turn started a process of concentration in the industry. Marginal, less efficient producers were squeezed out. In the early 1960s, the average price of an integrated circuit was around 40 dollars, but by the end of the decade, the same circuit cost less than 2 dollars. Despite strategic public policies (which limited semiconductor supply), by 1980 the more than 30 producers of Silicon Valley's high-tech cluster had shrunk to seven.

Not every high-tech company was affected the same way. Intel, a spin-off of Fairchild, was founded in 1968 by Bob Noyce (the creator of integrated circuits) and Gordon Moore (Fairchild's R&D director, who became famous for his statement that the capacity of an integrated circuit was going to double every two years). By committing itself to mass production of memory chips, Intel aimed to achieve growth. In 1972, Intel placed a 1K DRAM standard memory chip (both erasable and rewritable) on the market, and this shortly became the company's premium product. From that moment on, Intel enjoyed continuous growth, thanks in part to the increasing success of the company's mass-produced microprocessors.

New organizational forms?

As should already be evident, the technologies of the Third Industrial Revolution had a significant impact on the strategies and structures of the companies that developed, marketed, and sold the new products and services. New technology did not weaken big business. Thanks to this technological revolution, large corporations became even more global, expanding their activities on a considerably larger scale than they had been able to in the past. A growing emphasis on technological and knowledge-intensive industries, characterized by heavy investment in R&D, created cultures of learning within these organizations. Investments in intangible capital, which previously had been the purview of big business, now became increasingly important to all companies in these new markets. The largest businesses had a head start because of their long-standing practices of, and capabilities in, knowledge management.

Large companies reaffirmed their importance, but the development of new sectors, products, and services caused changes in business strategies and behavior. Beginning in the early 1970s, adoption of new technologies forced the structural reorganization of the large enterprises. Frequently, decentralization became necessary, a development that rewarded the entrepreneurial role played by small- and medium-sized units of production (see Chapter 20).

In their seminal essay devoted to the role of big business in modern economic development, Alfred Chandler and Takashi Hikino argued that one of the ways large companies contributed to the growth of contemporary economies was through their ability to organize themselves into central "nodes." Each node functioned within a network of other companies. And with the growth of the global economy, these small- and medium-sized networks gradually expanded in size and importance.

As we saw with the earlier example of the zaibatsu, networks of firms linked by processes of informal coordination are not an historical novelty. The establishment in some industries of "vertical networks," or subcontractors organized around a single large firm, was a common form of business organization in the Second Industrial Revolution. This was the case even when internalization through vertical integration became popular. The Information Age and digital innovation brought a decline in information costs, which contributed to the formation of networks of producers who were coordinated by large companies: a significant example is provided by the pharmaceutical industry after the swing toward biotech. The Third Industrial Revolution increased organizational restructuring within large firms, encouraging higher degrees of decentralization within these groups. This process reached its peak around the year 2000.

Further reading

A.D. Chandler, Jr., *Inventing the Electronic Century: The Epic Story of the Consumer Electronics and Computer Science Industries*, Free Press, New York, 2001.

L. Galambos and J.E. Sewell, *Networks of Innovation: Vaccine Development at Merck, Sharp & Dohme, and Mulford, 1895–1995*, Cambridge University Press, Cambridge, 1995.

F. Malerba, *The Semiconductor Business: The Economics of Rapid Growth and Decline*, University of Wisconsin Press, Madison, WI, 1985.

D.C. Mowery and N. Rosenberg, *Paths of Innovation: Technological Change in 20th-Century America*, Cambridge University Press, Cambridge, 1998.

R.R. Nelson (ed.), *National Innovation Systems: A Comparative Analysis*, Oxford University Press, New York, 1993.

G.P. Pisano, *Science Business: The Promise, the Reality, and the Future of Biotech*, Harvard Business School Press, Boston, 2006.

V.W. Ruttan, *Is War Necessary for Economic Growth? Military Procurement and Technology Development*, Oxford University Press, New York, 2006.

Appendix

Table 13.1 US production of semiconductors bought by Defense, 1955–1968

Year	Total semiconductors production, million dollars	Production of semiconductors bought by Defense, million dollars	Production oriented to defense purchase, % of total
1955	40	15	38
1956	90	32	36
1957	151	54	36
1958	210	81	39
1959	396	180	45
1960	542	258	48
1961	565	222	39
1962	575	223	39
1963	610	211	35
1964	676	192	28
1965	884	247	28
1966	1,123	298	27
1967	1,107	303	27
1968	1,159	294	25

Source: Adapted from Nathan Rosenberg and David Mowery, *Paths of Innovation: Technological Change in 20th-Century America*, Cambridge University Press, Cambridge, 1998.

Table 13.2 US integrated-circuit production and prices and the importance of the defense market, 1962–1968

Year	Total production, millions of dollars	Average price per integrated circuit, dollars	Defense production share of total,[a] %
1962	4	50.0	100
1963	16	31.6	94
1964	41	18.5	85
1965	79	8.33	72
1966	148	5.05	53
1967	228	3.32	43
1968	312	2.33	37

Source: Adapted from Nathan Rosenberg and David Mowery, *Paths of Innovation: Technological Change in 20th-Century America*, Cambridge University Press, Cambridge, 1998.

Note

a   Defense production includes devices produced for the Department of Defense, Atomic Energy Commission, Central Intelligence Agency, Federal Aviation Agency, and NASA.

Table 13.3 Aircraft production by countries in the 1930s

	1933	1936	1939
France	600	890	3,163
Germany	368	5,112	8,295
Italy	500	1,000	2,000
Japan	766	1,181	4,467
United Kingdom	633	1,677	7,940
United States	466	1,141	21,195
USSR	2,595	3,578	10,382

Source: Adapted from Christopher Freeman and Francisco Louçã, *As Time Goes By: From the Industrial Revolution to the Information Revolution*, Oxford University Press, Oxford, 2001, p. 286.

14 American hegemony and its aftermath

By the time World War II had come to an end, America had been the world's leading economic power for many decades. No nation had done better than the United States in seizing and expanding the opportunities introduced by the Second Industrial Revolution. US business took full advantage of an extended era of transformational innovations characterized by high capital intensity, elevated use of energy, continuous and efficient manufacturing processes, mass distribution, and substantial economies of scale and scope. Already at the beginning of the twentieth century, the key sectors in America—metallurgy, machinery, chemicals, electricity, and electrochemicals—were dominated by large-sized firms. If compared with the situation of British firms at the same time, the outcome in the United States was very different. In fact, in the United States, the birth and growth of large corporations in most industries where technology made it possible (both in industrial products and in goods destined for mass consumption) was greatly favored by the wide availability of natural factors (land for agriculture, forests, underground resources), by an uncommon dynamism of the internal market (the result, in part, of a significant demographic boom brought on by waves of immigrants combined with a growth in per capita income), by antitrust policies that impeded collusion, and by the diffusion of a culture that was well suited to business and organizational change.

The American challenge

Not even the political and economic turmoil of the first half of the twentieth century had jeopardized the American supremacy—an advantage that was substantially increased after World War II. Thanks to the war, American firms benefited from government economic assistance that was given to reinforce national defense and which ended up stimulating already enormous productive capacity. Government assistance also included new resources for research. This was combined with the arrival of first-rate scientists who escaped persecution and war in their home nations by fleeing to America. First the war and then the Cold War stimulated demand for technologically advanced products in fields such as air transportation, electronics, synthetic materials, and pharmaceuticals; all were products that could be used or easily transformed for civilian use. Likewise, millions of men who had been trained to fight the war upon their return to America enrolled in large numbers in training programs designed to help them reenter the workforce. During the 1950s and 1960s, threatened by competition from the Soviet Union, the government continued to make substantial investments in training and scientific research. In this way, the United States continued to strengthen what was already a cutting-edge educational system, especially in the research universities. The network of infrastructures for transportation, telecommunications, and the manufacturing and distribution of energy was highly developed in the United States. Growth was sustained by an abundance of capital that made interest rates low, a market demand oriented toward mass consumption of standardized goods, and an abundant supply of entrepreneurs eager to take advantage of the so-called American Century.

While war-torn Europe and Japan were still suffering a dearth of basic goods, the United States was a consumer's paradise. Consumption was further enhanced by America's modern channels of distribution—including self-service and fast food—combined with heavy advertising on both radio and the ever more popular television. America by the beginning of the 1960s had only a few sectors (e.g., clothing and furniture) where it was not one of the leading manufacturers on a worldwide level. The country led not only in cutting-edge sectors such as semiconductors and computers but also in less technologically advanced industries such as transportation and packaged consumer goods. The United States was the most aggressive player in industries such as office machinery, generators for electricity, and telecommunications, while it was leading the world in innovations in the defense industry, in entertainment and recreation sectors, and in high-level management consulting.

This superiority on a variety of fronts was reflected in consumer demand for all kinds of goods that reinforced America's dominant position and strongly stimulated innovation. What was most impressive, especially in the two decades immediately following the war, was the climate of confidence that could be found around the country. This culture pushed America toward new undertakings and made its entrepreneurs willing to take on risky new challenges. Even though the internal market had once been so vast and dynamic as to limit the amount of internationalization pursued by firms, there were now increasing investments and operations abroad. Sure of their technical and organizational superiority, American corporations pushed back against those nations that tried to place political obstacles in their way. Able to count on cultural hegemony in the Western world—English was now becoming the universal language of business—American investments abroad reached a level after 1960 which encouraged other nations to express growing concern about the "American challenge" to their national institutions and values.[1]

The first signs of decline and the new wave of mergers and acquisitions in the 1960s

America's economic strength seemed irrepressible, but still, during the 1950s, some faint hints of a slowdown could be detected: there were lower volumes of investment as well as only a slight increase in productivity and per capita income when compared with other countries. In fact, glimmers of a new era of intense competition started to show, and Americans were not prepared for this. Their firms had grown accustomed to enjoying virtually unchallenged success. Companies such as General Motors and Radio Corporation of America (RCA) were world leaders, larger economically than most of the nations of the world. Inside the United States, consumer demand was relatively stable. Although American confidence in its scientific and technological resources was shaken when the Soviets launched their Sputnik, US business appeared to be on track to maintain its position as the world's most innovative system.

All too soon for Americans, however, the recovery of the European economy and the rebirth of Japan's business—both had received massive help and technology transfers from America after the war—made for fierce foreign competition. Entrepreneurs and managers in many industries were disoriented by the changes in the 1960s. Business leaders who boasted an MBA acquired at a leading institution found it hard to adjust to global competition. Convinced of their ability to manage any kind of company in any sector, they responded to the new situation in different ways. Some chose to intensify research, looking for better processes and products. Others sought out opportunities for investing and profiting in fields where the competition appeared to be less fierce. They did this even though their firms had no technical–organizational advantages in the new enterprises. Thus, there were sometimes mergers and acquisitions (M&A) based on no rational criteria from a purely technological perspective.

Other factors pushed many firms toward new forms of diversification. After the approval of the Celler–Kefauver law of 1950, antitrust policies made horizontal and vertical integration in their industry more difficult. Meanwhile, tax policy became more benevolent to M&A. Businesses saw in diversification a strategy that promised to stabilize their revenue and profits, and they saw no obvious limits on the types of businesses they could enter. The emerging information revolution seemed to supply managers with the tools to control the most disparate investments. By the end of the 1960s, the path to growth via M&A was wide open and well trod. The number of these deals exploded—from 2,000 in 1965 to more than 6,000 4 years later—but, probably, the most significant fact was that, in the 10-year period 1963–1972, many of the M&A that were completed involved diversification that was not based on a common technology or market. In the period between 1973 and 1977, M&A that brought about this kind of diversification were half of the total.

The parabola of the conglomerate

Out of this flood of M&A (the third in America's history after that of the early 1900s and then the other wave in the 1920s) came a new type of enterprise—the conglomerate. The conglomerate was different from the multidivisional firm as its distinguishing feature was the choice to operate in a number of sectors that were unrelated. In 1968 alone, 4,400 corporations disappeared in the United

States because of M&A; many of these deals involved conglomerates such as Litton Industries that operated in sectors as varied as office machinery, shipyard construction, restaurants, canned foodstuffs, and consulting for government organizations. Textron is another important example. The firm started up in 1923 in the textile industry, but after the war, it entered into new fields, thanks to mergers that took place primarily in the 1950s and 1960s. In 1963, after divesting its textile activities, annual sales at Textron included 35 percent in aerospace products, 20 percent in heavy machinery, 16 percent in consumer goods, 17 percent in metals, and 12 percent in agricultural chemicals.

Diversification was a common goal of corporate strategy in American firms throughout the twentieth century. Searching for economies of scope, protection against declining demand, and opportunities to jack up their revenues and profits, businesses acquired firms that were already operative or launched new firms in industry sectors closely correlated to their existing business. This kind of orientation did not change much even during the Depression of the 1930s—when firms aimed at developing profitable lines of business in correlated areas to make up for the drop in demand for their traditional products. Nor did it change when the war effort in the 1940s cut back on the production of some consumer goods so as to favor conversion to military products.

But the level and type of diversification during the 1950s and 1960s was an anomaly, as it was based on an extraordinary economic situation the United States was enjoying at the time. By 1950, industrial manufacturing had grown to account for 45 percent of the world's production, whereas three decades earlier, it only accounted for 25 percent of world production (at the eve of the twenty-first century, it would also drop back to this same level). America's firms enjoyed significant profits. However, putting those profits to good use was a serious challenge for top management. A portion of the profits was distributed to shareholders in the form of larger dividends, but in the 1950s, as in the previous decade, shareholders were almost always the affluent, and their preference was for long-term growth of their investments rather than dividends that were subjected to high taxation rates. Top executives in many US firms thus had access to considerable sums of money to be used for investments that would be both profitable over the long term and a source of growth.

Many US firms took advantage of postwar reconstruction to expand into international markets in the decade starting in the late 1940s. Investing in activities abroad—distribution networks, warehouses, assembly plants, and industrial factories—promised good profits as well as stable growth. But not all sectors were suitable for internationalization projects and some of the firms that had found opportunities abroad had other ways of investing profits that were not returned to investors.

This was especially true for firms operating in sectors that were undergoing an incredible growth phase in the 1950s such as IBM and Xerox. Companies like these extended operations abroad, and their profits were also put to use in the construction of cutting-edge research and development (R&D) centers and in hiring a large number of scientists and engineers for these new laboratories. The leading pharmaceutical manufacturers pursued a similar path, initially reinvesting the profits generated by innovation, increased domestic demand, and exports to increase the amount of R&D that would focus on finding new medicines. Other sectors such as aerospace and electronics followed the same path.

Nevertheless, there were companies that operated in mature industries, and for which investments abroad or new R&D efforts did not have much appeal. These sectors included heavy metals and some standardized consumer goods that continued to be made with traditional technologies. In the boom enjoyed by the United States in the postwar period, even these firms were able to make good profits, but their future prospects were a source of concern for top management. Their leaders concentrated on developing strategies that would continue to work as the economies of Europe and Asia were once again growing. That competition was already starting to edge into US markets. In the 1950s and 1960s, managers in the most important companies operating in mature sectors used the profits that were not returned to investors in new kinds of diversification strategies that would involve unrelated sectors that enjoyed high growth rates. This was usually done by purchasing controlling shares in companies that were already operative or exchanging shares with the other firm.

Armco Steel is a good example of the firms that adopted this strategy. The company was established in 1900, and over time became one of the most important vertically integrated steel manufacturers in the United States. It enjoyed good times both during the war and during the postwar reconstruction era in Europe, but by the end of the 1950s, this favorable period was coming to an end. Armco, together with other steel manufacturers, came face to face with the reality that demand for steel was stagnating. Company leaders decided to embark on a policy of diversification over the next 20 years. After an initial period of expansion in correlated sectors—purchasing plants that produced oil refinery equipment and launching the manufacture of specialized steel made with new technologies—the diversification process then started to take them into fields further and further away from their original business. An insurance company was purchased with the idea that they could insure their own activities and later extend the service to other industrial firms. With the expansion of the American economy, sectors such as insurance and finance were very promising, so Armco decided to extend its investments into other fields of finance. At the end of the 1960s, it began leasing manufacturing assets such as machinery, airplanes, ships, and railroad equipment; it also entered the real estate industry. By the end of the decade, 40 percent of its sales were in fields entirely unrelated to steel.

Armco was not an isolated case. Another firm operating in a mature industry that embarked on a strategy of diversification that would bring it into unrelated sectors and transform it into a conglomerate was General Mills. Created in 1928 as the result of a merger of seven firms that together formed the world's largest producer of flour, General Mills acquired more than a dozen additional companies, becoming world leader in the manufacture and distribution of flours as well as boxed foods. In the 1940s, the firm started to produce war materials, and on the basis of this experience, General Mills' managers decided that the company had sufficient skills to grow outside its core businesses. In the postwar period, General Mills continued to work in the defense sector, producing electronics for the Army as well as small household appliances. It also bought some chemical plants.

Naturally, there were other factors that favored the growth of conglomerates. One of these was increasing fiscal pressure on firms' earnings, and by the mid-1960s, global competition was driving down profits in a number of industries. The possibility of saving on taxes became an attractive reason to pursue a strategy of conglomeration. International mining or petroleum companies could take advantage of tax credits abroad to purchase new foreign firms where the profits were not subject to heavy taxation. Using a similar logic, often it was possible to use one firm's profits to compensate for the losses of a recently acquired firm.

Developments in management science also encouraged conglomeration in the United States. It had its origins in the application of mathematical models that had been created for use during the war period. These concepts and methods developed during World War II were later applied with vigor to management problems in the private sector. Assessing investment projects, evaluating forms for financing, choosing a site for a plant, controlling production, and managing warehouse inventory were all problems that could now be solved by applying mathematical methods of control. To do this efficiently, a systematic use of computers became necessary. This transformation of management science produced new managers who were convinced of their ability to solve any type of business problem by applying the new techniques. Able to be used in any situation, the new tools of managerial science promised to reduce the costs of unrelated acquisitions and enable the acquirer to run them more efficiently.

In the 1960s, the conglomerate was often at the center of discussion—and often not in favorable terms—in specialized periodicals. Subject to much criticism was the transformation of top executives of the conglomerates from their previous role of exercising overall responsibility for the efficiency of manufacturing and distributing goods of correlated sectors to their new role in which their primary concern was the financial returns to be expected from investments in the various, disparate entities making up the corporation. Among the first to defend the conglomerate model were management scholars, many of whom were on the teaching staffs of prestigious business schools. They focused their attention on what seemed to be the strong points of conglomerates when compared with other forms of enterprise. The first was the reduction in risk: the results of the different units were negatively correlated, making it possible to achieve more stable returns and aggregate profits. A second feature was the lower cost of capital, given that a conglomerate could raise equity or debt at a lower cost than a single business. Yet another aspect involved managerial resources that could now be put to better use: the conglomerate could hire costly experts which smaller firms could not afford; and top management's talents and special skills could be put to better use among a larger number of businesses. Advocates of the conglomerate were supported by the data from 1958 to 1966, when this model clearly had excellent results. A subset of 58 multibusiness firms that operated in the late 1950s and early 1960s showed impressive results: annual sales grew by 17 percent, more than twice that of the average manufacturing firm in the United States while profits grew at a 10 percent per annum rate (vs. the 6.7 percent average of firms in Standard & Poor's).

Nevertheless, the golden years did not last long. The 1970s were a period of economic crisis for many countries, including the United States. By the end of the decade, the nation languished in stagflation: high unemployment, no productivity increases, high interest rates, and growing inflation. Not even the largest American corporations were spared the enormous economic problems that plagued the nation and the world; US conglomerates had the dubious distinction of being some of the first to have to deal with the economic slowdown. It was becoming progressively more difficult to manage companies that operated in highly diversified sectors. Managers, as the skeptics had foreseen, were incapable of concentrating their attention on the financial aspects of a business without regard to the conditions of the industry as a whole or to the specific problems of their products. They discovered that it was not so easy to blend together different businesses: each had its own distinct corporate culture, with different ways of doing things and, more importantly, different ways of coping with the markets in which they operated.

Some of the big problems could be traced to the administrative structures created by the conglomerate's management. Often they were quite different from those of the traditional multidivisional firm. While businesses that had diversified into closely related fields had set up structures based on key functions such as production, marketing, and R&D, the conglomerates had seldom followed this pattern. The headquarters of a conglomerate was relatively small and was focused almost exclusively on controlling functions such as finance and acquiring new businesses. Functions related to specific products and processes were left to be managed by the acquired companies.

Heads of conglomerates were only able to deal with their responsibilities by relying on statistical analyses that never seemed to capture the special complexity of firms that were decentralized, multisectorial, and multidivisional. As growth continued, the divisions started to diversify up to the point where firms such as General Electric or International Telephone and Telegraph (ITT) were managing more than 150 profit centers. At this point, return on investment (ROI), the guiding star of American managers, was transformed from being a starting point for discussion among managers to being an objective measure of performance that could not be challenged. New systems for forecasting were created, where one axis assessed return while the other calculated risk, and the time horizon of managers was shortened significantly.

Supervision from headquarters was reduced to little more than establishing objectives for the various units and assessing the results obtained on a quantitative basis. The system came to be known as "management by numbers." Not even these new methodologies could, however, incorporate all the relevant aspects of performance; some could not be quantified. The resulting inefficiency of management in functions such as control, coordination, and allocation of resources for future development became apparent. The growing separation between top management of the conglomerate and middle management of the divisions was a problem; the latter were the foot soldiers fighting in the front line for market share and profits. Not all of these firms failed, but by the beginning of the 1970s, the decline of the American conglomerate was serious. The reasons were many but two stood out: (1) a top management that was either incompetent or unable to understand the technological processes and the various markets in which the conglomerate's companies operated and (2) the near impossible task of governing aggregates based on dozens and dozens of divisions. There emerged in the 1980s a deep sense that profound restructuring needed to be undertaken so as to allow firms to compete successfully with European and Asian companies.

The conglomerate's impact on the US business system in the 1960s and 1970s was especially detrimental. Even if there were not many full-blown conglomerates, their overall importance was significant, given the popularity of these kinds of investments in the largest corporations in the United States. By the mid-1970s, they represented 8 percent of the top 200 firms and about 21 percent of the first 500 firms in America. Many other companies had a small package of conglomerate investments along with more traditional operations. An excellent example is provided by the saga of RCA that had been created in 1919 by the pioneering firms in radio and radio broadcasting—General Electric, Westinghouse, Western Electric, and American Marconi—with the objective of sharing all the patents they owned. At the beginning of the 1930s, after having incorporated the plants for radio manufacture previously managed by their single owners, RCA became an independent firm and under its energetic CEO, David Sarnoff, the company quickly integrated its structures for manufacture and design while also increasing marketing and making substantial investments in R&D.

RCA was able to take full advantage of the demand that came about during World War II, thanks in part to the wealth of patents it had inherited together with new patents acquired via the firm's important research centers. Many of the new patents were not related to the company's original product line but concerned radar, sonar, and other electronic devices. After the war, the arrival of the transistor and the first modern computers, combined with the progress made in developing sophisticated navigational and military instrumentation, helped to transform RCA into one of the largest American corporations. RCA began to diversify into the manufacture of other types of electronic instrumentation as well as becoming a first mover in the new industry of television: first, it developed the technology necessary for black and white transmissions, and later, it brought out the first commercial color televisions.

The end of the 1960s represented both the apogee of RCA's boom and the beginning of its decline. David Sarnoff retired in 1970 and his son, Robert, took the reins. The younger Sarnoff made his own mark on the company's strategic direction by setting off a process of growth via diversification into new sectors that were often far removed from consumer electronics. The reasons at the base of this change in strategy were varied: an antitrust decree of 1958 required RCA and other firms in the sector to make their patents available to competitors, while pressure from European and Japanese rivals was intensifying.

But certainly the most important reason for RCA's problems was the desire to maintain the high profit levels that first had been attained when they held a monopolistic position in radio technology and later with the development and commercialization of televisions. In the period from 1968 through 1974, RCA tried to achieve its profit goals by acquiring Hertz (automobile rentals), Banquet (frozen foods), Coronet (carpeting), the publisher Random House, and other smaller firms. In this way, RCA became a conglomerate of incredible dimensions— the original business of electronics now amounted to less than a quarter of total sales—and it quickly entered into a spiral of crises both industrial and financial. By the second half of the 1970s, after the intensive buying spree, the company was heavily in debt and unable to respond quickly to the growing threat posed by European and—most especially—Japanese manufacturers. The firm's answer to the crisis was to cut costs and sell off parts of the company, but most of these actions affected only the electronics division. Meanwhile, an attempt was made to restart the diversification strategy in 1978 by purchasing the financial holding Commercial Investment Trust (CIT).

RCA's heavy level of indebtedness (up from 1.1 billion dollars in 1975 to 2.6 billion dollars by 1981) combined with the progressive deterioration of its R&D in electronic consumer goods (e.g., the launch of Stereo 8 audiocassettes and the VideoDisc system) brought the company down. After it was sold to General Electric in 1986, the new owner broke up RCA and dismantled or divested the single segments. In the latter case, RCA plants still producing electronics were sold to European firms such as Thomson or Philips or Japanese companies such as Sony and Panasonic. After more than 40 years as the dominant player in consumer electronics in the United States, RCA had developed a strategy of diversification that failed to make up for its shortcomings in innovation. This whole sector disappeared from American industry.

At the beginning, financiers, bankers, shareholders, executives, and workers benefited from the strategies of diversification that brought about the creation of conglomerates and near-conglomerates. Ultimately, however, the outcome of their actions was to weaken the long-term prospects of the firms and the industries affected. Thus, a movement of restructuring began in the 1980s. The intention was to reduce the broad spectrum of activities or even return completely to a firm's core business so as to recover some of the terrain lost in global competition.

In some cases, this occurred as a result of a serious corporate crisis as happened with Armco. The company, thanks to a diversification program, had reached a significantly better performance level than that of other American steel producers in the 1970s. By the beginning of the next decade, however, it had entered a tailspin as a crisis in the steel sector coincided with a crisis in the oil industry. Armco's situation was aggravated by the collapse of some of its businesses' financial services as a result of too much exposure in the insurance market. In 1982, Armco closed with a heavy loss of 345 million dollars (the previous year it had reported earnings of 294 million dollars). Over the course of the next 12 months, the company reduced its workforce by 23 percent, cut costs by 50 percent, reduced dividends by 55 percent, and divested 500 million dollars of plants at a loss. To survive, Armco underwent a drastic restructuring and "weight loss" program that lasted until the 1990s. The company returned to concentrating on its core business, steel, and focused its production on specialty steels.

In other cases, the decision to pursue a strategy of deconglomeration was made independently by management with the intention of increasing profits and the overall efficiency of the firm. Between the late 1970s and the early 1980s, for example, General Mills changed direction and decided to focus on its core business of food. In a 5-year period starting in 1983, it sold off all nonfood activities, bringing in more than 500 million dollars and returning to a product line very similar to that of three decades earlier. General Mills made only one exception to this tactic, staying in the restaurant business, as it offered strong correlations with the core business.

Even a voluntary restructuring like General Mills' should be seen as a consequence of the new business climate of the 1980s. Management scholars and consultants pointed the finger at inefficient managers, while institutional investors grew increasingly important; the latter pushed for better returns and threatened to launch hostile actions with the help of corporate raiders.

Restructuring in the 1980s

The crisis of the conglomerates brought about the unusual phenomenon of divestitures. If in 1965 there was one for every 11 mergers, a decade later the ratio was one of two. Buying and selling companies or their major divisions became a flourishing business that offered, first to industrialists and then soon to the world of finance, great rewards. Among the causes of the takeover fever of the 1980s was the arrival of new institutional investors and their managers. Until 1950, slightly more than 4 percent of Americans owned stocks, as did insurance companies and banks. In the 1920s, pension funds and stock funds had been created, only to suffer the consequences of the Depression. However, after World War II, they returned with renewed force. These funds invested massive amounts in industry, and now, a manager's ability was measured simply by the returns he gained on stocks in the Standard & Poor's index of the 500 most important corporations on Wall Street. To achieve superior results, shares were sold and purchased continuously. In 1950, institutional investors held 8 percent of the shares on the market; by 1990, they accounted for 55–60 percent, while single investors held approximately 30–35 percent. The total volume of transactions exploded: from 500,000 in the early 1950s to 27.5 billion in 1985.

For the first time, there was a market for the control of businesses that were at times purchased by buyers who had no ties with what they bought. Diversification, divestiture, buying and selling, and seeking control of corporations brought about an important process of restructuring. Companies, in their entirety or only parts, were bought, sold, separated, and reassembled in ways that would have been unthinkable a few years earlier. "Deconglomeration" became as popular as diversification had been in the American Century.

The proponents were usually company managers who were looking to cut costs and increase profits. In the next decade, these kinds of operations reached a peak, but now, many were also purely speculative deals, undertaken by bankers and financiers who sought short-term profits without regard for how companies would be affected. In some cases, the excessive zeal of the dealmakers ended up damaging important parts of America's industrial system.

The full array of hostile takeovers, continuous restructurings, managerial buy-outs, and asset sales left not only many casualties but also many firms or parts of firms that went on to be successful as the US system recovered in the 1980s and 1990s. This was part of a major transition in which the United States was shifting, as the United Kingdom had earlier, from manufacturing to services. Where the United States continued to be successful was in the science-based activities in very high-tech, Third-Industrial-Revolution industries. In biotech and information technology, the largest US firms were continuing to benefit from a world-class research university system.

The United States still held a stronghold in fundamental sectors connected to aerospace, telecommunications, and computers, while its universities continued to be world-renown centers of research excellence. In addition, not all industry sectors were subjected to restructuring processes. In chemicals, for example, stagnant companies such as DuPont, Union Carbide, Dow Chemical, and Monsanto undertook programs focused on their organizations and product lines, removing themselves from basic sectors (like petrochemicals) and concentrating on specialties in which there was a higher value added—pharmaceuticals, bio-technologies, advanced materials—by acquiring smaller companies that had been pioneers in these fields. Giant firms such as IBM remade themselves, becoming wholly dedicated to high-end services in an industry the company had once dominated as a producer of equipment. In this way, the United States remained a key exporter and successfully faced intensified international competition. Thus, it cannot be said that the United States at the end of the twentieth century really resembled England at the end of the 1800s. The United States was still able to foster a myriad of companies in cutting-edge fields. The trip to that destination had been painful and was not over, but as of 2000, there were good grounds in US business for an optimistic prognosis.

Note

1 See Jean-Jacques Servan-Schreiber, *Le Défi américain*, Éditions Denoël, Paris, 1966 (subsequently issued as *American Challenge*, Hamilton, London, 1968).

Further reading

A.D. Chandler, Jr., "The Competitive Performance of U.S. Industrial Enterprises since World War II," *Business History Review*, 68, 1994, pp. 1–72.

G. Donaldson, *Corporate Restructuring: Managing the Change Process from Within*, Harvard Business School Press, Boston, 1994.

M. Jacobi, "The Conglomerate Corporation," in A.D. Chandler, Jr. and R.S. Tedlow (eds.), *The Coming of Managerial Capitalism*, Richard D. Irwin Publishers, Homewood, IL, 1985.

M.E. Porter, *The Competitive Advantage of Nations*, The Free Press, New York, 1998.

H.T. Johnson and R.S. Kaplan, *Relevance Lost: The Rise and Fall of Management Accounting*, Harvard Business School Press, Boston, 1987.

Appendix

Table 14.1 Distribution of world's largest industrial enterprises with more than 20,000 employees, by industry and country, 1973[a]

Group	Industry	United States	Outside the United States	Great Britain	West Germany	Japan	France	Others	Total
20	Food	22	17	13	0	1	1	2	39
21	Tobacco	3	4	3	1	0	0	0	7
22	Textiles	7	6	3	0	2	1	0	13
23	Apparel	6	0	0	0	0	0	0	6
24	Lumber	4	2	0	0	0	0	2	6
25	Furniture	0	0	0	0	0	0	0	0
26	Paper	7	3	3	0	0	0	0	10
27	Printing and publishing	0	0	0	0	0	0	0	0
28	Chemicals	24	28	4	5	3	6	10	52
29	Petroleum	14	12	2	0	0	2	8	26
30	Rubber	5	5	1	1	1	1	1	10
31	Leather	2	0	0	0	0	0	0	2
32	Stone, clay, and glass	7	8	3	0	0	3	2	15
33	Primary metals	13	35	2	9	5	4	15	48
34	Fabricated metals	8	6	5	1	0	0	0	14
35	Machinery	22	12	2	3	2	0	5	34
36	Electrical machinery	20	25	4	5	7	2	7	45
37	Transportation equipment	22	23	3	3	7	4	6	45
38	Instruments	4	1	0	0	0	0	1	5
39	Miscellaneous	2	0	0	0	0	0	0	2
	Conglomerate	19	3	2	1	0	0	0	22
	Total	211	190	50	29	28	24	58	401

Source: Adapted from Alfred D. Chandler, Jr., *Scale and Scope: The Dynamics of Industrial Capitalism*, Belknap Press, Cambridge, MA, 1990, p. 19.

Note

a Fortune's list only includes enterprises of noncommunist countries.

Table 14.2 Leverage buyouts in manufacturing by industry type, 1977–1987

	High-tech	Stable-tech		Low-tech	Total
		Long horizon	Short horizon		
Number of firms	5	13	22	36	76
Employment (000s)	46.5	42.7	272	367.6	728.8
R&D expenditures (millions, 1982 dollars)	63.8	37.2	285.8	71.2	458
Percent industry employment	0.7	0.7	15.5	6.8	3.7
Percent industry R&D	0.3	0.2	13.1	2.9	1.1

Source: Adapted from Alfred D. Chandler, Jr., "The Competitive Performance of U.S. Industrial Enterprises since World War II," *Business History Review*, 68, Spring 1994, pp. 70–72.

Table 14.3 Changes in world market share of US companies by major industry, 1960–1986

Industry	Percentage
Iron and steel	−58
Nonferrous metals	−47
Electrical equipment and electronics	−44
Chemicals	−38
Autos and trucks	−33
Tires and rubber	−26
Pharmaceuticals	−24
Textiles	−19
Petroleum products	−18
Computers and office equipment	−11
Industrial and farm equipment	−10
Food and beverage products	−8
Paper and paper products	−4
Aerospace	6

Source: Adapted from Alfred D. Chandler, Jr.,"The Competitive Performance of U.S. Industrial Enterprises since World War II," *Business History Review*, 68, Spring 1994, p. 72.

15 The Soviet Union
The antagonist

From the medieval era to Communism

The Union of Soviet Socialist Republics, the giant State that inherited the Russian Empire following the October Revolution of 1917, was undoubtedly the most radical challenge to the system of capitalism based on private ownership of the means of the production and the market—that is, the system that up until now has served as the framework of our analysis. The objective of Vladimir Lenin, founder of the Soviet State, and his Bolshevik followers, was to put into practice the theories of Karl Marx and Friedrich Engels. Marx and Engels saw capitalism as a form of exploitation that was unable, because of its unique social relations, to develop fully the potential of modern technology in a stable, equitable society. Following Marx's teachings, Lenin intended to create a new economic and social order, called "Communism," in which it would no longer be possible to obtain an economic advantage from the labor of workers. Production would be *shared* and not traded, and the outcome would be a class-less society where the motto was "from each according to his ability, to each according to his needs."

Marx and Engels believed that this grandiose project would work in some of the most advanced societies—those where industry had already taken on a pre-dominant role—and where the growth of equitable social relations was stifled. Given its simmering sentiments, this ideology was like lifting the cover of a boiling pot. The ideal candidate for this paradise on earth was England, the "workshop" of the world in the mid-1800s, or post-Bismarck Germany, or even the United States at the dawn of big business. Marx, however, took into consideration that Czarist Russia could also be a possible incubator of the Communist transformation. He had two reasons: first, Marx was fascinated by the communes that characterized the world of Russian peasants. The village community, known as the *obscina*, continued to govern social life in the countryside even after the serfs were freed. According to Marx, this form of Russian community was capable of easily transforming itself into modern Communism, avoiding therefore that which the German political thinker considered the "horrors of the Industrial Revolution." The second reason was the realization that capitalism had already spread around the world. If the proletarian revolution started in a nation at the heart of capitalism (England, central Europe, or the United States), Czarist Russia would then be able to pass quickly from the feudal medieval era to one of the most advanced forms of modernity. Lenin was a faithful follower of this vision, so much so that he declared that Socialism—the prelude to Communism and a stage where each would receive according to his labors—was made up of two halves: the political dimension found in Russia after power had been seized from the Czar and the economic half with Germany as its model. In the absence of an international revolution, Lenin was not convinced that a nation like Russia in the early twentieth century with its numerous peasant strongholds would be able to skip the stages of the model proposed by Marx; it was necessary, Lenin said, to pass through them before arriving at a society without class distinctions.

The Bolsheviks' seizure of power was to be justified by the fact that, by now, capitalism had become an enormous chain: by breaking the weakest link in Czarist Russia, it would be possible to break down the whole system. In 1919, even before the birth of the Union of Soviet Socialist Republics (1922), the *Comintern* (Communist International) was founded as a key instrument for creating a global revolution. Revolutionary movements had already materialized in various corners of Europe, including Hungary, Germany, and Italy, while the Red Army moved ahead as far as Warsaw's gates. But in the West, the revolution did not take off. After a stage defined as "War Communism," where the economy regressed to primitive levels based on requisition and barter and which marked the outset of a civil war that was won by the Bolsheviks, Lenin launched the "New Economic Policy" (NEP) in 1921. Under NEP, capitalism reappeared; in fact it was based on the so-called tax in kind. A peasant was no longer subject to requisition of the entire harvest, and once a duty (either in kind or in cash) had been paid, he would be free to sell the remainder of his crops.

In the same manner, initiatives by small enterprises in industry and commerce were tolerated. However, the large industrial firm was governed by a "trust," a grouping of firms by sector and geography. A high level of concentration already existed in Czarist Russia of the early 1900s; in 1910, factories with more than 500 workers accounted for 55 percent of Russia's manpower, whereas in the United States, this number was little more than 30 percent. Trusts in Czarist Russia were concentrated in sales of various products; this structure of enterprise separated their profits from the activities needed to produce the goods. Sectors where specific concentrations controlled as much as 60–75 percent of the activity included Prodamet (metals), Produgol (coal), Prodvagon (railcars), and Med (copper). Trusts were also present, but less extensive, in lighter industries. With this as its basis, in the 1922–1923 period, the Soviet Union created 421 trusts that extended into 90 percent of the State industries. One hundred forty of them had more than 1,000 employees, effectively accounting for 90 percent of the Soviet Union's workforce. The best of the former Russian empire's technical know-how was concentrated in these trusts, so much so that, around 1925, they produced about 80 percent of gross domestic output. Even if they were property of the State, the objective of the trusts was to make a profit. With the exception of works commissioned by the government, management was free to establish prices, including prices for work that resulted from labor union bargaining.

When compared with organizations in capitalist societies, Soviet trusts had two significant limits. First, only 20 percent of their profits was designated for new investments, whereas 80 percent was to be turned over to the State that, with these resources, made decisions regarding the creation of new production units. Second, over time, the trusts lost their marketing function. The "sales unions" were transformed into agencies supported by a state bureaucracy that controlled commerce in all the major industrial sectors. Management's role was reduced simply to assuring actual production. The nation's entrepreneurial abilities and organizational talents were sacrificed in those large corporations that were comparable with the enterprises and business groups that were born with the evolution of managerial capitalism.

The era of NEP was one of relative prosperity in the history of the Soviet Union. Still, some open questions remained, and the issues became more pressing upon Lenin's untimely death (after 2 years of grave illness) at the beginning of 1924. Now, three distinct factions came to the forefront within the Soviet Communist Party. The first was led by Lev Trotsky, a charismatic figure almost the peer of Lenin, thanks to his intelligence and abilities. Trotsky had created the Red Army, and he insisted on the need for permanent revolution via a continuous conflict with the capitalistic world. By the mid-1920s, this way of thinking seemed unrealistic both because of the strong reactions from the Western world and because of the state of a Communist Party burdened by internal issues. Spokesman for the second important faction was Nikolai Bukharin. Like Trotsky, Bukharin was an eloquent intellectual who imbued Lenin's ideas with substance. As explained earlier in this chapter, Lenin believed that, without an adequate phase of capitalistic development, it would be impossible for Russia to venture by itself into the form of Communism envisioned by Marx. Therefore, for Bukharin, it was important that NEP persevere, especially in regard to the peasant world in which private initiative was to be encouraged. He believed that peasants should not be penalized by a form of forced industrialization. Bukharin's concern for gradualism was well motivated, but over the long term, it was probably impossible to support his strategy if the idea was to maintain a single party system governed exclusively by the Communist Party. Groups of capitalists that were appearing once again in Russia would have certainly insisted on their own political representation. It was the third faction, that of Stalin, that predominated and was responsible for the next phase of the Soviet Union's history. Stalin clearly understood the limits of his rivals. Stalin's faction was in agreement with Trotsky that a cruel showdown with the capitalist world was inevitable, but they also believed that the Soviet Union would be able to deal with the capitalistic world only if it was an industrialized nation with a strong military. For Stalin, it was necessary that the agricultural sector be sacrificed by maintaining artificially low prices. Such an objective could only come to fruition by eliminating any form of capitalism in the countryside. Therefore, at the end of the 1920s, ownership of agricultural property reverted to collectives via a process that was often bloody.

Millions of peasants died in the process. At the same time, the "Market" was eliminated from industry, which then passed under the control of the "Plan."

The dictatorship under the Plan

The Plan (*Gosplan*) was entrusted to the highest level of the government and resembled the giant central office of a huge American corporation. The Gosplan was made up of various ministries that were responsible for industrial sectors. It established *what* and *how much* was to be produced as well as *which* technology would be used, *where* the plants would be situated, *how* prices would be fixed, and *what* salaries would be paid. Thus, the Gosplan essentially determined both all aspects of production and areas for future investment. The companies were grouped together in administrative units of territorial production (*glavk*) and no longer focused on profits but only on the manufacturing goals as established by the Gosplan. It was also the Gosplan that would establish the average price in a sector without consideration of the costs borne by a single manufacturer. This policy severed the relationship between prices for products and manufacturers. To actually realize such a huge project, the Gosplan put into place functional departments that corresponded, more or less, to those of a multifunctional or multiunit American firm at the beginning of the century. In this framework, the big Soviet firm was reduced to little more than a production unit that was neither allowed to decide what or how much to produce nor to establish manufacturing costs or exercise any kind of influence on the market. Not surprisingly, in Russian, the word "enterprise" is a synonym of the word "factory" and not of the word "company."

Of the three levels of management typically found in a Western company, Soviet enterprises only used one—on the lower level. Middle and top management were outside the firm; middle management was situated in the functional departments while top management was situated inside the Gosplan. One consequence of this type of arrangement was that enterprises in the Soviet Union were more fluid. They could, in fact, be closed or regrouped with other entities as occurs in a capitalist economy with operational units that are spun off or shut down. All this shifting, however, was a serious obstacle in the Soviet system to acquiring those organizational skills that were a winning feature of firms in market economies.

Nevertheless, it would be wrong to suggest that this form of organization kept the Soviet Union from becoming a major global industrial player. In the 1930–1950 period, the Soviet economy grew by double digits. Impressive production facilities such as the Gorki and Moscow works, the tractor factory in Stalingrad, and the heavy machinery plants in the Ural mountain region were created and were referred to as the "factories that manufactured factories." This same rigidly planned economy was at the basis of the nation's victory over Nazi Germany in World War II. Later, with some reforms that we will analyze, it was the same economy of the Plan that formed the background of the showdown between the Soviet Union and the United States during the era of the Cold War.

From armaments to the race into space, the Soviet Union had its own agenda. The first spacecraft (1957) and the first traveler into space (Yuri Gagarin, 1961) were from the Soviet Union. The economic Plan, with its increased availability of durable goods, also brought about a moderate level of well-being for most Soviet citizens. It became evident, however, that if this kind of rigid system was to produce a giant leap ahead, it was not the right way to achieve continuous and well-balanced progress involving both industrial and consumer goods. Especially clear were the limits of corporations that held no decision-making power. After Stalin's death and the rise to power of his successor, Nikita Khrushchev, an attempt was made to limit the concentration of decision making and the supervision of economic activities. Ministries that controlled various industrial sectors were replaced with territorial organizations of industrial management (*sovnarkhozy*). The goal of the reform was to give firms more integration and stability, but the real outcome was a push toward autarkical tendencies in various areas of the nation. A cutback in specialized production occurred, with resulting useless and dangerous duplications. At the same time, plants that relied on supplies originating in other regions encountered serious problems. In the 1950s, the country experimented with "production associations" as an alternative to the territorial *sovnarkhozy*. They first appeared in the Ukraine, then in Leningrad, before spreading out across the country. By merging plants and integrating production functions, these associations tended to take advantage in a more efficient way of economies of scale and secure a rationalization similar to what Western companies achieved.

The first unification of this kind took place in the Ukrainian city of Lvov where five previously independent shoe plants (each with its own production cycle) were merged. The outcome was a much larger factory where the manufacture of outsoles was concentrated; the remaining plants assembled the final product and each was specialized in a specific component. The entire system could rely on a laboratory that was focused on new products as well as on related services. These developments took place in the most important associations and, most especially, in those that operated in high-technology fields like Leningrad Optical & Mechanical Union (LOMO) in Leningrad, a producer of high-precision optical instruments. LOMO's manager calculated that, at the beginning of the 1960s, the plant logged significant savings, thanks to the concentration, specialization, and standardization of production and various other company functions.

"Production associations" were characterized by certain elements not found in Western enterprises, elements that limited their efficiency. The associations, in fact, held little decision-making power about issues such as salaries, hiring and firing of employees, and where investments would be made. In reality, the functional departments of the *Gosplan*, the *Gossnab*, and the *Gostekhnika* (responsible for supplying firms and assuring technological congruence of the finished products), the *Goskomstat* (stabilized prices), the *Goskomtrud* (oversaw work conditions and established compensation levels), and the *Gosstandard* (controlled product quality and standards) all held on to their powers.

There was a distinct contradiction between this nationwide oversight structure and the needs of the new organizations, which were the last typology of enterprise that came out of the Soviet economic Plan of the 1960s and 1970s. While they undoubtedly represented progress in the rationalization of manufacturing, other corporate functions remained weak—especially marketing—and there was a lasting inheritance from the stages of autarky and self-sufficiency. Unlike Western firms, the production associations showed a strong tendency to integrate both real manufacturing components (there were construction units, shops for repairs, printing plants) and social services (such as onsite nurseries or infirmaries) and even food supplies. Not even the reforms undertaken by Khrushchev's successor, the Soviet technocrat Alexei Kosygin, were able to shake off the oppressive legacy of the Plan.

The absence of a business community

In a brilliant essay on the evolution of the Soviet system by Andrei Yudanov, a Russian economist, emphasis is given to the fact that the Soviet Union was not lacking in big companies, but they were more likely to be considered "factories" rather than firms. Instead, what was entirely absent in the Soviet Union was that natural "community" of firms that, by pursuing competitive strategies that were completely different, gave solidity to the economic fabric of Western nations. Yudanov reminds us that, in medicine, a pathology is classified as either morphological or functional. In the first case, we are dealing with an organ that has been either damaged or is insufficiently developed. In the second case, instead, the organ itself is healthy but it is unable to correctly perform the functions with which it is associated. This is the situation in which the Soviet firm found itself; the only characteristic in common was its size.

In the West, there are four main types of strategy for a firm:

- focus on volume, that is, concentrating on mass-produced goods that attract customers with the right quality–price combination;
- search out a niche in which strength rests in the fact that a certain segment of consumers find the merchandise to be essential. In this case, a small market segment is sought, and these customers are assured a good part of the product quota;
- pursue a personalized strategy adapted for small-scale manufacturing, non-specialized but destined to satisfy any request of a market that is usually local. This type of strategy calls for great flexibility as it aims to obtain the highest profit margins possible;
- yet another alternative is a strategy to introduce some forms of radical innovation to the market. This last option is highly risky and requires specialization.

The Soviet Union adopted only one of these strategies: the big firm. However, it lacked the tools needed to convince consumers of the value of its products in the same manner practiced by Western firms. Henry Ford used to say that he was happy to sell his Model T to consumers in any color—as long as it was black. Ford, however, made up for the monotonous color choice with an extremely interesting price–quality ratio that grabbed the consumer's attention. Big business in the Soviet Union, instead, did not have this kind of an opportunity because prices and quality levels were determined by the Gosplan and its associated agencies. In the Soviet Union, small companies, that is, small factories, were active in much smaller numbers than was the case in the United States or in Germany. Still, the Soviet organizations behaved as big businesses even if they did not have the technology (which was extremely standardized), or the organization (that faithfully reproduced what was in place in much larger plants), or the flexibility that the West demanded from firms claiming to be oriented toward the needs of the single client. Also missing in the Soviet Union were some of those niche firms that were so highly valued in Western economies.

As an example, consider one of the best-known companies of our era: McDonald's. At the onset of its boom, the famous dispenser of hamburgers needed to purchase large quantities of a certain kind of cheddar cheese. The company asked Kraft to make a proposal, but they were turned down: for a food manufacturer of Kraft's significant dimensions, the quantity of cheese required by McDonald's was too small. Immediately McDonald's turned to a niche producer in Wisconsin, Schreiber, for an estimate. Accustomed to serving small niches, Schreiber secured a profitable deal with McDonald's and became the supplier for McDonald's famous cheeseburgers.

Also emblematic of a poorly articulated system was the paucity of small, innovative firms. Introducing an innovation in an extremely large firm is risky when considering the quantities and capital investments involved. An innovator is often a *persona non grata* in a big business. This happened regularly in the Soviet Union, where bureaucrats would clearly show diffidence toward new production methods or new products. They simply wanted to maintain the status quo in big firms, and the Plan rewarded this kind of stagnation.

The difference was, in part, that Western economies could count on having venture capital and large numbers of small experimental firms that led the way toward commercializing new products. Once they were successful in the marketplace, in the subsequent phase, either they would grow to a size sufficiently big for mass production or they would be bought up by big businesses that already had the structure and the necessary resources in place for manufacturing on a much larger scale. Interestingly, a number of manufacturing innovations that had their origins in the Soviet Union (e.g., continuous casting in the steel sector or the use of quick-fixing cement for construction) actually were put to best use in the West.

An inglorious end

The Plan's rigidity did not keep it from being effective in the early stages of forced industrialization and during the patriotic war against Nazi Germany. It was in these moments, in fact, that the totalitarian political regime—regardless of a vast and hateful system of repression—enjoyed a broad consensus. For example, conditions favoring social mobility were created. The children of plant workers and peasants became engineers (like Brezhnev and Kosygin) or law graduates (like Gorbachev). But as time went on, in moments that did not call for extraordinary mobility, the Plan revealed itself to be far inferior to the institution of the "Market" in any one of the various forms of capitalism. To function effectively, the Plan needed to be able to foresee everything, but this was impossible, and the process of correcting errors required a great deal of time. Victor Zaslavsky, a Russian sociologist, wrote of an incident in the 1960s when he assisted at a discussion about the Plan of the Russian Republic, the most important component of the Soviet Federation. At a certain point, the group dealt with the issue of producing elevators; it was decided that elevators were not really necessary and that the few that were truly needed could be purchased abroad. One of the collateral decisions was that no building should be taller than five stories; the outcome was the enormous extension of urban areas, which also meant much waste and high costs for the republic's infrastructures.[2] In such a rigid framework, illegal behavior and subterfuges became necessary. Subterfuges were usually covered by the so-called soft budget. If asked, the director of a firm or a factory would submit a request to the offices of the Plan for a sum larger than needed as the manager was always afraid of being left without supplies. To purchase stock not foreseen in the Plan (and hence illegally), "tolkaschi" operated. These were individuals who operated outside the usual channels, through corruption and personal connections, so as to secure all the resources a plant needed. This perpetual state of lawlessness meant that managers constantly ran the risk of severe sanctions, but the reality was that the illegal actions were the lubricant that assured the mechanism would work.

The end of the Soviet Union was marked by absurdities but, most especially, by tragic moments. Absurd were the demands of many plant directors who insisted on receiving prizes for having met production goals, regardless of either the characteristics or the quality of what was actually produced. The director of a shoe factory, for example, was not concerned by the fact that his plant had produced thousands of women's shoes with the heels attached in the front! Tragic, instead, were the gulags and the iron-fisted control over companies exercised by the various secret police forces: NKVD, Cheka, then the GPU, and later the KGB. This type of terrorism seems to be inevitable in a society where the State, the only employer, was authorized to determine the needs of citizens. Plekhanov's prophecy became a reality. At the beginning of the 1900s, this orthodox Marxist argued with Lenin that—in the actual social-economic conditions of Russia—the risk was that the real outcome would not be the construction of a Socialist society but, instead, an Incan empire. Few are the times in history that a political power has had the ability to determine economic relations and focus all of a society's forces of production. As evidenced by the Soviet Union, this kind of power was never likely to be put to good use, nor is it realistic today to imagine that such total control can actually be accomplished without dire consequences.

Notes

1 The Bolsheviks were a faction that held a majority position at the 1903 Congress of the Russian Social-Democratic Workers' Party.
2 See Victor Zaslavsky, *La Russia senza Soviet*, Ideazione Editrice, Rome, 1996, pp. 28–29.

Further reading

J.S. Berliner, *Factory and Manager in the USSR*, Harvard University Press, Cambridge, MA, 1957.
D. Granick, *The Management of the Industrial Firm in the USSR: A Study in Soviet Economic Planning*, Columbia University Press, New York, 1954.
G. Guroff and F. Carstensen (eds.), *Entrepreneurship in Imperial Russia and the Soviet Union*, Princeton University Press, Princeton, NJ, 1983.
J. Kornai, *The Socialist System: The Political Economy of Communism*, Princeton University Press, Princeton, NJ, 1992.
A. Yudanov, "USSR: Large Enterprises in the USSR—The Functional Disorder," in A.D. Chandler, Jr., F. Amatori, and T. Hikino (eds.), *Big Business and the Wealth of Nations*, Cambridge University Press, Cambridge, 1997, pp. 397–433.

Appendix

Table 15.1 Achievements of the Soviet planning system, 1928–1940

	1928	*1937*	*1940*
Annual growth rate 1928–1937			
GDP (1937 prices)	—	5.1	—
Per capita GDP	—	3.9	—
Agriculture (1958 prices)	—	1.1	—
Manufacturing (1937 prices)	—	11.3	—
Sectoral GDP composition (%)			
Agriculture	49	31	29
Manufacturing	28	45	45
Services	23	24	26
Transformation of the manufacturing sector (%)			
Heavy industry	31	63	—
Light industry	69	34	—
GDP structure (%)			
Private consumption	82	55	49
Public services	5	11	11
Public administration and defense	3	11	21
Investment	10	23	19

Source: Adapted from P.R. Gregory and R.C. Stuart, *Soviet Economics Structure and Performance*, Harper & Row, New York, 1986, tab. 10 and 16.

Table 15.2 Soviet employment and population, 1913–1990 (000s at midyear)

	1913	1950	1978	1990
Farming	51,450	35,726	29,740	27,239
Industry	5,900	15,317	36,064	35,286
Other	11,250	30,100	62,350	70,021
Total employment	68,600	81,143	128,154	132,546
Total population	156,192	180,050	261,253	289,350

Source: Adapted from Angus Maddison, "Measuring the Performance of a Communist Command Economy: An Assessment of CIA Estimates for the USSR," *Review of Income and Wealth*, September 1998, p. 314.

16 Japan

The challenger

Although Japan had successfully followed a quick path to economic modernization, at the outbreak of World War II the Asian nation was not yet on par with Europe and the United States. This was because Japan was late in undertaking the first steps toward industrialization. Consider, for example, the automobile industry. In the mid-1930s, the United States produced two million cars each year, England manufactured 286,000, in Germany 150,000 cars rolled down the line each year, whereas Japan produced only a sixth of that amount (and a portion of those 25,000 automobiles were either manufactured in the Japanese plants of Ford and General Motors or were simple three-wheeled vehicles). It was only after World War II that the nation's entrepreneurs created an industrial structure competitive with the strongest businesses in the United States and Europe. Then Japan's firms were finally able to enter the realm of international oligopolies as top players.

The evolution of industrial groups in Japan: from the zaibatsu to the keiretsu

Even though the zaibatsu (see Chapter 9) were formally dissolved in 1945 by General Douglas MacArthur, Supreme Commander of the Allied Powers, as a step in the direction of "economic democratization," groups made up of firms with informal ties continued to operate in the same way. In the decades following World War II, two new forms of group organization appeared; they differed on the basis of the direction of the ties (horizontal vs. vertical) between the various businesses that made up the group, but both forms are known by the same name: *keiretsu*.

The first form, known as the *kynyuu keiretsu* (horizontal groups), was made up by grouping competitive firms that operated in different sectors of industry, trade, and finance; they were connected to each other by a complex network of interlocking shares. The kynyuu keiretsu were typical of the Japanese industrial structure, both for the nature of the relationships between companies in the group and for the influence that these groups had within the Japanese economy. In 1990, it is estimated that the companies connected to the eight giant horizontal keiretsu accounted for 27.2 percent of the nation's capital as well as almost 17 percent of the sales of Japanese businesses. The biggest kynyuu keiretsu were effectively the re-creation (on a different organizational basis) of the main zaibatsu that operated in prewar Japan. In the latter, the structure of the shareholding ties was actually the first element in their cohesion: the founders' families participated directly—and indirectly via the capital of the financial holding of the group, which they also entirely owned—in the major subsidiary firms, thus being able to coordinate the group's key activities. In addition to the shares owned directly by the family and the financing company in command, an exchange of shares between subsidiary firms assured that control of the majority shares remained inside the group. Dissolving the zaibatsu brought about the elimination of a system of control centered on financial holdings and forced out the families/founders who had to transfer ownership of their shares by placing them in the market. The reforms undertaken by the Allied Powers thus created broader equity ownership in Japan.

Still, with the outbreak of the Korean War in 1950, American foreign policy changed; Japan was now seen as a bastion of the West in the Far East. It was preferable not to show bitter opposition to the country's traditions, so the process of economic democratization was softened. For example, the anti-monopoly law was suppressed; the law (instituted in 1947) prohibited the possession of packages of shares by corporations, effectively making it impossible for firms to be interlinked by ownership.

With a return to sovereignty in 1952, the Japanese government reversed the policies instituted during the country's occupation, as they were perceived as an obstacle to rapid economic reconstruction and accelerated growth. The new trend encouraged a return to the system of horizontal links between firms. A new type of actor for the reconstruction of the groups emerged: the large house banks that also had been part of the zaibatsu in the past. During the liquidation process of a firm, the shares not held by small investors were bought up by the banks and later resold to financial institutions (insurance, real estate holdings, etc.) and other corporations. Thanks to the banks, groups were able to reconfigure themselves via interlinked shareholdings and thus reestablish ties similar to those of the zaibatsu, minus the family element. This is how the three major horizontal keiretsu that still exist today—Mitsubishi, Mitsui, and Sumitomo—had their origins. In these groups, the vertical structure was replaced by a horizontal one in which the ties between the companies of the group were maintained not only because of the cross-shareholdings but also via an integration of management groups, of loans within the keiretsu, and of a structure for coordination through periodic meetings that was a sort of "club" made up of the presidents of the largest companies of the group.

A network of intertwined shareholdings traced the existing ties between the firms of the ex-zaibatsu and between the firms and the group bank; these holdings could guarantee a high level of shareholder stabilization for the horizontal keiretsu because no single shareholder (or syndicate) could unilaterally control the strategic or operating decisions of the affiliated companies. On the other hand, control of the keiretsu was exercised in an informal way because there was no central body to which management of the group was delegated. The same club of presidents operated more as a place where information was shared and diffused than as a mechanism that coordinated operations of the individual firms. Often the nature of the ties among the firms affiliated with a horizontal keiretsu can best be described as a relationship of interdependence that was apparent in a wide range of situations: not only in the reciprocal support between managers of the various firms but also, for example, in the financial support given for important investments by single firms as well as assistance given to the associated companies in times of crisis. The ability of firms in the group to act in a coordinated manner was not based, after all, only on the network of cross-shareholdings. With its highly fractured ownership structure and with no permanent form of centralized control, each investor might have had a great incentive to break away from the arrangements of reciprocal cooperation. But this did not happen in the kynyuu keiretsu. This was because not only was there a relationship of mutual trust based on an exchange of shareholdings but also because, from the very outset, the keiretsu was created within a tight network of financial, commercial, and personal ties. Each group was characterized not only by cross-shareholdings but also by the level of debt that the single firms had with the affiliated financial institutions, by internal commercial transactions, and by the reciprocal exchange of managers between the firms.

As mentioned earlier, an important role—a sort of "glue"—was created by the group's bank of reference ("main bank"). This institution was entrusted with information regarding the daily management of the firms (a position that it held in common with other shareholders) and could exert a direct influence on management's investment decisions given its role as principal lender to the businesses of the group. There were also situations in which the bank could intervene directly, the most common being to assist insolvent companies with actions that ranged from changing management to granting additional loans or dealing with redundancy by transferring employees to other affiliated businesses. All these were possible in part because the Japanese government had no qualms about shareholders and creditors being one and the same. This meant that the bank (in its role as creditor-shareholder) could intervene more efficiently in the case of an insolvent firm. The main bank's importance is further evident in the decisive role it played between the late 1960s and the early 1970s in the birth of a new type of keiretsu that was no longer simply a continuation—in a varied form—of the old zaibatsu. The most important of these "new" horizontal keiretsu were the Fuyo, Sanwa, and Dai-Ichi groups. They were created because of the initiative of a bank that pushed a group of firms to band together. Of course that financial institution then took on the role of "main bank" of the newly established keiretsu.

The principal function of the kynyuu keiretsu was not so much to guarantee an increase in business volume or search out new entrepreneurial opportunities. Rather, the keiretsu's key purpose was to assure stability of decision-making and organizational structures inside the affiliated firms. The horizontal keiretsu showed itself to be a powerful tool for introducing and maintaining the managerial firm in the Japanese economy. Cross-shareholdings and other forms of interdependence between businesses assured not only that the firms would be protected from hostile attempts to be acquired but also guaranteed a certain type of autonomy to the managers vis-à-vis the shareholders. The internal hierarchical organization was stabilized.

It is symptomatic that—even though Japanese legislation assigned the right to nominate board members (the highest decision-making body in a firm) to the company's shareholders in the course of a general assembly—the reality was that members of the board were chosen by other board members who sought them out within the company's management and co-opted them into the board. Shareholder meetings were merely an occasion to ratify the board's decisions. Even if the board was formally seen as independent of management, in practice it was both an integral part of management and one of its strongest supporters.

In the Japanese firm, management responded to shareholders in a limited manner because the latter actually had little say in appointing the corporation's leadership. At the heart of management's position of superiority over shareholders was the common sentiment in Japan that firms, especially large firms, do not belong to shareholders but to the employees (managers and workers), and thus the latter should have a greater say in decision making and in how earnings should be distributed. In Japanese society, it is not the shareholder who controls the firm but the workers themselves by virtue of the fact that, when they joined the firm (at least in critical sectors), the workers effectively agreed to dedicate their entire working lives to the firm.

This philosophy of "lifetime employment" dominated the Japanese model of labor organization and industrial relationships at least until the early 1990s when the country entered a downward spiral of economic difficulties that undermined the traditional model. In exchange for a guarantee of lifetime employment (if a firm in the group was in trouble, its employees were transferred to another company in the keiretsu) and welfare benefits (given out at the level of the firm and distributed to the families of employees) that increased over time, the keiretsu's companies could count on a disciplined workforce that was both loyal and highly motivated. This was one of the secrets of the success of Japanese industry in international competition.

The notable stability of institutional assets and the virtuous relationship between capital and work in the kynyuu keiretsu do not, however, mean that Japanese capitalism was necessarily well regulated. Competition between horizontal groups was lively and unlike the vision of some American and European scholars who saw the keiretsu as a form of archipelago closed to the outside world. Undoubtedly ties, traditions, and a habit of working together all favored a growth of internal transactions within the group. But there were economic limits on that sort of relationship. Let us consider the top six horizontal groups: sales between firms of the groups were not particularly high. In 1981, they accounted for 20.4 percent in manufacturing companies and 7 percent in commercial firms. In the same period, purchases were 12.4 percent and 18.2 percent, respectively.

The Japanese attitude toward working in groups did not lead, as some might have expected, into collusive behavior or a suffocation of competition but, rather, ended up showing itself to be an incredible tool for increasing efficiency and the competitive stance of a firm. This can be seen in the second type of organization of company groups that developed in Japan in the 1950s and 1960s. The *kigyoo keiretsu* was a vertical grouping of businesses, made up of a head group—usually a very large manufacturing company—and tens (if not hundreds) of related companies that operated as suppliers of most of the components and the semiworked goods purchased by the group leader to whom they were connected by consolidated commercial relationships and, in some cases, by cross-shareholdings.

The relationship of vertical groups as developed by the kigyoo keiretsu can be seen in the active ties in the Japanese automotive industry between suppliers and the manufacturer. The latter benefited greatly from the intense competition between suppliers because each supplier wanted to establish a more stable relationship without necessarily formalizing it in a legal manner. This type of vertical organization was very different than the rigid integration pursued by other automobile manufacturers in the West (especially in the United States). Japanese auto manufacturers were smaller in size and far less vertically integrated than their American counterparts. In the mid-1980s, Japanese automobile firms bought on average about 75 percent of their components for auto assembly, whereas American manufacturers barely purchased 50 percent.

Vertical groups: Toyota Motors

Probably the most outstanding example of the Japanese tendency to "buy" rather than "make" is Toyota Motors[1] that bought from other firms (automobile parts, components, and various services) about 80 percent of the final value of its automobiles. The company's secret was the vast network of connected firms that were joined together in an association of suppliers led by Toyota. At the end of the 1970s, it had 168 first-level suppliers that worked directly with the auto manufacturer, 5,437 second-level suppliers that manufactured components for the first-level suppliers, and 41,703 suppliers at the third level (most were small family-run businesses) whose output was destined for the second-level suppliers. Toyota's number of both regular and occasional suppliers was increased because rarely did the company want to allow a single supplier or associated firm to produce a specific component. Instead, many suppliers were put into a situation of having to compete with others for producing the same component; this allowed Toyota to compare both prices and the quality of products manufactured. The biggest suppliers were not considered, unlike in the United States, as the specialized divisions of the final assembler. In 1980, for example, Toyota Auto Body assembled more than 400,000 automobiles and trucks for Toyota Motors, but it also produced 300,000 more vehicles that were commercialized under its own brand. Regardless of the close ties between them, Toyota Auto Body does not have a long-term contract with Toyota Motors; instead, the two have a straightforward relationship of reciprocal dependence based on unwritten rules.

The lack of long-term agreements did not present a risk to Toyota and actually was a source of some important advantages: any increase in the costs of manpower or raw materials was borne by the suppliers while, at the same time, there was an implicit agreement that over time the prices that Toyota paid for the components would decrease. And these were not the only advantages: quality control was the responsibility of suppliers, and this was the backbone of Toyota's success—as the firm did not need to inspect the parts and components it purchased, Toyota could adopt its famous "just-in-time" production system that allowed for small stocks of components in its warehouses and an increased production level. Toyota Motors could be certain that the parts and components it purchased were of good quality because the component manufacturers and the subassemblers could not risk losing one of the world's top automobile manufacturers as a client. The suppliers had invested too much in this relationship: locating their factories nearby, setting up plants, machinery, and even set the number of employees hired so as to produce what Toyota would need. They were so intrinsically linked to Toyota that there was only one way to be in a winning position: by carefully following the rules established by the main company or accepting the fact that the privileged relationship would cease. Either a supplier was able to provide Toyota with the quality it wanted at the time it needed it and at the lowest price possible or it would no longer be a member of the Toyota "family."

Suppliers fought not just to remain in the "family" but also to ascend the hierarchy. In fact, there was a fundamental difference between suppliers who manufactured to order on the basis of specific requirements and projects of Toyota Motors and those who were equipped with design and production know-how, so that they were capable of taking an idea from Toyota and designing the component as well as setting up the assembly line themselves. These companies were eager to rise up in the ranks of the suppliers for two reasons: first, the higher up a firm was in the hierarchy, the greater were its profits (higher value added), especially if it designed the parts and components; the second reason was that the most important suppliers received more orders because they designed and produced components for many different vehicle lines. The maximum goal for a supplier was to become an independent company with its own brand and distribution channels. Toyota Auto Body and Nippon Denso, given their very specific and specialized know-how, are two excellent examples.

Power was not evenly balanced between the main company and the suppliers. The company that produced automobiles knew that an alternative source of supplies could easily be found, and the assembler determined when, which, and how many components were needed. Still, the suppliers also secured some important advantages under this system: lower labor costs, greater productivity in the stages of specialized production that they oversaw, and managerial hierarchies that were smaller and less subjected to the rigidities of bureaucratic formalism. Each firm in the corporate hierarchy tried to do its very best—producing goods of the highest quality at the lowest possible price—and, in this way, maintain or even better its position within the group. As a result, Japanese companies affiliated within a kigyoo keiretsu showed signs of being more capable of adapting to unexpected market changes than firms in the Western world. The smaller size and the greater specialization of Japanese firms translated into a significant competitive advantage over the long run. Toyota Motors and the Toyota group were, from this point of view, an excellent example of the competitive advantage that could be achieved by a particular style of Japanese organization. The advantage was due to the lower level of formal integration coupled with higher levels of coordination and cooperation that helped the group adapt to transformations in markets as well as technologies.

The role of the State

The State played an essential role in maintaining and increasing the competitive position of many industrial sectors in Japan, most especially those that were export oriented. The Ministry of International Trade and Industry (MITI), after examining the errors of the past, had adopted more selective criteria for support and quickly scored some important successes on the international level. One of the most important examples of the ministry and business working together was the incredible growth of the Japanese steel sector.

MITI's primary objective in the postwar period was to accumulate foreign currency to finance the reconstruction of a nation that up to that point had been dependent on foreigners. From this perspective, steel was seen as a strategic product because it offered more value added than typical exports such as textiles. At the same time, steel was also an important component of Japan's reconstruction and growth in subsequent years. MITI's problem was not to decide whether it was worthwhile for Japan to develop the steel industry but, rather, how it would be possible to reach this goal. The first step was to separate—from the viewpoint of strategies to adopt—the purely internal operations from the world market for steel. MITI's bureaucrats started to see the global market not just as the place to dump excess production but, rather, as a true competitive arena for the Japanese steel industry. Until the export strategy was fully functional, however, it was necessary that the internal market continue to play an important role. Japan's domestic market was tightly regulated, with demand and prices carefully controlled by the government. MITI's idea was to transform this internal market into a type of incubator for the growth of the steel industry until it was able to compete effectively overseas.

MITI changed the economic scenario by permitting managers of the Japanese steel industry to make their own investment decisions. The principal actions were three. First, protectionism became more rigorous: imports from abroad were banned to prevent price competition and lower domestic production. Second, a new system for supporting prices was put into place so as to free companies from the dangerous effects of economic fluctuations. Finally, in what was probably the most innovative tool of industrial policy created by state bureaucrats, MITI created a system that linked permits to expand manufacturing capacity to past results.

The ministry's policy was based on a central premise: the only way to reduce costs over the long term and acquire a greater share of the international market was by higher levels of production, an essential prerequisite for the growth of the steel industry. Japanese firms responded to this incentive by competing on a cutthroat basis, constantly updating and rationalizing their plants so as to gain the right to increase their production levels.

MITI's control over investment decisions for the steel industry in Japan was extremely strong, and it stayed that way until at least the late 1970s. The tool for this was simple—a very well-designed policy of state subsidies. Investments in new manufacturing capacity were carefully coordinated according to market demand in both Japan and abroad. During the first decades after the war, MITI concentrated state subsidies and distributed them to only a handful of companies. For example, in the 1951–1956 period, 72 percent of the subsidies were distributed among only 4 of the 44 firms operating in the steel industry, and this only happened after each of the four had adhered to the rigid requirements of productivity and efficiency fixed by the ministry.

In the 1960s, MITI's authority to guide investment decisions started to wane, but it never disappeared completely. In fact, MITI helped steel companies to develop a system of autoregulation and to coordination of their investments. It was an "informal" system, best known for the "Monday Club" when managers from the most important steel companies would gather for their weekly appointment with representatives of the ministry. During these get-togethers, for which minutes were never taken and apparently no records were kept, they would discuss prices and investments. MITI continued its role as coordinator not via new, formal legislation but, rather, via "recommendations." Almost always the principal topic for discussion during these meetings was expanding manufacturing capacity. This was negotiated with the others on the basis of criteria established by MITI as regarded expectations of market shares, efficiency of existing factories, and potential international demand. To acquire the right to construct a new plant, a company needed to show that it was already operating the most modern and efficient plants possible. All these induced managers of the steel industry to abandon a logic based on analyzing marginal costs—that is, continuing to use obsolete plant technologies as long as the marginal costs of the old plant were inferior to the cost of constructing a new, more efficient one. They set off on a race to see which firm could build the biggest and most modern factory. The objective was not to become the most profitable in the short term but, instead, to pursue a significant increase in productivity in the long term.

The secret to this system was in the special kind of economic environment that MITI had built, a system in which recommendations—though not obligatory—were almost always adopted. In fact, given the system in which they had to operate, the only rational behavior for managers was that of heavy investments in modernization so as to keep both their market share and their firm's standing in the steel industry. The largest firms were kept busy with the construction of enormous plants that were capable of the most radical rationalization of production (around 1980, there were some plants that were capable of manufacturing as much as 10 million tons of steel per year). This was done without concern for costs over the short term and with a strong dedication to preventing obsolescence. A good example of this was the steel industry's reaction to the technological change affecting it in the 1960s. In 1960, the sector had undertaken a gigantic plan of investments so as to achieve government goals that called for tripling steel production over the course of the decade. Japanese firms started making heavy investments in plants and traditional machinery. Suddenly, they found themselves facing rapid transformations in manufacturing technologies, whereas the ideal plant size became bigger and bigger. Unlike firms in Western nations that faced the same dilemma, the Japanese decided to disassemble plants and machinery only recently acquired and to replace them with more modern machinery. In 1960, for example, 150 Martin-Siemens ovens were in operation in Japan, with more than half of them installed only in the previous 10 years. By 1980, all the Martin-Siemens ovens in Japan had been replaced with modern oxygen ovens that were considered more efficient. Kawasaki offered another example: in 1964, when the company demolished six enormous ovens that had been constructed between 1952 and 1961 and replaced them with more modern technology.

This philosophy of knocking down and reconstructing became a distinctive characteristic of the Japanese steel industry. In the mid-1970s, Nippon Kohan, the country's second largest steel firm, decided to dismantle a fully operative plant that manufactured 5.5 million tons and replace it with a new, almost entirely automated plant that could produce 6 million tons each year. In a quick sweep, Nippon Kohan threw away 20 years of investments to construct this new plant that only slightly increased production. Decisions such as this can only be understood if one considers the particular type of environment in which steel industry managers worked. The industry was both protected and heavily competitive at the same time; short-term profits were downplayed in favor of production increases over the long term. The results were striking and left little room for ambiguity. In 1943, Japan manufactured 8.5 million tons of steel, whereas the United States could boast more than ten times that figure (89 million tons). But although four decades later the two nations were producing similar amounts (115 million tons each), the difference was that the United States needed to import an additional 20 percent to meet national demand, whereas Japan, thanks to the size and efficiency of its plants, was able to export 22 million tons of what it produced.

Not all companies responded in the same way to MITI's recommendations. For example, in 1955, opposition by the industrialists led to the failure of the nation's "plan for a people's automobile." The plan included a state subsidy for the single company that would be able to manufacture on a vast scale a low-cost vehicle with a 350- to 500-cc motor. A similar failure occurred in the mid-1960s when an attempt was made to merge nine automotive firms so as to create a "national champion" able to compete with the American giants. In that period, MITI was also unable to put a halt to the proliferation of ethylene plants and to the creation of a dangerously high level of excess capacity in this section of the chemical industry. In the end, where there was excessive government control, the large Japanese corporation was able to come up with the means to oppose the State.

The Japanese "miracle"

Japanese capitalism was managerial as well as competitive—just as in America. Japan's economy in its most dynamic aspects was marked by lively competition, so much so that, in various critical industrial sectors, it was rare to find domination by only one or two firms. A key component of competition was the vast internal market—the country counted 120 million inhabitants at the beginning of the 1980s—and was culturally homogeneous. It was, moreover, characterized by an attitude of "knock down and reconstruct" that reflected the rapid and continuous growth for two decades after 1950. Firms had then thrown themselves into an impressive investment campaign. In April 1951, Toyota (with capital of only 418 million yen) embarked on a 5-year project of plant renovation that would cost 6 billion yen. Between 1957 and 1969, the Toshiba group, embattled in a serious rivalry with Hitachi for which of the two would enter the field of household appliances, increased its investments in fixed capital from 5.6 to 29.5 billion yen, a somewhat dangerous step given that the entirety of its activities in 1957 was estimated to be worth approximately 9.6 billion yen. Equally challenging was the decision by Kawasaki Iron and Steel in the 1950–1954 period to build modern full-cycle plants at a cost of 18 billion yen. Of course, it could not do anything less in light of what its competitors, Yawata and Fuji, were doing. This massive push for growth had its origins in a cohesive-corporate culture encompassing entrepreneurs, managers, and workers, a culture that had emerged after bitter conflicts in the postwar period. As Hidemasa Morikawa wrote:

> The top-level decision makers in large postwar industrial enterprises were salaried managers promoted from inside and founders. Both led their enterprises to vigorous investment in equipment from about 1950 on. What these two types of managers had in common was extensive experience with the unique internal skills network that had been built up within Japanese industrial enterprises from an early period, well before the war . . . When the top management of Japan's large industrial enterprises in roughly 1950 decided to embark on large-scale equipment investments far out of proportion to their limited managerial resources, they were motivated by more than the logic of industrial success and strategic intent. These top managers were certain that the managers, engineers, and workers they themselves had trained would, in a competitive environment, improve their product-specific and company-specific skills, form a tightly knit network, and readily accept the new equipment and technology they were introducing . . . It was that confidence that led to their daring investment programs.
>
> (1997: 321)

The culmination was Japan's new role as a global leader in sectors such as steel, automobiles, consumer electronics, office machinery, electronic components, and machinery for data analysis and telecommunications. The country was less competitive in some sectors, probably for reasons that were in part "cultural." For example, in the pharmaceutical industry and manufacture of software where, in addition to cooperation and specific skills, the ability to innovate and to be creative were of crucial importance, Japan lost to its rivals in America and Europe. In other industries, including construction, food production, paper, and base chemicals, the presence of cartels and excessive protection from competition by the State seem to have played a negative role. Despite these difficulties, Japan's forward thrust in the decades following its defeat in World War II was something almost miraculous. In a prolonged phase of dynamism between 1954 and 1971, the nation's GNP grew at an annual rate of 10.1 percent. Thus, by the end of the century, the nation whose per capita income in the postwar years had been 50 percent of that in Italy had become the second largest economic power in the world with only the United States able to boast a higher per capita income.

Note

1 The story of Toyota Motors had its start in 1933 when Toyoda Automatic Loom, a manufacturer of looms for the textile industry, decided to open a new division for the manufacture of automobiles under the leadership of Kiichiro Toyoda (see Chapter 12).

Further reading

R.P. Dore, *Taking Japan Seriously: A Confucian Perspective on Leading Economic Issues*, Stanford University Press, Stanford, 1987.

M. Fruin, *The Japanese Enterprise System—Competitive Strategies and Cooperative Structures*, Clarendon Press, Oxford, 1992.

T. McCraw (ed.), *America versus Japan: A Comparative Study of Business–Government Relations Conducted at Harvard*, Harvard Business School Press, Boston, 1986.

H. Morikawa, "Japan: Increasing Organizational Capabilities of Large Industrial Enterprises, 1880s–1980s," in A.D. Chandler, Jr., F. Amatori, and T. Hikino (eds.), *Big Business and the Wealth of Nations*, Cambridge University Press, Cambridge, 1997.

H. Odagiri, *Growth through Competition, Competition through Growth: Strategic Management and the Economy in Japan*, Clarendon Press, Oxford, 1992.

T. Shiba and M. Shimotani (eds.), *Beyond the Firm—Business Groups in International and Historical Perspective*, Fuji Conference Series II, Oxford University Press, Oxford, 1997.

Appendix

Table 16.1 Ten zaibatsu combines designated by the Holding Companies Liquidation Commission (HCLC) for dissolution

Zaibatsu	Number of subsidiaries in 1937	Number of subsidiaries in 1946	Paid-in capital as % of Japan's 1946 total
Mitsui	101	294	9.4
Mitsubishi	73	241	8.3
Sumitomo	34	166	5.2
Yasuda	44	60	1.6
Total of top 4	*252*	*761*	*24.5*

(Continued)

Table 16.1 (Continued)

Zaibatsu	Number of subsidiaries in 1937	Number of subsidiaries in 1946	Paid-in capital as % of Japan's 1946 total
Nissan	77	179	5.3
Asano	50	59	1.8
Furukawa	19	53	1.5
Okura	51	58	1
Nakajima	—	68	0.6
Nomura	—	19	0.5
Total of next 6	*197*	*436*	*10.7*
Total of top 10 zaibatsu	449	1,197	35.2

Source: Adapted from Randall K. Mork, *A History of Corporate Governance around the World: Family Business Groups to Professional Managers*, University of Chicago Press, Chicago, 2007, p. 375.

Table 16.2 Growth of real gross domestic product (GDP) in five countries (1953–1987)

Period	Japan	United States	United Kingdom	West Germany	France
Annual growth rate of real GDP					
1953–1963	8.28	2.8	2.78	6.22	5.02
1963–1973	9.12	3.83	3.22	4.38	5.15
1973–1987	3.67	2.48	1.63	1.79	2.12
1953–1987	6.63	2.97	2.43	3.85	3.86
Annual growth rate of real GDP in purchasing power parity					
1950–1960	7.26	1.33	2.27	6.76	3.54
1960–1973	8.45	2.8	2.53	3.59	4.63
1973–1985	2.79	1.27	1.13	1.91	1.47
Adjusted annual growth rate of real GDP in purchasing power parity					
1950–1960	5.29	2.86	2.71	6.27	3.6
1960–1973	7.29	3.97	2.78	4.05	5.03
1973–1985	2.53	2.16	1.03	2.48	1.97

Source: Adapted from Hiroyuki Odagiri, *Growth through Competition, Competition through Growth: Strategic Management and the Economy in Japan*, Clarendon Press, Oxford, 1992, p. 235.

17 Hybrid Europe

The Harvard project

In the early 1970s, Harvard Business School's (HBS) Research Division started an ambitious field project to analyze the strategies and structures of the largest corporations in Europe in a comparative perspective. The research focused on four European countries (the United Kingdom, Germany, France, and Italy) that had been experiencing two decades of economic growth. HBS scholars were thus observing Continental Europe at the apex of its postwar economic "miracle." The principal European nations had reached stable levels of development in economic and social terms. Their industrial systems were now populated by large companies, both privately owned and State controlled, in the capital-intensive industries of the Second Industrial Revolution, and European multinationals were successfully present in international markets.

The purpose of the Harvard project was to verify if the diffusion of large-scale enterprise had been accompanied by organizational modernization as well. To investigate this issue, researchers took a careful look at the features of the large managerial corporations in Europe, comparing them with the US model, which at that time was considered the benchmark.

They studied the period from 1950 to 1970 and focused on the top 100 companies in each country by turnover, ranking them by the strategy of diversification adopted (single, dominant, related, not related), and by organizational structure ("U-form," "M-form," and—in order to take into account what was a distinctive European feature—"Holding," which was characterized by limited managerial coordination of the subsidiaries). The expected outcome of the project was clear: researchers believed that they would find an inevitable similarity between European and American styles of business, both in strategy and in organizational structure.

Diversification and multidivisionalization in Europe

The empirical evidence available to the Harvard research team seemed to confirm the success of diversification strategies among large corporations. Accompanying changes in organizational structure usually showed a shift toward the M-form. In 1950, only one-quarter of the top 100 UK corporations had diversified their activities, but by 1960, a deep change had taken place. Diversification and the multibusiness organizational forms were spreading rapidly; by 1970, multibusiness forms had been adopted by more than 70 percent of the largest British companies. Similar systems were evident in Germany and even in France (notoriously a very traditionalist country) where corporations adopting multidivisional structures grew from 6 percent in 1950 to more than 50 percent in 1970. The Harvard team had identified a radical shift, similar to the one that had occurred by 1970 in Italy where 48 of the top 100 firms had adopted multidivisional structures.

This shift was partially due to the "Americanization" of European culture, which extended to include managerial culture. The origins of this trend lay in the modernization and growth of European economies in the years following World War II. The European Recovery Program (known widely as the Marshall Plan after US Secretary of State George Marshall who proposed it) was set up with the purpose of providing European countries with the resources necessary to speed up the reconstruction of their economies and set a strong, ideological barrier against the Soviet Union. The plan, which started in 1948 and lasted 4 years, was based on a massive inflow of financial and technical resources in the form of machinery, machine tools and components, other goods, and raw materials. The Marshall Plan transferred 12.5 billion dollars to European countries, with the exception of Spain, Finland, and, obviously, the Union of Soviet Socialist Republics and the other nations under Soviet dominance. Given its ideological and political purposes, the program was not welcomed everywhere. It was accompanied by strong American pressures to dismantle European barriers to trade, international finance, and investments that had been set up during the interwar period, as well as the widespread cartels and price-fixing agreements among large companies (see Chapter 13).

Western European companies benefited. In addition to the inflow of raw materials, goods, and machinery, Europeans became familiar with the techniques of American organizations as well as US technical and scientific knowledge. Part of the Marshall Plan was the "U.S. Technical Assistance and Productivity Mission," whose core idea was to make European industry as efficient as American producers. Even if not relevant in terms of budget (which amounted to a small fraction— 1.5 percent—of total aid), the Mission was responsible for the diffusion of American techniques and practices. US managers and businessmen traveled to Europe, bringing information about organizations and control systems, whereas Europeans crossed the Atlantic to learn the "American way."

This first big step in a broader process of Americanization took place in Europe that was quickly recovering after the war and entering into a period of intense change. In France, workers in the primary sector made up 37.6 percent of the total workforce in 1936; roughly three decades later (1968), this percentage had fallen to 15 percent, while members of the industrial workforce increased from 30 percent to 40 percent. These figures were similar to other Western European countries. The average annual rate of growth of gross domestic product (GDP) between 1950 and 1970 was 2.7 percent for Great Britain, 5.1 percent for France,

6.7 percent for Germany, and 5.8 percent for Italy. Following policies aimed at opening markets and abolishing trade barriers—two pillars of Americanization—the period from 1950 to 1970 was marked by a progressive increase in market size and a dynamism that demonstrated the efficiency of the smoothly functioning national and international financial systems.

Companies were encouraged to undertake consolidation strategies, so that they could benefit from economies of scale and then invest in new plants and production techniques. Technological advances were characteristic of almost all sectors but could be seen most clearly in automobiles and other consumer goods and, particularly, in high-tech industries: synthetic fibers, plastics, and electronics. The economic expansion of Europe generated growing employment, the intensification of welfare policies by national governments, and, above all, increases in the purchasing power needed for the introduction of mass production and distribution.

The lively market competition generated by these concurrent phenomena was fueled by several trade agreements, which culminated in the creation of the European Common Market (ECM). After the Rome Treaty of 1957, the creation of a continental-sized market was the logical consequence of the free-trade policies advocated by the Americans since the end of the conflict. Widespread decartelization was accompanied by the growth and strengthening of the European first movers. Steady growth in demand (in both qualitative and quantitative terms) not only opened new spaces for existing producers but also offered opportunities for challengers, some of whom were growing through diversification. This was true in almost all branches of manufacturing, from steel to automotives, from food processing to chemicals, pharmaceuticals, and rubber, from household appliances and machine tools to mass retailing. European economic growth, fostered by the creation, for the first time, of an integrated continental economic space, provided European firms the necessary basis for mass production. The Fordist philosophy and Taylorist methods of work organization became widespread among large European firms.

The enlargement and new-found dynamism of the European market had other consequences. One was the growing inflow of US direct investments in Europe. American companies were attracted by the increasing demand and the weakness, for some years after the war, of domestic competitors in many European industries. The birth of the European single market played a significant role in this process, since in some cases US companies were worried by the possibility that protectionist policies would be employed against non-European firms. European governments, to a varying extent, undertook systematic policies of tax reduction and incentives in order to attract foreign (basically US) investments and technology. In some cases, these policies were used to fill a knowledge gap and in others to foster industrialization and employment in depressed areas as, for instance, in the case of southern Italy. According to Harm Schröter (2005), in 1950, US foreign direct investments (FDIs) in Europe were about 15 percent of the world total, a percentage that grew steadily, reaching 21 percent in 1960 and nearly 31.5 percent in 1970.

The impact of US multinationals on European economies, however, went far beyond the inflow of capital: American companies brought new technologies, new products, new organizational forms, and new marketing techniques into Europe. With increasing Americanization came new actors in the economic land-scape, for instance consulting firms such as McKinsey, which implemented and diffused modern organizational structures at their client companies.

Increasingly, large domestic companies—both private and State-owned—found in the US multinationals suitable partners to fill technological gaps through business ventures and agreements. FDI inflows and internal growth brought the European "national champions" face-to-face with a serious new challenge, that is, the challenge of adapting their structural features to the requirements of the new market situation. They had to develop an adequate managerial class and transform their existing organizational structures to cope with expanding bound-aries and diversification strategies.

Deviations

Contrary to the expectations of the Harvard researchers, the adoption of the M-form occurred rather randomly in Western Europe. The full adoption of a "real" multidivisional structure seldom took place in the United Kingdom. Because of senior managers' unwillingness to delegate their power and responsi-bilities, even at operational levels, the process of reorganization was impeded. In Germany, the Harvard research team detected a different behavioral trend among senior managers who were willing and able to dedicate themselves to strategic planning, just as managers in the United States had done. But in Germany, there was little independence in divisional management, and companies placed a very low emphasis on marketing; there was also very little correlation between man-agement pay and division performance.

During the years of the "European miracle," the holding structure continued to spread rapidly, although the pace of change varied from country to country. In the United Kingdom, a modified M-form structure without centralized or coordinated leadership was widespread. In Germany, the predominant family-controlled con-glomerates allowed each subsidiary high degrees of autonomy. A loose organiza-tional structure was more suited to the French model, which was characterized by a strong and pervasive State presence. In France, top managements of each com-pany had their own relationships with bureaucrats, civil servants, and politicians. The Italian model combined two extremes: anarchy was tolerated in the periphery of the organization, while autocratic decisions were taken at the central level. In Italy, holding companies also were fronts for family-run pyramidal structures, set up to channel financial resources from the market; this allowed these family busi-nesses to maintain firm control over the whole group with a limited investment of personal resources.

European divergence from the US model was in sum a consequence of national differences in ownership structures and managerial cultures. State and family ownership (see Chapter 11) meant a high degree of ownership concentration, enforced through the widespread use of control-enhancing mechanisms, such as pyramid schemes, shareholders' agreements, and cross-shareholder, dual-class shares. It is worth noting that, after World War II, the United Kingdom was the only European country with a truly efficient stock market, and many British business owners finally had started to loosen control over their companies. The United Kingdom was also the first European country to allow an international market for corporate control (i.e., control of a majority of a firm's shares) to develop along American lines.

The European method of doing business had long been marked by unique styles of culture and management. US-style business schools were in operation in Europe during the 1960s, but most European managers were hardly comparable, professionally, with their American counterparts. Many of Europe's top managers were hampered by a marked lack of "soft skills," which made it difficult for them to envision long-term strategies. This was combined with a European training system inclined more toward academic theory than empirical evidence. The leaders of the main European companies were inclined to deeply involve themselves in the day-to-day operations of their corporations, but frequently this limited their ability to plan for the long term and control all the divisions of their companies. The Harvard research team found that European managers placed a heavy emphasis on the production side of business and had little interest in marketing.

Divergence between the US and European models also arose out of each region's distinctive patterns of productive specialization. The European emphasis on craft skill and labor-intensive industry was relevant to ownership patterns and diversification strategies. Families and individuals could easily manage enterprises because the average size of each of these companies was generally smaller than that of their American counterparts. At the beginning of the 1970s, turnover of the largest British firm was less than half that of the United States' largest firm; in Germany and Italy, this proportion was one-fifth, and in France only one-tenth. The size of the domestic market still mattered, but with globalization, this should have imposed less of a constraint on the European corporations.

The divide of the 1980s

Notwithstanding continental specificities in terms of ownership structures, average dimensions of firms, organizational patterns, and managerial roles and capabilities, a slow, progressive adoption of the multidivisional structure took place in Europe starting more intensely around the same time the Harvard researchers completed their survey. Ironically, the affirmation of the M-form in Europe took place in the same years in which—as mentioned in Chapter 14—US corporations were rethinking their competitive strategies and starting to reduce their degree of diversification. This was especially the case among US firms that had moved from diversification into conglomeration strategies.

According to Richard Whittington and Michael Mayer, authors of a comprehensive study of the 100 largest corporations in Britain, Germany, and France in the period 1985–1995, there was a notable increase in multibusiness strategies, especially in companies that had adopted a conglomeration logic. There was a decline in single-business or dominant-activity strategies. The scholars' findings reinforced the patterns identified by the Harvard research team in the 1970s. Diversification strategies and the adoption of multidivisional structures were continuing to dominate business, albeit with strong national differences. In the United Kingdom, diversification was particularly evident in the mid-1990s. Nearly two-thirds of the top 100 companies there diversified into related fields, and 24 percent diversified into unrelated fields; 25 years earlier, the same two categories had represented 57 percent and 6 percent of the whole sample. From an organizational point of view, the spread of diversification strategies mirrored the adoption of the M-form, which, in 1993, was used by approximately 90 percent of the largest British companies.

Germany showed different trends for the same period. Diversification strategies were popular in Germany, with a particular emphasis on the creation of conglomerates. But German companies tended to adopt the U-form organization with a holding-company structure.

France had a different pattern: the persistence of low diversification strategies (in the mid-1990s, 35 percent of the most important French firms were adopting strategies based on a single or a dominant activity model) or traditional patterns of diversification. In France, the functional structure was no longer in use, for it had been replaced by the M-form or, to a much lesser extent, the holding company.

In Italy, a country included in the Harvard project but not in Whittington and Mayer's analysis, major companies reacted to the economic slowdown of the 1970s by restructuring and divesting nonprofitable activities. This process, however, did not stop the trend toward diversification, which was accelerated by the adoption of aggressive financial strategies using highly leveraged policies. During the privatizations that occurred in the 1990s, some of the most important Italian firms diversified their activities by purchasing the most profitable State assets. This strategy was accompanied by the gradual introduction of M-form structures. The percentage of Italy's top 100 companies that adopted strategies of both related and nonrelated diversification rose from 47 percent in 1978 to 61 percent in 1988 and then 65 percent in 1998. Over the same period, the number of firms adopting M-form structures increased from 49 to 60 percent. Meanwhile, the number of companies that adopted U-form structures decreased (U-form was used by 40 percent of companies in 1978 but only 32 percent in 1998), whereas holding companies retained their popularity.

"Activist States"

As noted earlier, another relevant feature brought out by the Harvard researchers concerned the main corporations' ownership patterns. Together with families and financial institutions, European States were directly involved as corporate owners in manufacturing and services. The interventionist policies (see Chapter 11) of the interwar years had in fact been followed even after the conflict. During the steady growth of the 1950s and 1960s almost everywhere in Europe, direct ownership had been coupled with a widespread tendency toward planning and centralized coordination of the privately owned sector. Western Europe's "activist States" initiated, at the end of the reconstruction years, massive programs of intervention in the economy. "Soft" instruments were widely adopted. Credit provisions by State-controlled financial institutions, as well as subsidies, purchase orders, and tax exemptions, were employed. Sometimes, these policies managed to attract foreign capital to be invested in the country. In Britain and France, industrial policies often close to those adopted in Eastern Europe's planned economies behind the "iron curtain" were undertaken. A telling example was the French *Commissariat General au Plan*, established in 1946 under the leadership of the influential French statesman Jean Monnet to coordinate the reconstruction effort and foster modernization of the French economy.

State intervention—which mainly took the form of investments by the public sector—was justified in many ways, among which were Keynesian countercyclical policies to sustain demand and employment. In many industries, and especially in capital- and technology-intensive ones, the public sector soon became the main customer for private enterprises. State-owned enterprises (SOEs) and public agencies became another distinctive component of the "mixed economies" of Western Europe. Partially—or more often fully—under government control, these corporations played a relevant role in industries considered as essential for a modern economy—for instance, steel, energy, telecommunications, and transport. The public contributions went beyond the realization and management of key infrastructures and beyond also their contributions to their nations' total fixed investments (which was in any case significant, on average 30–40 percent of the total in the principal European economies from the second half of the 1950s to the mid-1960s). According to some estimates, the State also played a central role in promoting research and development (R&D). Through the laboratories of the State-controlled companies, European governments financed almost 50 percent of the R&D budget of their respective countries, making a fundamental contribution to technological advancement.

State-controlled companies were often the outcome of the nationalization of private assets. Nationalization policies spread quickly among European countries after war. In Britain, the Labour Party started a massive process of nationalization in 1946, which included coal mines, canals, and railways. Electricity came under State control immediately after. In 1948, steel, airports, airlines, and motorways followed, and finally, the Bank of England, together with flagship companies such as BP and Rolls Royce. France went down the same path. Starting in 1947 almost the whole energy sector—coal, gas, and electricity—fell into public hands. The main banks were nationalized as well, together with the insurance companies. Nationalization continued as the State took over air transport, mining, and a national champion such as Renault. State ownership was present, although to a lesser extent, in Germany as well. At the beginning of the 1950s, the majority of gas, aluminum, electricity, automobiles, and iron was produced by companies controlled directly or indirectly by the State.

Italy and Spain had created huge State-owned concerns before the war when the Institute for Industrial Reconstruction (IRI, 1933) (see Chapter 11) in Italy and Instituto Nacional de Industria (INI, 1941) in Spain were organized. They set out to manage the vast public shareholdings in almost all branches of manufacturing. After the war in both countries, these State-controlled conglomerates remained active. In Italy, IRI generated the major part of output in the steel sector and shipbuilding and had considerable market shares in electricity and heavy mechanics, as it also controlled the main banks of the country. IRI further expanded its activity in various directions in mechanical equipment and automotives, cement, motorways, and telephones. In energy, before nationalizing the whole electric industry in 1962, the Italian State supported the creation of a vertically integrated energy group in natural gas and oil refining, the Ente Nazionale Idrocarburi (ENI). ENI started operations in 1953 under the leadership of Enrico Mattei, a charismatic civil servant, former entrepreneur, and Christian-democrat partisan. In Spain, the State had control over almost all the capital-intensive industries, from steel to shipbuilding, from chemicals to automotives. The banking sector was also State controlled. State ownership grew, too, in smaller European countries, from Scandinavia to Portugal and Greece.

Obviously, such a diffusion of State ownership among European countries had an impact on the strategies, behaviors, and organizational choices of Europe's big business. As instruments to pursue anticyclical policies, the State-controlled enterprises had to orient their competitive strategies to compromise between efficiency and social goals. The same can be said as far as organizational structures are considered. They had to be designed to balance power centralization with the management of conglomerates that were sometimes enormous. This very often resulted in the wide adoption of the H-form.

The presence of "State entrepreneurship" in Europe steadily spread from the 1950s onward, for about 30 years. It was only at the beginning of the 1980s that external pressures and internal inefficiencies (which will be analyzed in more detail in the following chapters) started to undercut this vast complex of State ownership. Germany had begun to get rid of SOEs at an early date, but the rest of Europe had not followed until the 1980s. From the beginning of that decade, however, privatization spread, starting from the country that had inaugurated the postwar policy of State involvement in the economy, Britain. France followed in the second half of the decade and then, from the early 1990s, Italy and Spain also changed course.

The process of privatization differed from country to country, with consequently different impacts on the strategies and, above all, organizational and ownership structures of the formerly State-controlled companies and other European corporations. The process in Europe lasted for nearly 15 years and has yet to be completed. It was carried on in different ways depending on the constraints the governments had when the process started. In the United Kingdom, privatization policies resulted in the emergence of US-style public companies. Among shareholders, the presence of institutional investors (insurance companies, pension funds, and mutual funds) was pervasive. In 1963, institutional investors controlled about one-third of the capital in UK-listed companies, and by the year

2000, that percentage had risen to 56 percent. The pervasiveness of institutional investors' ownership makes the British case slightly different from the American one. In the United Kingdom, the control over enterprises and their management was—and still is, today—exercised by a few dozen fund managers through informal channels, and the control was accomplished through direct influence on the shareholder meetings. The United Kingdom's model of management and ownership combined concentrated ownership with tight control over management and an emphasis on the maximization of shareholder value.

In France, the models of ownership and control only partially changed while privatization policies were being implemented under conservative governments. The privatization of the banking system between 1986 and 1993 was followed by a second wave of privatizations in manufacturing and services. The French, unlike the British, opted for a "soft" privatization process from the beginning. The French aimed to avoid foreign ownership in strategic and capital-intensive industries. The privatization process was carried out therefore by handpicking a "core" of stable financial and industrial French investors—called the *noyau dur*—to stabilize and protect management and make strategic decisions. The outcome was a lasting and concentrated pattern of ownership. The French State maintained control of an important number of large enterprises, mainly in natural monopolies or in strategic industries. Either directly or through private entrepreneurs, these companies are linked to key political leaders through informal relationships.

In Italy, the main purpose of privatization was not to create public companies; many companies in fact were sold in private arrangements to individuals, families, or foreign groups. During the 1990s, the traditional features of Italian-style capitalism remained, at least as far as private companies were concerned, essentially intact. Even today, the pyramidal group headed by a holding company is still the rule among large corporations, both listed and unlisted. This confirms the Italian tendency toward a model of concentrated ownership.

Notwithstanding the intense push toward privatization in most European countries, the State retained an important role in many industries, acting as either an owner or controller of corporate assets. The State continued to employ control-enhancing mechanisms such as the "golden share"—that is, a privileged State shareholding bearing special rights that could be used to influence the management of the enterprise. Recent research shows that, by the year 2000, many countries belonging to the Organisation for Economic Co-operation and Development (OECD) had retained governmental control in more than 60 percent of the formally privatized enterprises.

A "European corporation"?

Understanding ownership and management is crucial when interpreting the dynamics of strategy and structure. Stakeholders and main controllers influence the strategy, structure, and efficiency of enterprise; thus, they also influence the national economic system. Past theories about business organization maintained that there were three types of ownership inconsistent with strategies of diversification: personal/familial, State, and bank.

These theorists believed that individuals and families tended to resist the decentralization and delegation of power characterized by M-form structures. It was thought beyond the ability of family-run enterprise to manage the complexity of diversification. Multidivisional structures create, by definition, an internal market of capital and resources, which works through internal price transfers, capital allocations, and financial flows among the divisions. These same structures were thought to challenge banks and prevent them from monopolizing the allocation of capital to corporations. Finally, the State— historically an important owner-controller in Continental Europe—was believed to prefer U-form organizational structures and holdings (which strengthened close control) over M-form.

However, current evidence seems to challenge these assumptions. The business structures that prevail in Europe today are heavily concentrated and based on a mixture of State, bank, and personal control; this is coupled with the pervasive strategy of diversification on the part of most large European companies.

The impact of ownership concentration on performance is less clear. According to some research, these effects have been quite positive, particularly when shareholders are families or individuals who are active in the boardroom. This is a perspective that calls into serious question the conventional view about the inefficiency of a family-based control model.

Some have argued that the absence of an adequate regulatory framework has reduced the efficiency of European firms. Under this rubric, firms have problems creating and distributing value to their shareholders and particularly to minority shareholders. This type of analysis is not convincing to those who believe in a direct relationship between diversification strategies, the adoption of multibusiness organizational structures, and positive performances both at the firm level and at that of the national economic system. Evidence from Europe seems to reinforce this approach to the relative efficiency of Europe's distinctive organizational structures. After more than 50 years, it may well be true that there is not enough "institutional perversity"—a term coined by Whittington and Mayer—to support new organizational forms. But the European experience shows two things. First, "nationality" counts. Diversification and multidivisionals, even if they are popular, are not always the most efficient strategies and structures. Firms that are focused on a single business seem to be just as efficient as those characterized by a high degree of diversification. Second, history seems to confirm the presence of a distinctly European model of diversification and of management— and thus distinctly successful European firms of various types.

One of these types is the multidivisional network. In this case, the M-form is replaced by a federation of small and aggressive "entrepreneurial businesses." In the case of the Swedish company Asea Brown Boveri (ABB), neither the considerable size of the company nor its degree of diversification were significant; the company was both large and diverse. But its success was due to the peculiar organizational structure that ABB's management designed and developed. ABB brought together a number of the entrepreneurial organizations that seemed to thrive in dynamic, evolving markets. In the United States, this was the case in Silicon Valley. This may indeed be a wave of the future, as well as another peculiarity of the European business setting.

In Europe, there are plenty of the large diversified M-form corporations on which Chandler's paradigm focused. But there are also many European variations on business forms. The peculiarities of the "European large corporation" were accompanied by the persistence (to a different extent in different countries) of business systems alternative to mass production: industrial districts and local production systems characterized by the clustering in a defined area of a high number of small firms, each one highly specialized in performing one or a few phases of the production process. Characterized by a diffuse entrepreneurship, a strong social cohesion resulting in low "transaction costs," and a high degree of flexibility and creativity, industrial districts have played a key role in sustaining the economic performances of industries, regions, and even countries.

Probably, the most significant example in this respect is Italy, where the diffuse presence of industrial districts particularly in the northeastern and central regions was the basis of the relatively good performance of the Italian economy during the 1970s, achieved notwithstanding the difficulties of the nation's large firms. The structure of industrial districts, based on flexible small firms and a fragmented production process, was particularly suitable for the manufacture and distribution of specialized and customized goods—such as machinery and machine tools—or of products for the person (from footwear to textiles, from jewels to leather goods) or the home (tiles, furniture, ceramics). The productive specialization of industrial districts thus heavily influenced the nation's "competitive advantage," which from the 1970s onward was increasingly based on "Made in Italy" products that accounted for the vast majority of the country's exports.

If the Italian industrial districts with their informal kind of cooperation are one of the distinctive features of the European business system, similar importance should be given to the cooperative capitalism that characterized Germany in the decades following World War II. The pillars of Europe's strongest economy were the coordinating role exercised by the universal banks and its business associations brought together with a form of cooperative industrial relations known as "codetermination" (i.e., a representation of labor present in the supervisory boards of firms with more than 2,000 employees). German capitalism—which relied on a highly skilled labor force—continued to be export oriented, as it was at the beginning of the twentieth century, especially in sectors such as heavy machinery and chemicals. Even if German firms did not quickly embrace the information age or the swing to biotech, remaining stuck in the Second Industrial Revolution, we must recognize that, already in the late 1950s, Germany had rid itself of its major SOEs (Volkswagen being a good example).

The European hybrid business system thus offers an intriguing alternative to the US model, just as the Japanese system does. Each of these models offers distinctive strengths and weaknesses. They clearly overlap: the Americanization of Europe ensured that there would be many enterprises that closely resembled their

American competitors. But the differences persisted and are important. The H-form did not disappear. The M-form did not make it impossible for the multidivisional-network businesses to prosper. The State backed away from business but did not yield its power completely, even as SOEs were privatized and traditional regulations relaxed. Europeans can take a full measure of satisfaction with this outcome, especially since the Great Recession of 2007–2010 swept from America through the global economy. "One Size Fits All" is not always a good policy, either for business, for individual entrepreneurs, or for national economies.

Further reading

D.F. Channon, *The Strategy and Structure of British Enterprise*, Macmillan, London, 1973.

G.P. Dyas and H.T. Tanheiser, *The Emerging European Enterprise: Strategy and Structure in French and German Industry*, Macmillan, London, 1974.

M. Piore and C. Sabel, *The Second Industrial Divide: Possibilities for Prosperity*, Basic Books, New York, 1984.

H. Schröter, *Americanization of the European Economy: A Compact Survey of American Economic Influence in Europe Since the 1880s*, Springer, Dordrecht, 2005.

P.A. Toninelli, *The Rise and Fall of State-Owned Enterprise in the Western World*, Cambridge University Press, Cambridge, 2000.

R. Whittington and M. Mayer, *The European Corporation: Strategy, Structure and Social Science*, Oxford University Press, Oxford, 2000.

Appendix

Table 17.1 Percentages of firms by structure, strategy, and ownership[a]

	France		Germany		United Kingdom	
	1983	*1993*	*1983*	*1993*	*1983*	*1993*
Nonmultidivisional	31.1	24.2	43.3	30.2	10.6	10.5
Single business	24.3	19.7	18.3	12.7	6.7	4.5
Dominant business	18.9	21.2	18.3	9.5	22.7	13.4
Related diversified	43.2	45.5	43.3	52.4	54.7	56.7
Unrelated diversified	13	13.6	20	25.4	16	25.4
Bank ownership	5.4	13.6	18.3	20.6	0	5.9
Government ownership	28.4	24.4	10	9.5	6.7	1.5
Personal ownership	44.6	42.4	53.3	46	8	4.5
Number of firms	74	66	60	63	75	67

Source: Adapted from M. Mayer and R. Whittington (2004), "Economics, Politics and Nations: Resistance to the Multidivisional Form in France, Germany and the United Kingdom, 1983–1993," *Journal of Management Studies*, 41 (7), p. 1070.

Note

a   Beneficiary and nominee shareholders in France and the United Kingdom; proxy shares excluded for Germany.

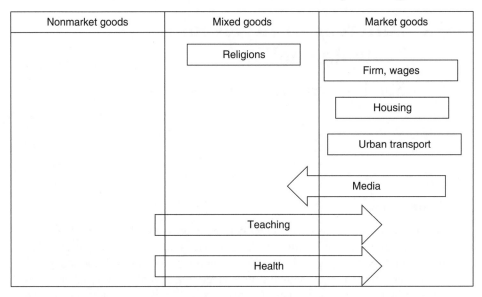

Figure 17.1 The role of the market in the "neo-American model"

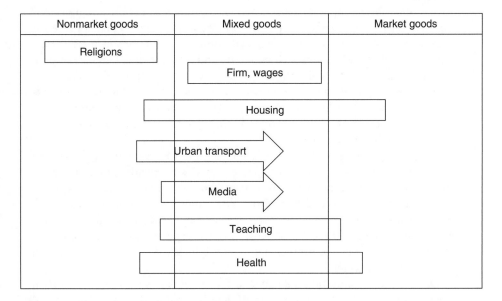

Figure 17.2 The role of the market in the "Rhine model"

18 Different strategies for "catching up"

South Korea and Argentina

South Korea

By the end of the 1970s, it was clear that the expression "Third World" was no longer an adequate description of the countries that were neither of the West nor in the Soviet Communist bloc. These nations had followed too many different paths to be lumped in one simple category. To most, the socialist model seemed increasingly inadequate for ensuring well-being and social emancipation. Likewise, having the good luck to possess precious natural resources—as was the case in the Organization of the Petroleum Exporting Countries (OPEC)—was also insufficient to guarantee stable prosperity. Then there were nations in areas such as equatorial Africa or in the Indian subcontinent overwhelmed by the disproportion between population and available resources. Still others, for example in Latin America, continued to be affected by sociopolitical turmoil that rendered ephemeral those growth phases that appeared at first to be signs of a takeoff. At the same time, small nations in the Far East such as South Korea, Taiwan, Hong Kong, and Singapore had embarked on a unique form of economic development that mixed state interventions and competition in a style attuned to a global marketplace. This outcome was unexpected, as many had believed that, after the US defeat in Indochina, these nations would all be hit by the "domino effect" and fall victim to the irrepressible advance of Communism.

In search of diversity, we will now turn to South Korea and Argentina, two nations that were initially slow to modernize and were clearly on the fringes of the critical core of capitalism. Then, they had completely different economic performances in the second half of the past century. By the mid-1990s, South Korea had created a productive and stable economy based on strong national industrial champions. By contrast, Argentina had experienced alternating phases of success and economic decline and, over the long run, had failed to create a strong industrial sector.

Despite these contrasting outcomes, the two nations were similar in certain regards. First of all, the characteristics of their internal markets and their limited dimensions meant that, in both countries, big corporations were based on diversified groups because it was almost impossible to take advantage of economies of scale. Second, in both nations, there were authoritarian political regimes capable of bringing together economic resources and piloting them toward their choices without any form of opposition. Those choices were, however, different in the two nations. Both the economic policies of their governments and the behavior of the controlling big business groups were very different, and this is the key to understanding their different performances.

Among the Asian nations that were capable of rapid economic development in the past century, South Korea (described by Massachusetts Institute of Technology [MIT] professor Alice Amsden as "Asia's next giant") truly stands out. A Japanese colony until 1945 and a nation without natural resources, South Korea in the immediate postwar period had a stunted industrial sector. The largest factories were concentrated in the northern part of the peninsula, which was separated from the rest of the country and controlled by a Communist government. The war that followed an invasion from North Korea further retarded development in the South. Nevertheless, by the 1970s, South Korea was experiencing an economic takeoff based on a series of economic policies aimed at favoring the growth of exports while, at the same time, placing restrictions on imports and foreign direct investments. Seeking to jump-start the economy, South Korea's leaders chose not to focus on light, labor-intensive sectors in which it would have the advantage of low labor costs. Recognizing that this advantage would shrink in the medium to long term, South Korea adopted a more difficult approach. It also rejected an inflationary policy that might eventually destabilize the economy and social structure. The government also decided not to opt for the massive entrance of foreign firms, a choice that would have quickly accelerated development at the price of offending Koreans' sense of independence and national pride. In the 1950s, there was so much hostility toward multinationals that they were only allowed to enter the country in partnership with local firms and in minority shareholdings.

An authoritarian State, supported by the military, could make these hard choices in part because its citizens seemed content with a society characterized by a relatively egalitarian distribution of wealth. Unlike the government in Argentina, the South Korean government only rarely intervened directly to take on the role of entrepreneur. The only State industrial firm in Korea was Pohang Iron and Steel Company (POSCO). Instead, the State dedicated itself to a series of actions intended to support private industry. It subsidized firms; it protected them by applying high tariffs and granted them credit at favorable terms; and it stifled labor conflicts. In exchange, it demanded that plants be constructed according to the highest international standards and that Korean firms strive for economies of scale so as to compete successfully on the export front.

Even though there were incidents of corruption, the Korean State operated through a strong bureaucracy, free of pressure from outside groups and capable of getting businesses to adhere to the commitments made, especially the objectives established for sales abroad. In fact, a company that failed to reach the performance objectives established would stop receiving subsidies, and any measures of protection established in its favor would be removed. The nation initially focused its efforts on sectors that were not trailblazing industries such as air transportation, specialized chemicals, or telecommunications—sectors in which Korea possessed no significant economic resources or adequate technical and scientific know-how. Instead, the country concentrated on sectors with high capital intensity and well-defined technologies. This included fields such as automobiles, shipbuilding, and cement.

Korea paid special attention to the production stage and the quality of labor in the factory. Both public and private leaders understood that they had to import all the technologies necessary for development and would not be able to purchase them ready to put into use. To accomplish this, significant resources were invested in training technicians and workers; as a result, Korean workers are among the most highly trained in the world. All young engineers who intended to take on managerial roles were expected to pass a long apprenticeship inside a factory.

Until now, we have only addressed the relationship between State and enterprise. Let us shift our attention to the groups of firms, the *chaebol*, that were controlled by family owners who usually worked in tandem with their managerial hierarchies. Like the Japanese keiretsu, the chaebol diversified their activities into unrelated sectors but, unlike Japan, the law in Korea prohibited groups from owning banks. Financial institutions were considered to be public property, and this seems to have been a way for the State to hold tightly the reins of credit policy. As in many latecomer nations, the origins of unrelated diversification can be found in the fact that firms, given the limits of the internal market, needed exports to realize economies of scale. They also needed to avoid the risk (in mature sectors where the majority of the firms operated) of obsolete technology.

The needs that were imposed by the government should also be considered. When the government decided to develop a new sector, it preferred to entrust the project to a big group with experience in realizing large-scale initiatives. This is what happened in the naval ship construction sector in 1971 when the State gave the project to Hyundai Construction, leader in the field of civil engineering, rather than entrusting it to seven small shipyards. Hyundai and Samsung were two of the largest chaebol. The first, initially operating in the construction industry, grew rapidly in the 1950s thanks to some important projects (including the first bridge on the Han River, the international airport of Kimp'o, and the Seoul–Pusan highway) commissioned by General Park's government. Hyundai began to diversify into unrelated fields in the 1960s when it entered sectors such as steel and petroleum refineries. Thanks to its performance and the support it received from State efforts to develop heavy industry, Hyundai became a highly diversified chaebol and experienced rapid growth.

Combining public funding, State protection, and foreign technology imports, Hyundai and the other chaebol entered into sectors such as automobiles, aluminum, and ship construction in the 1970s and then into electronics, elevators, robotics, and informational and publishing services in the following decade. In the years following the Korean War, Samsung, originally a commercial entity, diversified into sugar refining, textiles, and insurance. Unlike Hyundai, Samsung received few of the State benefits related to policies promoting heavy industry. It did receive important benefits from having its share of the internal market protected; strengthened in this way, it was able to concentrate on products with a high potential for export. As happened with Hyundai, unrelated diversification became a distinctive characteristic for Samsung; in 1965, the company started producing fertilizers. Shortly thereafter, it entered other fields, including electronics, shipbuilding, chemicals, petrochemicals, construction, and aerospace. By the mid-1990s, Samsung had become the world's largest producer of semiconductors. With the growth of their economic activities and increased tendency to export, both Hyundai and Samsung started expanding abroad by opening subsidiaries. The branches that they opened in China and other nations of the Far East were planned as a way of lowering production costs, whereas those in the United States and Europe were a way of bypassing commercial barriers.

Korea was able to combine a strong State that promoted growth and forced companies to compete on a global basis with private enterprises that devoted substantial attention to efficiencies in production and distribution in their highly diversified operations. Between 1962 and 1979, the country's gross national product (GNP) grew at an average annual rate of 8.9 percent, whereas exports in the same period reached 39.9 percent of GNP. By the end of the 1970s, Korean investments in machinery and equipment represented 13.5 percent of GNP; the same type of investment in Japan represented 4.7 percent of its GNP; in the United States, it was 3.9 percent, and practically the same in Germany (3.8 percent). The rapidity of Korea's progress was truly impressive: by the beginning of the twenty-first century, a nation that only a few decades earlier had been classified as "backward" was the world's top producer of ships, sixth in steel production, fifth in automobiles, and second as assembler of semiconductors.

The system was unusually successful, but it was not without its weak points. For example, small- and medium-sized enterprises (SMEs) were much less dynamic than their counterparts in other industrialized nations, and the policies of Korea—founded on a form of economic growth driven by the chaebol—inhibited the development of the SMEs. According to recent data, the performance of Korea's SMEs was poor because of their outdated technology.

Another weak point of the system was the risky policy of bank financing during the tumultuous process of industrialization; together with the international economic context, this made the situation in Korea especially difficult during the Asian crisis of 1997–1998. The list of SMEs, banks, and chaebol that failed was long, and the same fate awaited the country's fourth largest chaebol, Daewoo, in the summer of 1998. With the failure of Daewoo, Korea became an object of concern in the international business community.

Nevertheless, Korea had made massive strides in the process of industrialization. Notwithstanding the crisis and the slowdown in the 1990s (during which average growth still hovered around 7 percent), by the end of the century, the "Little Giant" had become the 11th largest economy in the world. Although it only had a population of 45 million, it ranked just behind the most advanced Western nations, Japan, and countries with much larger populations such as China and Brazil.

Argentina

The story of twentieth-century Argentina, which unlike South Korea could boast of extensive natural resources, was characterized by substantial political instability and significant errors in economic policy. As a result, the nation's industrial development was slow, uneven, and incomplete over the long term.

At the end of the nineteenth century and in the first decades of the 1900s, Argentina was already fully integrated into the world's economy and ranked sixth in per capita income. Unfortunately, this era of prosperity did not provide a solid foundation for a long-run industrialization process. The country had many advantages. Like the United States, it had vast lands for agriculture and its food products enjoyed great success in world markets. The earnings from this sector could have been used to make further investments in industrial activities, but Argentina's ruling class kept policy oriented firmly in favor of their own narrow self-interests; they were overly cautious when thinking about the nation's further development. Not even the construction of railways, which in other developed nations had made an important contribution to the growth of industry and modern corporations, was successful in stimulating the growth of local industries. While the railroad network transformed segmented local markets into an integrated national market, the scarcity of raw materials and legislation that constrained the potential for imports of capital, machinery, and even human resources from abroad did not favor the growth of national large-scale industries such as steel and transportation vehicles.

The crisis of the 1930s opened the way to a series of economic policies oriented toward substituting products made locally for imports; in the following decades, various tools were utilized to support different sectors as well as actors in the Argentinian economy. The saying "*todo lo que se mueve se promueve*" (everything in motion is in promotion) captured well the mentality of Argentina's governments, which, over the course of the twentieth century, heavily intervened in the economy by granting protectionistic measures and resources to those entrepreneurs who exercised the most pressure via lobbying. Almost all kinds of firms (large private diversified groups, foreign multinationals, State enterprises, and small- or medium-sized firms) benefited from this system, but the support did follow a consistent course, and it did not encourage industry.

At the beginning of the 1900s, the largest industrial activities in Argentina were almost exclusively big diversified business groups owned by families, similar to Japan's zaibatsu or Korea's chaebol. Many of these *grupos* were in the hands of immigrants, and they had grown because of their ability to produce and export agricultural products. Most had been able to integrate their banks into the group. In an area where access to long-term credit was severely limited, this last factor turned out to be a key advantage. It made it possible for some of these groups to obtain funding for investments in numerous activities, often very diversified. One example is the *Banco d'Italia y Rio de la Plata*, a business created by a group of

Italian immigrants who operated in the banking and trading industries and moved into the manufacturing of frozen meats, matches, paper, textiles, and chemicals. Another was the *Bunge y Born* group, created in 1884 by some Belgian entrepreneurs who were especially active in the processing of cereals and industries such as olive oil production, textiles, chemicals, and metallurgy. Foreign multinationals, especially British at the outset, became important protagonists of local business groups starting in the late 1800s. In the early 1900s, in a sector such as meat canning, Argentinian groups found themselves facing heavy competition from British & Argentina Meat Co. Important American operators such as Armour and Swift were quick to follow. Due to a booming local economy, a number of multinationals set up plants in Argentina in the 1920s and came through the economic crisis of the 1930s in good shape. The industrial sectors most affected by foreign competitors were those that were capital intensive and characteristic of the Second Industrial Revolution: chemicals and pharmaceuticals (Duperial, Parke Davis, Bayer, Colgate-Palmolive, Union Carbide, Johnson, Upjohn, and Abbott), rubber (Pirelli, Firestone, and Goodyear), metallurgy and machinery (Argentrac, Armco, and Pechiney), and foodstuffs (Fleischmann, Quaker, and Adams).

With Juan Domingo Perón's rise to power in 1946, government policies favored two important actors in the Argentinian economy: State-owned firms and small local companies. The State created state-owned enterprises (SOEs) not only to achieve economic goals but also for social and military purposes; the intention was to develop important national "champions" in strategic sectors and areas connected to national defense such as steel, petrochemicals, automobiles, and air transportation. The government also protected small firms, seeking to reinforce local initiatives that in the early part of the twentieth century had been suppressed. State support for SMEs, like the creation of SOEs, was part of an intensive effort to replace imports and close off those multinationals that had acquired a strong position in the national economy. When the economy began to slow down in the 1950s, the State once again changed direction, trying to establish a delicate balance between neo-liberalism and nationalism. If, on the one hand, the activities of multinationals continued to be regulated, on the other hand, the government actively encouraged the selective arrival of some, especially American firms, by granting them numerous incentives. Argentina erected high protectionistic tariffs, while excluding imported capital assets from the duties. For those who set up new plants, there were guarantees of special terms and few bureaucratic obstacles. As a result, according to 1963 census data, a quarter of Argentina's industrial production came from foreign firms with half of that from firms that had only been operative in the country for less than 15 years. Even this strong, specific support, however, was unable to foster an efficient industrial system in Argentina; when the economy stagnated in the mid-1970s, the nation's firms entered a period of crisis. Thus began a process of "deindustrialization," which entailed a massive reduction in output. During this process, the government was forced once again to reassess its policies and objectives; it chose to favor the nation's big diversified groups, organizations that had been forgotten for many years.

By the end of the 1980s, there were few signs of the flourishing economy of a century earlier. The various types of companies that had developed inside Argentina appeared to have completely failed, as had the government's economic policies. The country was in miserable shape. The big Argentinian diversified groups that had animated the first stages of industrialization and that had become fashionable again in the 1970s were unable to reach the necessarily high levels of innovation and efficiency to compete in the global economy. Unlike the Korean chaebol, Argentina's grupos had not been able to accumulate essential technological competencies and organizational capacities, preferring instead to focus their energies on lobbying the government rather than increasing efficiency. Foreign multinationals, even if over time they introduced some of the more recent technological, organizational, and managerial innovations, were subjected to the frequently changing winds of government policies. They also had to contend with the hostility of public opinion and the limitations of the domestic market. For most multinationals, it was impossible to reach the same performance levels achieved in other nations.

Argentina's SOEs (which, in 1975, numbered 8 in the top 50 industrial firms) also suffered from structural problems. They were not managed with the goal of low-cost output and suffered from the influence political factors had on management. The situation was further aggravated by the nation's political instability. As it turned out, the country's SMEs were not in much better shape because in many cases they did not know how to group themselves into suppliers for the big corporations or to focus on product niches so as to render themselves important actors in the nation's industrial economy.

The inability of Argentinian industries to be successful over the long term is primarily due to two factors. First, the limited dimensions of the internal market certainly did not foster the creation of an important group of large, efficient companies. As late as 1960, Argentina had barely one-third of Germany's population and one-quarter of those in the United States at the beginning of the 1900s. Second, the intense lobbying activity by private entrepreneurs had a negative impact on developing companies, potential competitors that would have improved the efficiency of their industries. The lobbying resulted in a series of policies that, in effect, wasted energy by encouraging companies to seek political solutions to their problems rather than achieving competitive advantages through innovation and low-cost operations. The government's long experience with import substitution was a failure. Tariff protection and subsidies encouraged the development of particular business groups, but in Argentina, the government used criteria designed more to obtain political consensus rather than international competitiveness. The results were thus unlike those achieved in Japan and, even more so, in Korea. Bent on developing an extensive "welfare state," the government promoted economic stability rather than economic growth. Firms were protected and backed by the government without regard to their performance; the State made no demands on the companies involved nor were these firms obliged to increase exports of their products. This system of protected and globally uncompetitive firms brought about a painful depression when international competition increased in the 1970s and 1980s. Argentina's industrial firms experienced a series of failures regardless of their dimensions, ownership structure, nationality, or management.

A good example of the impact of a limited domestic market can be seen in the history of the Argentinian automobile industry. Up until the 1950s, the market was in the hands of a small number of foreign multinationals—Ford, General Motors, Chrysler, and Fiat. In 1959, the government instituted a wide-ranging program of incentives and granted licenses to 22 firms (7 of which were foreign) to build automobiles in Argentina. But the market was not big enough for all the automobiles that were now produced, and the manufacturers were unable to reach a level of efficiency that would allow them to compete internationally. By 1970, all the private Argentinian automobile firms had ceased production, and the sector was completely controlled by SOEs and a handful of multinationals. But the writing was already on the wall if we consider that, at the sector's peak, 11 manufacturers produced a total of 293,742 automobiles, of which 274,831 were sold in the domestic market. The small dimensions of the market made it impossible for the subsidiaries of the American "Big Three" to stay competitive. When new government policies were adopted in 1976–1977 for liberalizing commerce and reinforcing the national currency, this brought about a drop in the cost of imported automobiles, especially those of Japanese manufacturers; companies such as General Motors and Citroen opted to stop producing automobiles in Argentina rather than attempt to increase efficiency levels so as to remain competitive.

Government policies also had a very negative effect on sectors that were dominated by SMEs. For example, in the wine sector, Argentinian producers decided to take advantage of a government policy promoting the substitution of imports with domestic output; the result was an unusual system that appeared to be based on a Fordist model. In the valleys below the Andes, vineyards set up enormous plants capable of producing large quantities of low-quality wine. They were trying to respond to three government objectives: create the maximum number of jobs possible, protect basic minimum earnings for growers, and supply sufficient table wine to meet the needs of Buenos Aires, Cordoba, and the other major cities of the nation. These policies conflicted with the aim of developing foreign markets for the country's wines.

Over the course of the 1990s, President Menem introduced a series of reforms designed to foster greater efficiency and innovation. These policies had an impact on every aspect of the Argentinian economy. In parallel with the transformation of the banking and financial services industry, the new order promoted the privatization of the most important State enterprises, the liberalization of sectors that had long been subjected to regulation, and the creation of Mercosur, a regional trade agreement between Argentina, Brazil, Paraguay, and Uruguay. Out of this new scenario came signs of entrepreneurial abilities that had been suppressed by the policy errors of earlier decades. Even if the majority of Argentinians and their businesses were not able to develop the technological skills and organizational capabilities needed to compete successfully on an international basis, there were some groups that stood out; they included Industrias Metalúrgicas Pescarmona, one of the largest corporations in the world specializing in the production of turbines and cranes; and the steel manufacturer, Techint, which, in the 1990s, was world leader in seamless tubes for transporting oil and gas. Even the automobile sector, after the disastrous situation of the past, was rapidly transformed in the 1990s, thanks to the liberalization brought about by the Mercosur agreement. It is still too early to evaluate the new program. Even if the South American accord convinced many Argentinian firms to think about markets much larger than the domestic one, we need to remember that Mercosur is a protectionistic bloc and its objective is to defend the interests of corporations and industries within its borders. In some cases, it has sought to defend inefficient companies in various sectors; it has also allowed a continuation of the policy of import substitution. Still, the bloc is an important step forward for a country such as Argentina, a nation hampered too long by national policies that hindered the full exploitation of its entrepreneurial, material, and financial resources.

Further reading

A. Amsden, *Asia's Next Giant: South Korea and Late Industrialization*, Oxford University Press, New York, 1989.

A. Amsden, *The Rise of "the Rest": Challenges to the West from Late-Industrializing Economies*, Oxford University Press, Oxford, 2001.

M.I. Barbero, "Argentina: Industrial Growth and Enterprise Organization, 1880s–1980s," in A.D. Chandler, Jr., F. Amatori, and T. Hikino (eds.), *Big Business and the Wealth of Nations*, Cambridge University Press, Cambridge, 1997.

M. Guillén, *The Limits of Convergence: Globalization and Organizational Change in Argentina, South Korea and Spain*, Princeton University Press, Princeton, NJ, 2001.

T. Hikino and A. Amsden, "Staying Behind, Stumbling Back, Sneaking Up, Soaring Ahead: Late Industrialization in Historical Perspective," in W. Baumol, R. Nelson, and E. Wolff (eds.), *Convergence of Productivity: Cross-Country Studies and Historical Evidence*, Oxford University Press, New York, 1994.

Appendix

Table 18.1 Agriculture and integration into the global economy: Argentina and South Korea, 1960 and 1990

	1960		1990	
	Argentina	*Korea*	*Argentina*	*Korea*
Importance of agriculture and fishing				
% of GPD	16.6	39.9	6.7	8.3
% of employment	15.2	75.6	12	18
% of exports	66.3	30.5	27.3	2.6
As % of GDP				
Exports	10.2	3.4	10	37.6
Imports	11.3	12.7	13.7	41.5
Exports plus imports	21.5	16.1	23.7	79.1

Source: Adapted from Mauro Guillén, *The Limits of Convergence*, Princeton University Press, Princeton, NJ, 2001, p. 34.

Table 18.2 Investments in machinery and equipment, Korea, Japan, the United States, and Germany, 1967–1987 (% of GNP)

Year	Korea	Japan	United States	West Germany
1967	5.3	6.8	4	4.7
1969	5.7	8.5	3.8	5.9
1971	6.5	7.4	3.4	5.6
1973	8.1	6.8	3.5	4.3
1975	7.8	5.5	3.6	3.6
1977	10.8	4.7	3.6	3.7
1979	13.5	4.7	3.9	3.8
1981	10.2	5.5	4.2	3.8
1983	9.6	5.4	3.6	3.5
1985	9.7	6.6	4.4	3.7
1987	11.8	6	3.9	—

Source: Adapted from Alice H. Amsden, "South Korea: Enterprising Groups and Entrepreneurial Government," in Alfred D. Chandler, Jr., Franco Amatori, and Takashi Hikino (eds.), *Big Business and the Wealth of Nations*, Cambridge University Press, Cambridge, 1997, p. 352.

Table 18.3 South Korean companies included in the Fortune Global 500 ranking, 2009

	Global 500 rank	*Revenues (million dollars)*
Samsung Electronics	40	110,350
LG	69	82,082
SK Holdings	72	80,810
Hyundai Motor	87	72,542
POSCO	199	37,976
GS Holdings	213	36,503
Korea Electric Power	305	28,712
Hyundai Heavy Industries	355	25,004
Hanwha	362	24,782
Samsung Life Insurance	367	24,420
Korea Gas	438	21,076
S-Oil	441	21,020
Doosan	471	19,494
Samsung C&T	495	18,635

Source: http://money.cnn.com/magazines/fortune/global500/2009/countries/SouthKorea.html. Last accessed October 6, 2010.

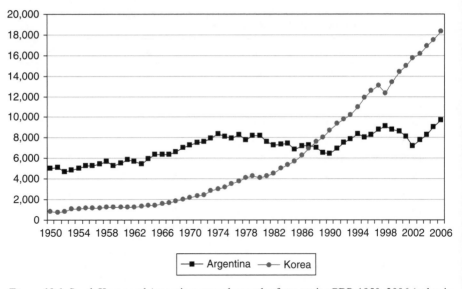

Figure 18.1 South Korea and Argentina: annual growth of per capita GDP, 1950–2006 (value in 1990 US dollars)

Source: adapted from Angus Maddison, *Statistics on World Population, GDP and Per Capita GDP, 1–2008 AD*, http://www.ggdc.net/maddison/; last accessed October 6, 2010.

Part VI
The globalization of today

19 Multinationals
Quid novi?

From the mid-1980s until the beginning of the new millennium, the total flow of foreign investments among developed, developing, and transition economies rose dramatically, from 1 to 4.5 percent of the world's gross domestic product (GDP). The vast majority of these investments took place from and in developed countries, but a similar, sharp rise was seen in peripheral countries where the process of globalization (which had started after World War II) was well underway.

Long-term trends

The considerable increase in international business activity, especially in investments directed toward the acquisition of income-generating assets abroad, was not new. Innovations in transportation and communication systems (see Chapter 7) had made the transfer of goods, individuals, money, and information across the globe much easier in the twentieth century, but following World War II, a new wave of globalization, economic integration, and intensification of cross-border investments swept through the world economy. In this framework, in which a crucial role was played by the absence of major conflicts between the developed nations, Western corporations intensified their investments abroad in an effort to replicate their competitive advantages in more dynamic and promising markets. These companies possessed superior technologies, organizational capabilities, and financial resources, and they used these advantages in foreign markets in both developed and developing nations. The creation of foreign subsidiaries was a long and complex process, however, and their efficiency depended on many elements including the free circulation of technology, knowledge, and capital.

The process of "multinationalization" involved all of the "advanced" industrialized economies. European and American investors made heavy investments in foreign countries, including the peripheral but quickly developing "old world" countries such as Russia, Scandinavia, and those in the Mediterranean. The investors and firms targeted Africa, Asia, and South America because of their large endowments of natural resources, especially those related to mining and oil. Here, the strategies of multinational expansion were driven by the desire to establish rigid control over the raw materials that were indispensable to the continuous production processes of the Second Industrial Revolution.

These fast-growing investment sites also attracted foreign funds in the service sector, in utilities such as electric energy production, water and gas distribution, and public transportation. The lack of technical expertise and capital in developing nations was coupled with an increasing demand for utilities and services, and this combination made these countries very attractive areas for investment by foreign entrepreneurs. Foreign companies usually financed their ventures with capital collected from their home nations. The practice of incorporating in a wealthy country, collecting capital, and other resources to be invested abroad gave rise to the widespread presence of international corporations that had not grown out of an existing domestic business. These were *free-standing companies*. Their total capital at the eve of World War I amounted to nearly 45 percent of the total world foreign direct investments (FDIs), and the amount invested grew tremendously after World War II.

Business leaders working in developing nations again attempted to replicate the Western strategies that had worked so well in their home countries. Their control of superior technology was the key component in this internationalization process, but branding, marketing, and even organization became increasingly important. Favorable political and economic conditions prevailed after World War II. The US dollar—to which world currencies were pegged under the Bretton Woods settlement—was overvalued and European businesses were temporarily weakened. This allowed many US companies to strengthen their presence abroad. The US position also became much stronger in the Western, developed countries. The spread of the "irresistible empire"—as US historian Victoria De Grazia has termed the process of Americanization in postwar Europe—was unchallenged until the beginning of the 1970s. In that year, the United States made half of all FDIs worldwide. Manufacturing, where US companies could most easily exploit their competitive advantages, became the target sector. As shown in Chapter 17, FDIs were an important vehicle for the Americanization of Europe, and US multinational companies were present in almost all industries in which organizational capabilities and superior technology gave them substantial advantages—from oil to chemicals and pharmaceuticals, from automotives to food and beverages, and even in modern services such as consulting and mass retailing.

Then gradually Europe began to build a new role in the process of international expansion. During the 1950s and 1960s, already, several European companies that had been able to recover quickly from wartime conflict were becoming competitive on an international scale. Thanks in some cases to their governments' support or even direct involvement, these European companies started to challenge US supremacy. The United States was sinking deeply into debt and was preoccupied with the war it was conducting in Vietnam. By the early 1970s, Germany and France started to invest directly abroad on a considerable scale. By that time, one-fifth of the total volume of foreign investments originated in European companies. The 1970s also witnessed the conspicuous growth in Japanese foreign investments in some industries, for instance automobiles or electronics. Companies such as

Toyota and Matsushita enjoyed substantial advantages as a result of their superior ability in managing the organization of the production process (see Chapter 12).

Multinational organizations

Using the popular multidivisional form of organization (M-form), the largest multinational companies were able, without further structural changes, to adapt rather easily to international expansion. As multinationals moved abroad, they opened subsidiaries, built totally new plants (i.e., "greenfield" facilities), or sought the support of local partners to reduce uncertainty and limit transaction costs. The M-form organizational structure normally allowed the multinationals' headquarters to maintain control over the operations of these foreign subsidiaries. Because research and development (R&D) was still usually conducted in the home country, the result was a hierarchical organization characterized by the strong dominance of the mother company over its foreign subsidiaries. The foreign subsidiaries had a relatively low degree of autonomy in planning their strategies, market approaches, and investment decisions in almost every branch of manufacturing and services. A good example is provided by the US oil producers, which from the interwar period started a massive policy of foreign investments to secure control over the natural resources they needed.

In Europe, large companies in countries characterized by relatively small domestic markets successfully developed commercial and investment strategies to take advantage of the international market. This was the case among many Dutch firms, including prominently such companies as Philips and Unilever (an Anglo-Dutch merger), and Swiss companies such as Nestlé. The latter had long been a major international firm. Only a year after its foundation (1866) by a German immigrant to Geneva, it had started to produce for customers in other European countries, primarily Germany and France. In other cases, companies started to establish subsidiaries abroad on the basis of strong technological advantages. For example, IBM, which had an established position in the US market for business machines, had long been a major multinational. In other cases, the main driver for the establishment of operations abroad was superior capability in marketing and sales. This was the case with Singer, whose sewing machines were already a truly global product. Singer was among the largest and most profitable corporations in the world.

The post-World War II internationalization strategies—now carried on through foreign investments and not simply via exports—have been analyzed by numerous scholars using many different interpretative frameworks. At the peak of the international expansion of US multinationals during the 1960s, Canadian scholar Stephen Hymer introduced the concept of "ownership advantage" to explain why domestic companies risked the uncertainties and costs of business activity abroad (see Chapter 9). In his view, multinationals were successful abroad because they possessed superior technological, organizational, financial, and marketing capabilities; these were the skills that they had first developed inside their "home" country. Harvard Business School professor Raymond Vernon tried to improve this theory by adding to it the product-life-cycle concept: thus, the decision to start up abroad stemmed from the normal, progressive saturation of a company's home market. Other, frequently more complex, explanations followed. In Europe, the Uppsala school considered the process of multinationalization to be the outcome of expertise accumulation as companies gradually learned to run their operations in domestic and then in foreign countries.

The most effective and still most influential paradigm was developed by John Dunning during the 1970s. Dunning's broad, eclectic framework analyzed the decision to establish operations abroad as a mixed, highly variable choice. He described certain advantages on which a foreign firm could rely, including the internal characteristics of the company, its capabilities, and assorted competencies that he labeled the "ownership advantages." Some incentives for the establishment of foreign operations were country specific, that is, generated by the resources found in the country "hosting" the investment. These he called the "location advantages." They ranged from the size and dynamism of the domestic market to the nature of the host country's infrastructures, political climate, and cultural attitudes. The shape taken by the foreign operations—from export activity to vertical integration through direct ownership of plants located abroad, that is, the degree of "internalization" of foreign operations—was, according to Dunning, explained by the necessity to reduce transaction costs and protect relevant strategic assets. The ownership–location–internalization (OLI) paradigm provided a complex, realistic interpretation of the process of internationalization of large firms at this time.

The 1970s

Multinationals, most of which were characterized by a high degree of centralization and focused tightly on exploiting their comparative advantages, started to change during the second half of the 1970s. Several transformations took place—one of them in the services sector. During the late 1970s and the 1980s, different types of services emerged. These were characterized by unique market strategies. Three areas of business that were particularly active in this new wave were finance, trade, and services to business. Finance and trade benefited from the intense wave of deregulation and liberalization, which accompanied this second wave of globalization, particularly from the mid-1980s onward. Services to business, including management consulting, expanded rapidly in these years. Together, finance, trade, and services to business activities came to represent roughly two-thirds of international investments in the service industry.

In addition to banks and insurance companies, retail firms began now to invest heavily in international operations. They quickly expanded their activity abroad, especially after liberalization began in Eastern Europe. Initially, many of these organizations continued to exploit the expertise and capabilities they had developed in their home country. But internationalization of retail forced companies to confront increasingly complex and varied cultures of consumption. Strategies of expansion had now to be planned more carefully in order to select the right approach to the market. For instance, during the 1950s, US investors had begun to target the Italian mass retail market, opening the first supermarket chains. In one important venture,

Supermarkets Italiani (the name was later changed to Esselunga), the investment took place in the form of a joint venture with some Italian entrepreneurs.

It was opposed, of course, by small shopkeepers and, consequently, by some local authorities and political parties, but the stores were attractive to Italian consumers. The management in this case successfully adapted the US model to the local situation, often in matters that seemed very small and inconsequential. For instance, shopping carts were smaller than in the United States, so that the stores' relative lack of contents was not accentuated. In addition, the décor was arranged so as to avoid any off-putting sense of prosperity that might prevent poorer people from entering stores whose appeal was based on low prices.

From the late 1970s on, business consulting was another area in which international investment expanded rapidly. The business of "consulting" began in the United States where companies sought sophisticated accounting and financial services. They also needed information about new practices in job organization and evaluation, in both their "home" offices and their offices abroad. The internationalization of consulting firms came, in large part, as a result of international business. But as satellite offices abroad began to create a local client base, they quickly accommodated to local conditions, adapting their programs to the characteristics of their foreign business clients and systems of political economy.

While the United States and its multinationals continued to play an important role in these changes, the 1970s marked the end of American dominance in many industries. As we saw in Chapter 14, some of the largest American firms were falling behind their international competition during the 1970s and 1980s. This was particularly true in the capital-intensive industries of the Second Industrial Revolution. The devaluation of the US currency posed a serious challenge to US firms, as did the technological progress being made by European and Asian businesses. By the end of the 1980s, American businesses had lost their position as the world's most active foreign investors.

At the beginning of the 1970s, the US share of world FDI was nearly 50 percent, with Europe at 40 percent. Thirty years later, at the beginning of the new millennium (i.e., in 2000), America's share had shrunk to 20 percent, whereas the European share remained almost stable. This shift in the relative importance of the United States in foreign investment was accompanied by an increase in international investment activity of other countries, namely Japan (during the 1970s and 1980s) and other East Asian nations such as Korea, Singapore, Hong Kong, and Taiwan (from the 1980s onward). According to statistics provided by the United Nations Conference on Trade and Development (UNCTAD), at the beginning of the 1970s "developing economies" (such as the Asian Tigers) possessed only a negligible share (close to zero) of FDI worldwide; just 10 years later, this share had risen dramatically to more than 12 percent.

Multinational novelties

The emergence of East Asian multinationals took place for reasons different from those underpinning the internationalization of US firms. Japanese and Asian companies expanded abroad—within Asia but also in the hypercompetitive US market—on the basis of advantages that frequently were not related to the possession of superior technology. Superior organizational capabilities, a virtuous relationship with their banking systems, the support of other companies, and state financial support made these achievements possible. In some cases (e.g., in Korea), the State explicitly made "internationalization"—meaning exports as well as foreign investment activity—one of the requirements for government credit, subvention, and protection. More recently, multinationals in emerging countries have been able to invest successfully abroad by using ethnic network relationships, by designing products particularly well suited to emerging markets, and by taking advantage of privileged access to untapped resources and markets. These companies have been so successful that they have even been able to expand in "advanced" economies, diffusing their brands on a global scale. This happened when the Chinese company Lenovo successfully acquired IBM's production facilities for personal computers and suddenly became one of the major players in the industry.

Companies such as these, often referred to as the "Dragon Multinationals," played a growing role in the globalization of business in the 1990s. Many of them had unique strategies for internationalization. Companies located in "newly industrialized countries" embraced internationalization because it allowed them to achieve competitive technological advantages that were unavailable at home. These corporations expanded internationally by establishing partnerships and joint ventures with foreign interests, not by purchasing foreign subsidiaries outright.

While East Asia has been particularly significant in recent years to international business, other emerging economies have slowly gained more important positions in the international economy. Starting in the year 2000, Russian, Brazilian, Chinese, and Indian multinationals were leveraging "advantages" similar to those that had ensured the success of the "Tigers" in the 1980s and 1990s. Superior knowledge of emerging markets, privileged access to resources and markets, governmental support, and the benefit of informal network relationships enabled them to move ahead along different business paths than those employed by Western corporations—and they did so with great success.

Changing strategies and structures

Since the late 1980s, multinational companies have adopted a variety of new organizational structures. Two scholars of international business, Chris Bartlett and Sumantra Ghoshal, have published extensively on this aspect of the evolution of multinational organizations. They identified four organizational models: the multinational firm, the international firm, the global firm, and the transnational firm. Of these, only the global firm (featuring weak subsidiaries closely related to the mother company, which was in full control of the organization's technology and knowledge) resembled the centralized structure typical of the "classic," US multinational that dominated international business in the decades immediately following World War II.

The other models—inspired by a real case, that of the successful turnaround of the Swedish multinational Asea Brown Boveri (ABB)—were developed in order to establish closer relationships with local markets. This development showed how successful multinationals used local subsidiaries creatively to control a relevant section of the value chain. They were thus able to attune their operations to local market conditions. The most "virtuous" model was the transnational one, which described a company operating in a network of largely independent subsidiaries, all different in their capabilities, which collaborated by exchanging knowledge and innovations. The original mother company in this setting exercised very loose control. This new style of globalization changed the behavior of many multinational companies.

The appreciation of different cultural patterns and the increasing value of non-Western knowledge thus deeply influenced the structure of these firms. This process of change was facilitated by new information and communication technologies. The Internet Revolution allowed multinational firms to organize themselves more efficiently by reducing one of the fundamental determinants of international integration: transaction (especially control) costs. These new technologies—along with considerable reductions in transportation costs—have allowed the value chain and the production process to fragment into smaller and more specialized companies. These small, specialized companies possess a high degree of independence and legal autonomy, and the new technology allows for an easier flow of information within the firm and among its customers and clients. "Network" organizational structures have become increasingly common among international firms, as have cross-border alliances. Cross-border activity by small- and medium-sized enterprises was made possible by this same technological revolution. These firms are now able to specialize and innovate successfully in world-sized markets. There are more and more examples of medium-sized businesses increasing their international activity.

The Italian case is particularly significant, especially in light of the traditionally low degree of international operations of the domestic corporations. During the past 15 years, a number of medium-sized firms, frequently originating in the fertile seedbed of industrial districts, achieved stable positions in worldwide market niches for specialized and customized products, from machine tools to chemical specialties. They were able to open new plants or engage in intense mergers and acquisitions (M&A) activity at a global level. These "pocket multinationals," as they have been labeled, are still (in the vast majority) family controlled and managed, demonstrating the opportunities introduced by the new technologies of communication and transport in the field of international business. A good example, for instance, is Mapei, a company with a turnover of 2 billion euros, which successfully exploits a global, specialized niche in the production of glues and adhesives for the building industry. The company, fully controlled by the founding family, is today run by the second and third generations. It underwent a process of international expansion through M&A, as well as greenfield investments, and today it is present in more than 40 countries with nearly 50 production plants and more than 5,300 employees.

The acceleration in the globalization process during the late 1980s and 1990s offered these companies the chance to expand their international operations in specialized areas of business. Other family companies in traditional businesses such as food and clothing have also expanded their international operations and presence, sometimes creating global brands. In this and other ways, international business has continued to evolve and grow. This is a business world far different than the one that existed in the immediate postwar years. No longer dominated by one style of firm headquartered in one of a small number of leading nations, the international business setting has experienced tremendous expansion and change.

Further reading

Geoffrey Jones, *The Evolution of International Business: An Introduction*, Routledge, London, 1996.
Geoffrey Jones, *Multinationals and Global Capitalism: From the Nineteenth to the Twenty-First Century*, Oxford University Press, Oxford, 2005.
Mira Wilkins, *The Maturing of Multinational Enterprise: American Business Abroad from 1914 to 1970*, Harvard University Press, Cambridge, MA, 1974.
Mira Wilkins and Harm Schröter (eds.), *The Free-Standing Firm in the World Economy, 1830–1996*, Oxford University Press, Oxford, 1998.

Appendix

Table 19.1 Top industrial companies in the world by total assets[a]

	1999 (billion euros)	2008 (billion euros)	Change (% in local currency)		1989 (billion euros)
Toyota Motor (Japan)	160.0	230.4	76.8	Royal Dutch Shell (Great Britain)	76.1
Royal Dutch Shell (Great Britain)	110.7	199.3	175.8	General Motors (United States)	75.6
CNPC (China)	—	165.5	—	Hitachi (Japan)	44.3
Gazprom (Russia)	—	173.6	—	Exxon (United States)	68.3
Exxon Mobil (United States)	139.1	159.6	59.0	IBM (United States)	62.2
Volkswagen (Germany)	66.7	155.6	133.5	Matsushita El. (Japan)	44.2
BP (United Kingdom)	85.4	149.5	168.4	Toyota Motor (Japan)	49.2
Daimler (Germany)	168.6	126.2	−24.9	Ford Motor (United States)	42.9
Total (France)	77.9	113.0	45.1	BP (United Kingdom)	40.4
Chevron (United States)	39.5	112.5	294.7	Fiat (Italy)	35.4

Source: Adapted from Mediobanca R&S, *Multinationals: Financial Aggregates, 2010*.

Note
a   Excluding intangibles.

20 New forms of enterprise

The season of the multibusiness conglomerate was followed by an equally intense phase of refocusing, reorganizing, and revitalizing in business. Spurred frequently by the same consulting firms that earlier had encouraged the adoption of diversification strategies, top management turned its attention toward programs aimed at improving business efficiency and performance. The resulting transition was also influenced by a new dynamism in the market for corporate control, dynamism that followed a few years of increased activity among raiders and leveraged-buyout companies willing to extract the breakup value resulting from the sale of conglomerate divisions (see Chapter 14).

During the 1990s, other dynamics of a very different nature influenced the strategies and the organizational structures of leading corporations. Once again, it was a shifting technology—combined with the possibility of designing new organizational architectures—that accelerated the process of transformation started during the previous decade. In many cases, the new technologies began "crumbling" the walls of the once monolithic, vertically integrated corporations that had dominated the first three-quarters of the century.

New technologies and big business

In this respect, an important element to be kept in mind is the sometimes "ambivalent" way in which the impact of the new technologies of the Third Industrial Revolution was experienced by modern big business. In a first phase, from the 1960s to the 1980s, efficiency gains and a rapid decline in transport and communication costs encouraged the geographical expansion of large companies as well as their degree of diversification. Multinational corporations and multibusiness firms largely benefited from an information revolution that allowed headquarters to exercise a closer control over business operations, even in very distant geographical areas. Thus, the first phase of technological change actually consolidated a trend already underway.

Measured in dollars (at current prices), global foreign direct investment (FDI) flows jumped from 13 billion dollars in 1970 to 54 billion dollars in 1980 to more than 207 billion dollars in 1990. Multinational companies expanded their borders, becoming truly global. From the 1970s onward, corporations such as Unilever in Europe, IBM in the United States, and Toyota in Japan were able to simultaneously carry on strategies of diversification and of increasing international investments as they expanded around the world (see Chapter 19). This dual strategy was possible in part because of the decrease taking place in the cost of control, a drop made possible thanks to new technologies. From the early 1980s, the technologies of the Third Industrial Revolution began to exert a huge impact on corporate structures, fostering a widespread reduction in the degree of vertical integration and in the optimal average size of the production unit.

This trend continued into the 1990s, affecting many of the "core industries" of the Second Industrial Revolution. Once dominated by large, vertically integrated enterprises characterized by a closely centralized control, these industries now became more decentralized. The result was that in several cases, for instance electricity production and some areas of chemicals, pharmaceuticals, engineering, electronics, and durables, there was a reduction in the scale of production, accompanied by an increasing diversification.

The decrease in the scale of production did not necessarily encourage disinvestment strategies. Instead, the effect was to enable a restructuring of the production process, a reorganization that decisively transformed apparently consolidated and even mature industries. In the case of cellular telephony, new, dynamic competitors emerged to challenge successfully the incumbent telephone companies. Deregulation and privatization accelerated this process. In other cases, the reduction in the optimal production scale allowed the companies to focus on previously unthinkable strategies of specialization. A significant example is the introduction of new technologies in steel production, which downsized considerably the minimum size of mills and allowed some producers to focus on the production of special steels so as to exploit profitable niches in the international market.

In other cases, vertically integrated firms discovered the benefits inherent in exploiting the market to buy goods and services once carefully kept inside the boundaries of the firm itself. One telling example is provided by IBM that, since the beginning of its history, had shown a marked tendency toward vertical integration, with all of the components necessary in recent decades for the "core business" of computing internally produced. Beginning in the early 1990s, IBM started to break from this rigid strategy, encouraging the various units to place their products, whether software or components, autonomously on the market. This process culminated for "Big Blue" (as the company was known) in the gradual shift of its strategic focus from the production of hardware and software to business and information-system consultancy.

Deverticalization, outsourcing, and hollowing-out

The new technologies, especially those improving transportation and communication, also influenced other aspects of business that cumulatively had a considerable impact on the internal structures of many large firms. The specialization process was accompanied by a diffuse tendency toward the "disintegration" of once vertically integrated structures. The boundaries of many of the main corporations also started to crumble under the pressure of outsourcing, a transition undertaken to save on both fixed and variable costs. The phenomenon was most evident in the mechanical, transportation, electronics, pharmaceutical, and chemical industries, all of which were once dominated by large, vertically integrated companies. Outsourcing was also a means of achieving increased innovation in several of these industries.

During the 1990s, it became a common practice for many automotive companies to outsource to suppliers significant portions of the production cycle. The pharmaceutical industry provides another interesting example of this process of decentralization. In this case, outsourcing included strategic activities such as the production of intermediates or even the administration of clinical trials; in some instances, pharmaceutical firms now relied on external partners who were willing to conclude detailed, long-term agreements with these large firms. One significant and quite recent example is provided by one of the world's largest pharmaceutical companies, AstraZeneca, which resulted from the merger in 1999 between the Swedish Astra AB and the British Zeneca PLC. The company refocused its business strategies, putting a strong emphasis on the development of new products. It invested more than 3 billion dollars per year in 12 research laboratories, but it also leveraged on the relationship with biotech companies and independent research centers.

Similar phenomena started to occur in sectors characterized by an especially high involvement in the new technologies, such as in consumer electronics and microelectronics. In these industries (as in the fashion and design industries), many producers kept close control over strategic functions such as design and marketing, while they outsourced production to external and specialized suppliers.

One consequence of these transformations has been, in some cases, a real "hollowing-out process" of once very large, tightly consolidated corporations. In those instances, this has had direct consequences for the whole industry's structure and operations. Market mechanisms have been increasingly substituted for those internalized, integrated processes characteristic of the large U-form and M-form bureaucratic organizations. Interestingly, "deverticalization" has not affected the volume of production flows, which remain significant: in 2009, Cisco—the US leader in network and communications equipment and one of the most significant examples of the restructuring process based on networking and outsourcing—ranked in 57th place among the top American companies, with nearly 40 billion dollars of revenue.

Networks and new organizational forms

To achieve a better understanding of the transformations described earlier, some clarifications are needed. The first concerns the nature of the actors involved in the processes of disintegration of vertically integrated structures. Outsourcing is based on specialized suppliers of components or services. These companies have developed unique skills and capabilities in the production of the specific items they feature and sometimes customize in many different ways; this makes them "general specialists," different from mere subcontractors and able to rely on competencies developed internally, while actively collaborating with the customer about the design, planning, and implementation of the final product or service. Significant examples of these relationships can be found in the field of electronic manufacturing services, or EMS, consisting in the production of components (for instance, printed circuit boards) and design and assembling of electronic systems.

The industry's world leader today is Flextronics, a US company with a turnover of nearly 30 billion dollars in 2008. The firm has sales and production facilities in 30 countries around the world. Founded in 1968, it grew steadily during the 1990s through a process of acquisition of specialized producers while building facilities, especially in Asia. Specialization in the case of Flextronics was accompanied by an increasingly wide coverage of the supply of components for many purposes. This strategy has made the US company the main supplier of some of the world's largest companies in consumer electronics including Casio, Dell, Ericsson, Hewlett-Packard, Microsoft, Motorola, Siemens, Sony-Ericsson, and Xerox.

Another aspect of the transformations occurring among the largest companies was a new organizational architecture that allowed the full exploitation of the advantages of decentralization. Modular products, characterized by components assembled through standardized interfaces, started to spread during the 1990s. One advantage of modularity is the fact that the process of innovation takes place inside each module. So long as the interfaces remain standardized, modularity expands the range of possible technological solutions for the system or product. Modular architectures allow, in addition, the development of final products only marginally subject to the logic of mass production.

The production of personal computers is probably the best example of a production process originally vertically integrated and then successfully transformed through the introduction of modular design. This has been at the origin of some sensational entrepreneurial successes, such as the well-known case of Dell, which based a substantial part of its successful business on the modular nature of personal computers (see Chapter 21). Even if the principles and benefits of modularity already existed and were well known to producers of other consumer goods (as, for instance, in stereo equipment and consumer electronics in general), the diffusion of standardized interfaces has been recently accelerating in many of the industries central to the Third Industrial Revolution. One significant example is the production of complex software, built on modules developed by specialized subcontractors. This enables a business to produce customized packages of software for particular uses.

The advent of modularity is one of many conditions allowing for the efficient operation of organizational forms fundamentally different from the large, vertically integrated enterprise. The main examples in this respect are business networks, defined as "groups of independent subjects linked by repeated cooperative relationship aimed at mutual benefit and that, during this process, develop 'learning communities'" (Fruin 2008: 255). The concept is a very broad one capturing different organizational typologies. The examples range from networks of sub-contracting, for instance those established between car manufacturers and small and medium independent producers of components, to the relationships among small firms inside the industrial districts, or even to the grouping of specialized suppliers around specific projects requiring sophisticated technologies and capabilities, for example in the development of open-source software. The processes of specialization and deverticalization described have had considerable impact on the strategic and structural characteristics of companies active in many industries of the "new economy." Even in many of the once vertically structured businesses of the Second Industrial Revolution, modularity and networks spread, profoundly changing competitive practices and the shape of the most dynamic competitors.

The process was, however, not without costs and potential problems. These soon became evident and started to affect the competitiveness of countries in which the process was taking place most intensely. Particularly significant is the case of the United States. Since the mid-1990s, major information and communication technology (ICT) companies have been reducing the size of their domestic work-force and thus increasing employment—frequently of skilled workers—abroad. At IBM, the percentage of US employees fell from 46 percent at the beginning of 2000 to 30 percent in 2008, at HP from 48 to 30 percent in the same period, whereas at Intel from 65 to 54 percent. ICT companies and general specialists were increasingly becoming global enterprises, relocating high added-value activities abroad and knowledge-intensive portions of their production chain to foreign facilities and eventually to foreign-skilled subcontractors. Flextronics, for instance, was once headquartered in California in the knowledge-intensive area of Silicon Valley; but now, the firm has moved to Singapore and, through its affiliated Multek, produces printed circuit boards in facilities located all over the world. According to some commentators, this process of "knowledge evaporation" has contributed to the decline in US competitiveness and the nation's ability to generate new and successful ventures in high-tech industries. The "collective capabilities" once clustered in areas such as Silicon Valley or the similar Route 128 area of Massachusetts have now in part relocated to other countries of the world, with the result that the US trade balance in high-tech products became increasingly negative from 2002 onward, reaching more than 50 billion dollars, about 7 percent of the whole deficit. The United States in 2007 was importing from China, Mexico, and Southeast Asia more than it exported in products related to life science, optoelectronics, information and communications, advanced materials, and nuclear technology.

Big business in the "New Economy" era

Inside the network and other forms of noncentralized production, a particularly delicate role is played by those in charge of coordinating the whole process. These actors are normally also the developers of the project at the core of the network itself. Companies such as Cisco or Dell assumed from the beginning the role of "hubs" engaged in building and managing networks of independent producers. Many of the companies that quickly achieved high rates of growth inside the technology-intensive industries of the Third Industrial Revolution are in effect exploiting the potential of decentralized structures. In the above-mentioned case of AstraZeneca, the company is involved in thousands of relationships and alliances, so much so that the company has introduced the role of "alliance manager" for the employees in charge of managing these complex and multiple relationships.

As this example indicates, instead of disappearing, the big corporation has been in many cases changing its organizational structure as well as its approach to the market and the process of innovation. Big business has assumed the role of coordination and distribution, while maintaining under control crucial functions such as research and development. The age of General Motors has given way to the age of Dell and Intel. It's a new world for business as well as the consumer.

Further reading

P. Di Maggio (ed.), *The Twenty-First-Century Firm: Changing Economic Organization in International Perspective*, Princeton University Press, Princeton, NJ, 2001.
M. Fruin, "Business Groups and Inter-Firm Networks," in G. Jones and J. Zeitlin (eds.), *The Oxford Handbook of Business History*, Oxford University Press, Oxford, 2008.
R. Langlois, *The Dynamics of Industrial Capitalism: Schumpeter, Chandler and the New Economy*, Oxford University Press, Oxford, 2007.
R. Langlois and P. Robertson, *Firms, Markets and Economic Change: A Dynamic Theory of Business Institutions*, Routledge, London, 1995.

Appendix

Table 20.1 Total number of electronic digital computers in use, 1950–1974

	United States	United Kingdom	France	West Germany	Japan
1950	2	3	0	0	0
1960	5,400	217	165	300	85
1970	74,060	6,269	5,460	7,000	8,800
1974	165,040	14,400	16,100	18,800	26,100

Source: Adapted from Thomas McCraw, *Creating Modern Capitalism*, Harvard University Press, Cambridge, MA, 1998, p. 355.

Table 20.2 Top ten computer firms worldwide, 1975 vs. 1994

1975	1994	1994 information technology (IT) revenues (billion dollars)
IBM	IBM	64.1
Burroughs	Fujitsu	21.3
Honeywell	Hewlett-Packard	19.2

(Continued)

Table 20.2 (Continued)

1975	1994	1994 information technology (IT) revenues (billion dollars)
Sperry	NEC	18.7
Control Data	Hitachi	13.7
NCR	Digital	13.5
Bull	AT&T	11.5
Digital	Compaq	10.9
ICL	EDS	10.1
Nixdorf	Toshiba	10

Source: Adapted from Thomas McCraw, *Creating Modern Capitalism*, Harvard University Press, Cambridge, MA, 1998, p. 394.

Table 20.3 Leading semiconductor (SC) manufacturers worldwide, 1988–1989

Rank		Company	1989 SC revenues (million dollars)	1989 market share (%)
1989	1988			
1	1	NEC	4,964	8.9
2	2	Toshiba	4,889	8.8
3	3	Hitachi	3,930	7
4	4	Motorola	3,322	5.9
5	6	Fujitsu	2,941	5.3
6	5	Texas Instruments	2,787	5
7	8	Mitsubishi	2,629	4.7
8	7	Intel	2,440	4.4
9	9	Matsushita	1,871	3.4
10	10	Philips	1,690	3
11	11	National	1,618	2.9
12	12	SGS-Thomson	1,301	2.3
13	18	Samsung	1,284	2.3
14	15	Sharp	1,230	2.2
15	20	Siemens	1,194	2.1
16	14	Sanyo	1,132	2
17	17	Oki	1,125	2
18	13	AMS	1,082	1.9
19	16	Sony	1,077	1.9
20	19	AT&T	873	1.6

Source: Adapted from Christopher Freeman and Francisco Louçã, *As Time Goes By: From the Industrial Revolution to the Information Revolution*, Oxford University Press, Oxford, 2001, p. 307.

21 The "roaring 1990s"

America is back

By the start of this new millennium, the United States was once again a global leader. A comparison among the world's largest economies at the time is telling: per capita income was 100 in the United States, when it was 75 in France, 74 in Japan, 72 in Britain, and 67 in Germany. Out of the top 500 corporations in the world ranked by turnover, more than 160 were based in the United States, the Japanese were fewer than 80, whereas Europeans accounted for about 100. Between 1995 and 2000, the annual income growth rate, per capita, exceeded 2 percent in the United States; this compared with 1.4 percent in Europe, with the exception of Spain, which had started in this period a process of modernization and industrial growth. Within one decade, American gross domestic product (GDP) had increased, in constant values, from 28,000 to 34,000 dollars per capita per year.

The prosperity of the 1990s was based on factors that were both intrinsic and extrinsic to the American economy. The United States was more prosperous than most other industrialized countries because of the vitality of an economic system that was able to create large numbers of new jobs: about 18 million between 1995 and 2005. This was similar to the rates of job creation in Europe, but with higher levels of productivity; and US productivity continued to increase about 2.5 percent per year during the decade. Most relevant was the fact that the United States had achieved solid leadership in nearly all of the most technologically advanced and research-intensive industries. At the beginning of the 1990s, the United States had more than 20 percent of world exports in industries such as aerospace, pharmaceuticals, computers, telecommunications equipment, machine tools, and precision machinery, the highest share among industrialized countries together with Japan. During the 1980s, the American world market share of technology-intensive industries held at around 25 percent; it exceeded 40 percent by the year 2000.

The size of the internal market, the pressures of foreign competition, and the presence of an efficient institutional framework and flexible capital markets were key contributors to American success. Public efforts in policies of procurement and support of intellectual property rights and scientific research helped to give the United States a large competitive advantage. In telecommunications equipment and computer manufacturing, the United States even managed to replace the world's leader, Japan.

American achievement was mirrored by a rise in the country's international trade and investment outflows. Knowledge-intensive service industries, such as telecommunications, financial services, and business services (including software design and healthcare), showed patterns similar to those of high-tech manufacturing. By the end of the 1990s, the American service industry accounted for nearly two-thirds of its GDP, whereas its turnover was about one-third of global turnover.

Just lucky?

Exogenous factors help to explain the American business system's success. Some of the constraints that had caused the economic slowdown during the 1970s and 1980s were lifted by the 1990s. The United States fully benefited from the opportunities created by an increase in world trade volume greater than had ever been seen before (see "New Globalization" in Chapter 13). The tensions in the international oil market, which had severely affected the most advanced world economies in the 1970s by increasing the cost of energy input, disappeared during the 1990s. When oil prices sank to half of those recorded during the previous decade, levels of inflation also dipped, eventually falling to less than 5 percent. In the United States, this positive trend was reflected in federal deficit spending. Meanwhile, increases in foreign trade helped America to control the trade balance deficit. The end of the Cold War, following the disintegration of the Soviet Union, also relaxed the need for additional federal spending in military and defense industries.

These favorable conditions were enhanced by the Clinton administration. Bill Clinton, a Democrat, made his guidelines for industrial policy clear during his presidential campaign. To support entrepreneurial creativity and thus to increase productivity and wealth, he believed that it was necessary to invest in adequate and efficient infrastructures, particularly broadband communications networks and other infrastructures. One of the main goals of his presidency was to control public spending (achieved also by maintaining the previous level of fiscal pressure), aiming ultimately at a further reduction of the US deficit. A lower level of public debt, in turn, meant lower interest rates. These decreases allowed the "new American economy" to boost private investments.

The New Economy

The exogenous processes described above created a favorable framework for a remarkable process of growth and entrepreneurial effervescence as the so-called New Economy took off. The progressive loss of labor-intensive industries guided new investments toward high value-added activities. Between 1992 and 2000, the contribution of fixed capital to manufacturing grew steadily from 13 percent to more than 18 percent of GDP. A relevant part of these new investments went to technology- and knowledge-intensive industries: information and communication technologies (ICT), electronics and microelectronics, computers and biotechnology, and especially toward Internet development, with notable effects on the whole economy. Labor productivity grew from 1 to 1.5 percent annually in the period from 1973 to 1994 to higher than 2.5 percent in 1995–2000.

The New Economy created a number of new jobs and start-ups, particularly in the ICT industry. According to some estimates, between 1985 and 1995, more than 15 million new jobs were created in companies with less than 100 employees, and around 1.3 million new businesses were organized every year.

An innovative financing instrument, venture capital, supported and sustained these initiatives in technology-intensive sectors. Venture capital firms had been operating before and had, since the early 1970s, fostered the growth of Silicon Valley's hundreds of new start-ups (see Chapter 20). Often founded by former practitioners in high-tech industries, these firms invested in small start-ups, betting on their entrepreneurial ideas and ability to grow successfully. Growth was crucial in order to get high returns on their investments and a consistent capital gain in the case of an Initial Public Offering (IPO), that is, of the decision to go public and list the shares of the company on the stock exchange.

When founded in the mid-1970s by two young hobbyists, Steve Jobs and Steve Wozniak, Apple was one among the many small start-ups in California, all of which needed capital to develop their founders' creative ideas. Immediately after the organization of the company, Steve Jobs approached a venture capital firm headed by a former employee of Intel, another high-tech firm. The investor was Mike Markkula, who understood Apple's potential and put around 90,000 dollars into the business. In this case, the venture capitalist not only provided money but also suggested that the founders hire professional managers to improve Apple's efficiency. To attract and retain skilled managers and engineers, committing them to the business, Apple introduced the practice of distributing stock options, that is, the opportunity to buy shares of the company at a low price in order to realize a capital gain if the share price grew. This helped deepen management's commitment to the start-up.

High-tech new businesses required significant financial resources because they were characterized by uncertain and delayed returns. Following a partial relaxation of the rules aimed at savings protection, institutional investors and pension funds started to invest their huge resources in the New Economy. At the end of the 1980s, 3 billion dollars had been invested in venture capital; almost half of this money came from institutional investors. The volume of venture capital investments continued to grow steadily during the 1990s. More than 5 billion dollars was invested in 1994 and more than 10 billion dollars just 2 years later. The majority of this money went to businesses developing ICT, software, e-commerce, and advanced services such as health care. By the year 2000, despite the fact that contraction of the New Economy was pending (and, some would argue, inevitable), venture capital funds maintained very high returns on their investments, in the order of 30–40 percent per year.

Despite the dramatic contraction of what was familiarly named the "dot.com bubble" in 2000, the New Economy revolutionized the competitive structures of entire industries, particularly those closely related to consumers. In August 1995, Netscape, a company that produced an "Internet browser" allowing any computer to navigate freely on the Internet, was successfully listed in NASDAQ, the stock exchange specializing in high-tech start-ups. The company, which had been founded just a year before under the name Mosaic Communication Corporation, was the creature of two computer experts, Jim Clark and Marc Andreessen. Netscape was an almost immediate success, and this kind of rapid growth demonstrated the enormous potential of the Internet market. It showed that this industry might actually revolutionize the system of retail sales and of global commercial transactions.

During the second half of the 1990s, many business initiatives were based on exploiting the potential of the Internet. In 1999, the Dow Jones Index reached a level three times higher than it had been at the beginning of the decade, while the NASDAQ jumped from 1,000 to 5,000 points. The New Economy suffered an abrupt slowdown starting in 2001, a crash that caused a wave of bankruptcies with unprecedented losses. Despite these losses, however, a number of the initiatives established in the 1990s—companies such as eBay, Amazon.com, America Online, Yahoo!, and Google—were able to benefit from this market collapse and actually consolidate their leadership positions.

The growth of the New Economy had important consequences in the field of telecommunications. Given an unprecedented expansion in the demand and volume of sales, investment in ICT grew exponentially. In the case of computers and office machinery, industry turnover jumped from 19 billion dollars in 1990 to 214 billion dollars in 2000 (in constant values). Communications networks, including fiber-optic networks, increased from 28 billion dollars in 1990 to more than 600 billion dollars in 2000.

Another feature of the New Economy was the introduction of radical change to industries that had been viewed as static. New technologies profoundly affected distribution, where the introduction of information technology (IT) into management of purchases, sales, and stocks reaffirmed the success of global corporations such as Wal-Mart. Another company that was able to take advantage of the new technology was Dell, which in 20 years recorded profits of several billion dollars. Dell was founded in 1984 by a young student at the University of Texas, in Austin, Michael Dell, who, after the first positive results, got a substantial amount of money—about 300,000 dollars—from his family. The idea at the origin of the start-up was to sell customized personal computers that would be assembled according to the requirements of the customers. The strategy was successful, and immediately after its IPO in June 1984, the company had a market capitalization of 30 million dollars. Dell initially sold its products directly to the consumers and through the existing selling network, that is, computer superstores. Eager to increase sales, Dell turned to a direct-to-consumer selling strategy, starting to sell computers on a website that customers could use to select the different components to be assembled and delivered directly to their homes.

At the core of Dell's success were the cost savings derived from the elimination of large inventories. In addition, while traditionally computer manufacturing had been characterized by mass production, Dell was able to take advantage of Internet and on-demand production that allowed it to combine the benefits of large-scale demand with the flexibility typical of modular products (see Chapter 20).

Re-engineering the large corporations

The New Economy was only one part of the recovery of the US business system in the 1990s. America's success in technologically intensive industries was achieved largely by the radical restructuring of corporations that had been at the edge of global economic leadership in the 1960s–1980s.

In the mid-1990s, two-thirds of the largest American industrial firms had undertaken radical processes of "re-engineering," a term that meant both huge layoffs and deep changes in strategies and organizational structures. As shown in Chapter 14, the origin of these transformations can be traced to the intense pressure that competition exerted on top management; revolutionary changes in the ownership of America's largest companies had transformed the relationship between shareholders (now most often large, organized interests) and managers.

The ability to adopt effective turnaround strategies made the difference among industry leaders. The example provided by two of the main industrial corporations, General Electric (GE) and Westinghouse, which for a long time were fierce competitors, is telling. While at the beginning of the 1970s the two companies ranked among the top 20 largest US corporations, 20 years later GE ranked in fifth place, whereas Westinghouse had slipped to 42nd position and was performing very badly. It was no longer in business at the beginning of the new millennium, a fate that many other US corporations suffered in these years. In the mid-1970s, both companies had a high degree of diversification from their core business, a strategy adopted from the 1960s onward. As we have seen, this kind of diversification was very popular in American business at that time. For a time, it was profitable.

But as competition became fierce, both companies recognized the urgent need for restructuring. The turnaround at Westinghouse brought, in the end, a further diversification in the risky (and noncore) business of lending in real estate and investment banking, investments that ultimately brought heavy losses.

At GE, since the beginning of the 1980s under the strong leadership of Jack Welch, things went very differently. Welch's strategy was to refocus GE on fewer—but profitable—activities. This meant huge layoffs (from 1980 to 1984, GE's total workforce shrank from more than 400,000 to 330,000), but it allowed management to concentrate efforts on businesses in which the company could gain the largest, or at least the second largest, share in the market. During the first half of the 1980s, GE sold around 100 businesses. With the funds obtained, Welch partially revamped old core businesses but also moved toward "new fields" such as services and hi-tech—the three overlapping circles that summarized his managerial philosophy. For more than 20 years (Welch stepped down early in the new century), GE moved toward the New Economy businesses and sophisticated services including financial services. The company was self-defined as "a diversified technology, services and manufacturing company" with more than 130 billion dollars of revenues worldwide.

GE's successful transformation symbolizes the radical changes occurring among the largest US companies. Forced to face the challenge of adapting to new rules of the competitive game, they either transformed themselves as GE did or suffered the fate of Westinghouse. The challenge also meant that even old and venerable incumbents with well-established brands were nevertheless in danger.

The New Economy created the opportunity for talented entrepreneurs to emerge and quickly build large corporate empires. People such as Bill Gates at Microsoft, Steve Jobs at Apple, Jeff Bezos at Amazon, and Andy Grove at Intel were able to take advantage of the best opportunities provided by the New Economy. What made their success stories possible, and their companies' growth so fast, were some elements that characterized this new form of entrepreneurship. First, science and hi-tech knowledge were at the core of all these successful initiatives. New Economy entrepreneurs were most likely students studying computer science or electronics (such as Dell, Jobs, and Gates), university graduates (such as Bezos), or academicians and scientists such as the Intel cofounders. Gordon Moore was a chemist, and Bob Noyce, a physicist, whereas Andy Grove, who joined them immediately after, was a chemical engineer. Technical knowledge gave these entrepreneurs the capability to single out new market segments with a huge potential for expansion, something that old-economy, established firms were not able to provide.

Second, as already stressed, efficient instruments were now available to direct appropriate financial resources into these projects in their early stages, under the form of venture capital firms, often founded, headed, and managed by former technicians or entrepreneurs who used part of their personal wealth to finance other initiatives of which they were able to see the potential success. An example of this alliance between science and "skilled capital" is provided by the early history of Genentech, which successfully started its activity in the totally new field of biotechnology—another of the New Economy dynamic industries—in 1976. Its founders were a scientist, Herbert W. Boyer (at the time professor of biochemistry and biophysics at the University of California in San Francisco, where he was also the director of the graduate program in genetics), who was a pioneer in recombinant DNA technology, and a venture capitalist, Robert Swanson, who was convinced of the market potential of the breakthrough technology Boyer had mastered. Swanson's strong commitment to the initiative certainly derived not only from entrepreneurial intuition but also from the fact that he had an undergraduate degree in chemistry from the Massachusetts Institute of Technology (MIT) as well as a masters in management from MIT's Sloan School of Management.

Highly innovative firms of the New Economy, which were increasingly going public after a start-up process funded through the committed venture capital firms, became more and more attractive for investors in the stock market. In the second half of the 1990s, there was a sharp increase in the level of speculative activity, which created a real "bubble" just at the turn of the century. Between 1998 and 2000, the NASDAQ Index, which included companies such as Microsoft and Intel, rose by nearly 150 percent in just 2 years, before abruptly dropping during the two following years, returning to the same level it was at in early 1998. This was the other side of the innovation coin in America's brand of capitalism.

Investors' capitalism

At the beginning of the 1990s, shares of the largest US corporations held by institutional investors exceeded those that were in the hands of individuals and households. By the year 2000, mutual funds, pension funds, and insurance companies held in their portfolios more than half of all equity issued in the US market and controlled about 70 percent of the total capital of the largest American companies, or at least those in Fortune's ranking.

This new "constituency" had very different expectations than private shareholders. Mutual and pension funds were oriented toward the short-term maximization of shareholder value. Before the 1970s, institutional investors, who had been increasingly active since the interwar period, tended to favor bonds. Inflationary pressures following the oil shocks and the end of monetary stability redirected their interests toward the stock market. As mentioned earlier, institutional investors had a relevant role in the late 1980s and during the 1990s because of the pressure they put on management and the financial resources they provided New Economy businesses. Venture capital and private equity funds that supported the expansion of Silicon Valley start-ups thus channeled a high amount of the capital now available from institutional investors (in general, pension funds). In addition, during the 1980s, institutional investors provided the resources needed to finance leveraged buyouts (see Chapter 14) that benefited from the high returns of subsequent breakups.

Although it was rare for any single fund to hold a very large stake in a single company (after 1974, the Employee Retirement Income Security Act, or ERISA, regulated the activity of pension funds limiting the extent of their single investments and imposing risk diversification), institutional investors as an aggregate had considerable influence. At the end of the 1980s, about one-fourth of the capital of the world's major companies was in their hands.

Fund managers closely scrutinized the standards of performance of the enterprises in which they had invested and, consequently, judged the appropriateness of management's behavior. Particular concerns arose about the autocratic behavior of some top executives, the practice of not distributing profits, and the diversification strategies, especially those resulting in conglomerate structures. When profits were not sustained after diversification and when inefficiencies prevailed, the resulting stock market losses—which could be as much as 20 percent of a company's capital—prompted quick responses from institutional investors.

The pension and insurance fund managers now agreed with the consultants that these firms needed to identify and preserve their "core competences." All this was done in the name of efficiency and higher profits and wealth, meaning "value" for the shareholders. Driven by these pressures and by waves of hostile takeovers in the 1980s, top management in large companies was forced to refocus their efforts and those of their firms. By the mid-1990s, two-thirds of the companies surveyed by Fortune once again were concentrating their activities within a single industry. Between the 1980s and 1990s, the average level of diversification was reduced by approximately 30 percent.

The search for efficiency and value creation was carried on also through improvements in operations, which were frequently made possible by the introduction of automation systems. New procedures, such as Total Quality Management and outsourcing practices, were based on new communication technologies, and in their turn affected information sharing and knowledge diffusion within the organization. The most radical changes occurred in relationships between managers and shareholders. The philosophy of "shareholder value" drove most of the decisions, behaviors, and strategies of the management of major companies, and undoubtedly, this had some positive effects in terms of efficiency, recovery, and transparency. The emphasis on "value creation" was often accompanied by new ways to establish appropriate incentives for management, such as stock option plans. Companies increasingly directed increasing amounts of the wealth they created to shareholders, both in the form of dividends and through stock repurchases, which had the twofold benefit of keeping the price of the stock high and leaving managers to benefit from their stock options.

Not infrequently, the new rules of the game and the new corporate governance requirements resulted in strong incentives for managers to adopt policies aimed at increasing equity value in the short term. All too many executives emphasized dividend distribution while severely cutting the companies' capability of generating internal resources for investment and growth strategies. In some cases, the necessity to provide investors with high, constant, and secure flows of earnings brought top management to adopt illegal practices that resulted in frauds followed by huge failures and scandals. In 2001, with revenues of about 100 billion dollars, Enron, one of the most celebrated US companies in the field of energy and communications, filed for bankruptcy after it was reported that its huge profits were in large part the result of complex accounting fraud. The result of the failure was substantial losses for shareholders and creditors and obviously for a large number of employees; the scandal also took down Arthur Andersen, one of the world's leading accounting and consulting firms, as it had been negligent in auditing Enron's balance sheets and may indeed have been complicit with the company's mismanagement practices.

The "Enron scandal" and others that affected big companies such as Tyco International and WorldCom so outraged public opinion that the US government decided to enhance the regulation of public companies' corporate governance. Congress passed and the president signed (2002) a new federal law, the "Corporate and Auditing Accountability and Responsibility Act," known as Sarbanes–Oxley, Sarbox, or SOX. Although the new law did not yield all of the results anticipated by Congress, it accurately reflected a growing public concern that America's largest companies lacked the kind of direct and energetic regulation needed to protect investors, workers, and their communities. That sentiment would again well up when the country's banks ran into trouble in 2007 and 2008.

Further reading

W. Lazonick, "The New Economy Business Model and the Crisis of U.S. Capitalism," *Capitalism and Society*, 4 (2), 2009. Available HTTP: http://www.bepress.com/cas/vol4/iss2/

R.N. McCauley, J. Ruud, and F. Iacono, *Dodging Bullets: Changing U.S. Corporate Capital Structure in the 1980s and 1990s*, MIT Press, Cambridge, MA, 1999.

N. Nohria, D. Dyer, and F. Dalzell, *Changing Fortunes: Remaking the Industrial Corporation*, Wiley, New York, 2002.

M. Useem, *Investor Capitalism: How Money Managers Are Changing the Face of Corporate America*, Basic Books, New York, 1999.

W. Wells, *American Capitalism, 1945–2000: Continuity and Change from Mass Production to the Information Society*, Dee, Chicago, 2003.

Appendix

Table 21.1 Research and development investments in US industries, 1990

	R&D expenditures (millions of dollars)	R&D expenditures as a percentage of net sales	Number of R&D and engineers (thousands)
Food, kindred, and tobacco products	1,308	0.5	8.8
Textiles and apparel	242	0.4	—
Lumber, wood products, and furniture	160	0.7	—
Paper	715	0.8	—
Chemicals	12,277	5.6	78.9
Chemicals—industrial chemicals	4,272	4.7	—
Chemicals—drugs and pharmaceuticals	5,366	9.3	33.5
Chemicals—other chemicals	2,646	3.7	22.4
Petroleum refining and extraction	2,133	1	10.2
Rubber products	730	1.7	—
Stone, clay, and glass products	894	2.4	8.6
Primary metals	801	1	—
Primary metals—ferrous metals and products	245	0.5	—
Primary metals—nonferrous metals and products	556	1.5	3.4
Fabricated metal products	644	1	—

Source: Adapted from Alfred D. Chandler, Jr. and T. Hikino, "The Large Industrial Enterprise and the Dynamics of Modern Economic Growth," in Alfred D. Chandler, Jr., Franco Amatori, and Takashi Hikino (eds.), *Big Business and the Wealth of Nations*, Cambridge University Press, Cambridge, 1997, p. 48.

Table 21.2 Distribution by nation of the world's 500 largest industrial enterprises, 1962 and 1993 (ranked by sales)

	1962	*1993*
Developed market economies (except Japan)		
United States	298	160
Great Britain	55	43
Germany	36	32
France	27	26
Sweden	8	12
Australia	2	10
Switzerland	6	9
The Netherlands	5	9
Canada	13	7
Italy	7	7
Belgium	3	4
Spain	0	3
Norway	0	3
Finland	0	3
Austria	1	2
Others	0	3
Total developed market economies	461	333
Japan	31	135
Late-industrializing countries		
South Korea	0	11
South Africa	2	4
India	1	5
Mexico	1	3
Turkey	0	3
Others	0	6
Total late-industrializing economies	4	32
Total	496	500

Source: Adapted from Alfred D. Chandler, Jr. and T. Hikino, "The Large Industrial Enterprise and the Dynamics of Modern Economic Growth," in Alfred D. Chandler, Jr., Franco Amatori, and Takashi Hikino (eds.), *Big Business and the Wealth of Nations*, Cambridge University Press, Cambridge, 1997, p. 53.

22 Slowing down

Europe and Japan

The growth of the US economy during the 1990s was remarkable, but this expansion seems even more exceptional when it is compared with the European or Japanese economic performance in the same period. During the 1980s, the gross domestic product (GDP) gap between America and its two challengers had been shrinking. During the following decade, however, the situation changed significantly. According to the statistics provided by the United Nations Conference on Trade and Development (UNCTAD), in the 1990s almost all the main European economies became less competitive. By the year 2000, the average per capita income in the European Union was only 70 percent of that in the United States. European and Japanese decline derived from a number of factors, many of which were related to the structures of the two economic systems, structures that had once allowed them to challenge American economic power successfully.

Europe for sale

The international political framework was deeply transformed between the late 1980s and the early 1990s, and these alterations affected the economic performance of the leading European countries. This was particularly true for Germany, immersed in a welcome but extremely expensive process of political reunification. In Italy, the problems were profoundly structural. The country's social, economic, and political framework came into serious question as a series of scandals revealed a dense network of bribery and corruption involving leading entrepreneurs, managers, and politicians. The crisis profoundly shocked the political system that had characterized the country since the end of World War II.

There were different sorts of questions throughout Europe as the slowdown prompted serious doubts about the economic and social model on which Europe had built its prosperity in the decades following the conflict. All of the postwar European countries had developed and implemented highly redistributive welfare systems based on full employment and (with the exception of West Germany) pervasive state-ownership in strategic industries such as energy, transport, and utilities. This "Rhine" or Continental European style of capitalism based on consistent deficit spending had been successful in achieving growth and satisfactory levels of employment, but it apparently was no longer sustainable by the 1980s.

The first pillar of European-style capitalism to crumble under the pressure of the cyclical slowdown was the diffuse state ownership common to almost all the economies of Continental Europe (see Chapter 17). Starting at the end of the 1970s and steadily growing in number and amount, during the second half of the 1980s privatizations spread across all over Europe. In Britain, France, and a few years later in Italy and Spain, the extent of State ownership in banking and insurance, manufacturing, and services began to decline, sometimes radically. This process of privatization took place even in so-called "natural" monopolies. In Britain, the once pervasive system of State ownership almost entirely disappeared. The state-owned enterprises (SOEs) that survived were severely challenged.

During the period from the early 1980s to the beginning of the millennium, more than 1,000 privatization deals were concluded in Western Europe. The total amount of capital involved was more than 600 billion dollars, nearly 50 percent of the world's total. Britain alone accounted for almost one-fourth of this amount. This was a stunning economic transformation with significant implications for European society and politics.

Privatization programs were undertaken with different purposes and carried out in different ways. As we noted in Chapter 17, Britain employed a radical privatization technique based on massive sell-offs that virtually wiped out the State presence; the remaining "natural monopolies" were put under the supervision of public authorities and "watchdogs." In France and Italy, the reduction of state ownership did not mean the reduction of ownership concentration. Often, while reducing its direct ownership, the State tried to keep some form of control over the privatized companies. In some instances, the governments used smaller stakes, defined as golden shares, and other artifices, including informal and personal relationships, to keep the State involved in decision-making. The private entrepreneurs acquired their companies through a system of auctions and sometimes through private deals. In Spain, the retreat of the State from direct intervention, pervasive under the regime of Generalissimo Franco, took place through the 1980s and 1990s, with revenues involved of around 50 billion dollars. Germany, which, compared with other European countries, had a far lower level of direct State ownership, was nonetheless engaged in extensive privatization during the reunification. To align the two economies, Germany had to sell the state-controlled assets of the former East German communist government.

The retreat of the European States from the direct ownership of big companies had to be forcefully accompanied by policies of market liberalization. Private companies now were allowed to enter markets once characterized by close political control over natural monopolies. These liberalizations normally involved the creation of supervisory authorities in charge of monitoring the market and the efficiency of services provided to consumers.

Privatization policies deeply transformed the ownership structure of the largest corporations in many European economies, but these processes were only occasionally accompanied by radical changes in the other economic, fiscal, and industrial policies of European governments. The persistence of high deficits and high levels of taxation to finance expensive welfare economies hampered private consumption. The impact was only partially compensated for by public investment. Simultaneously, rigidity in the labor and financial markets slowed the creation of new business initiatives in Europe. All this occurred while America's economy was taking off.

American and European economies continued to differ in their intrinsic structures. The US recovery of the 1990s (see Chapter 21) was based largely on the dynamism of the digital economy whereas, in general, Europe persisted in relying largely on mid-tech, and in some cases low-tech, industries. This was due to the basic features of some of the leading Continental countries. It was particularly evident in the case of Italy, where the manufacturing sector was largely composed of mid-tech, capital-intensive industries and small, low-tech firms in textiles, clothing, footwear, furniture, and other "Made in Italy" products. These industries, which during the 1980s and 1990s accounted for a vast section of the country's exports and value-added production, represented a significant component of the nation's "competitive advantage."

At the beginning of the new millennium, the high-tech industries accounted for 35 percent of all manufacturing activities in the United States in terms of their contribution to value added. This percentage was only 13.5 percent in Europe and about 15 percent in Japan. One of the pillars of welfare capitalism, that is the protection of the workforce, made the European manufacturing sector increasingly vulnerable to the competitive challenges of newly industrialized countries. The newcomers frequently had the advantage of comparatively low-cost labor and minimal welfare expenses. Europe also suffered because its labor productivity was not increasing, particularly when compared with the United States. According to some calculations, between 1995 and 2000 the United States' hourly labor productivity rate grew by more than 2.5 percent annually, whereas the average rate of increase in the major European countries was far lower.

The loss of European competitiveness, especially if compared with emerging economies, is evident when one looks at the trend in the balance of payments. Almost everywhere, with the exception of Germany, the balance became negative during the 1990s.

In several cases, European nations lost their "competitive advantage" under the challenging pressure of globalization. This was true in Britain and France and also in Italy, which during the 1970s and 1980s emphasized a specialization model based on small firms clustered in industrial districts; the Italian focus was on the flexible and specialized production of "Made in Italy" products such as apparel. The model was so successful that Michael Porter in *The Competitive Advantage of Nations* (1990) titled his chapter on the country "Surging Italy." Indeed, the Italian economy was able to keep a positive trade balance for almost all the 1990s, notwithstanding huge deficits in high-tech industries and, above all, energy products. From the end of the decade, however, Italy started to suffer harsh competition in its most successful industries as Chinese competitors moved into these sectors of global markets. The trade balance for Italy became increasingly negative.

Japan and the "lost decade"

The year 1989 was crucial for a Japanese economy which had experienced a long phase of steady growth starting in the 1960s. The Japanese economic model continued to be based on four pillars: industrial policies encouraging domestic firms to increase their competitiveness in foreign markets; the presence of the keiretsu, with its dense network of cross-shareholdings and the informal ties; a participative model of industrial relations, reinforced in many cases by the practice of lifetime employment; and, finally, an efficient banking system based on the practice of "inside lending" because each main bank was closely linked to one of the keiretsu.

The Japanese model allowed businesses to formulate solid, long-term investment strategies, but neither the State nor the businesses were able to transform that basic model when the economic environment shifted radically in the 1980s and 1990s. At this point, Japan found itself trapped in a deep economic stagnation which lasted for over a decade. The origins of the crisis are to be found in the burst of a speculative real estate bubble which had been steadily inflating between the end of 1985 and the last months of 1989. In less than 4 years, Japan's stock market indices more than tripled, while the value of land for residential and commercial use increased almost fourfold. The increase in speculative activity had its origins in several concurrent elements. The most important one was the expansive monetary policy undertaken by Japan's central bank during the second half of the 1980s. To support domestic demand, the Japanese central bank cut the discount rate from 5 percent to 2.5 percent in 1987. This move was accompanied by a policy of revaluing the yen, a measure influenced by US politics that aimed at putting a limit to America's steadily growing trade deficit. Meanwhile, low interest rates made a huge amount of "easy money" available for speculation.

The resulting problems were magnified by ongoing deregulation in the financial sector, a deregulation intended to increase the competition inside a traditionally rigid banking system. Banks started to invest more aggressively, financing real estate speculation. The real estate bubble burst when the Bank of Japan, fearing a growing inflation, decided to change the discount rate. At the same time, Japan's Ministry of Finance tried to limit the involvement of banks in real estate speculation. As a consequence, the Japanese stock exchange contracted sharply—in 12 months the Nikkei index lost half of its value—and simultaneously real estate prices abruptly collapsed.

As a result, private consumption and investment in Japan stagnated from 1990 to 2000, and this coincided with a prolonged deflation. Unemployment rose steadily during the decade, passing from 2 to 6 percent yearly. This percentage was perceived as particularly high because the country had been accustomed to full employment since the immediate postwar years.

The crisis had important consequences for the overall architecture of the Japanese capitalist model. All the social, political, and cultural foundations of the country's success were heavily challenged.

Banks' distress

As the Japanese bubble burst, the main banks of the keiretsu suffered heavy losses. Between 5 and 10 percent of all loans issued during the second half of the 1980s defaulted. The damages were immediately transmitted to the manufacturing industry, which lost the main banks' vital support. These difficulties brought about a major process of consolidation inside the financial sector. The number of very large banks dropped from seven to four: Mizuho, Mitsubishi Tokyo, Sumitomo Mitsui, and United Financial of Japan (UFJ).

The decline in the banks' support and confidence brought managers increasingly to emphasize cost reduction and profitability, market shares, and revenues. At the same time they were searching for additional sources of finance alternative to the traditional ones. For instance, Japanese firms showed a much higher propensity to recur to foreign capital. Its presence grew steadily during the 1990s; at the beginning of the new millennium, foreign investors (mainly institutional investors such as mutual and pension funds) controlled nearly one-fifth of the shares of the largest Japanese listed companies, a proportion never seen in the past. As could be expected, foreign investors were putting increasing pressure on managers to improve the still poor disclosure practices in use among the largest companies. Thus, they were challenging another of the main foundations of Japanese capitalism, that is, its cooperative and collusive practices. The need to ensure a constant flow of external resources from abroad impacted also the State institutions—primarily, the Ministry of International Trade and Industry (MITI) (now known as METI—Ministry of Economy, Trade and Industry)—which were encouraging the adoption of disclosure practices. Japan was changing, although some scholars contend that the nation's corporate finance model is still today largely bank-tied, with the proportion of bank loans in corporate funding largely exceeding 60 percent (compared with 40 percent for the United States).

Unwinding the keiretsu?

Following the crisis in the financial sector, the large Japanese keiretsu were forced to introduce some changes in their approach to capital markets and corporate governance. One undisputable legacy of the crisis has been a decreasing intensity of mutual cross-shareholdings among companies. During the 1990s, the dense network of cross-shareholdings linking banks with companies and companies among themselves—one of the distinctive characteristics of Japanese capitalism—was gradually cut back. Cross-shareholdings shifted from nearly 20 percent to 11 percent of the total share capital among the largest Japanese business groups.

As a consequence of the crisis, the leading manufacturing industries, including automobiles and consumer electronics, found themselves in serious difficulties due to over-production and debt. Even established companies, for instance

Nissan, were forced to seek the support of foreign capital. This in turn compelled their managements to undertake radical restructuring processes, particularly as far as disclosure and corporate governance practices were concerned. The presence of foreign capital and institutional investors had in many cases pushed senior management to pursue a more "shareholder-value" attitude, quite different from the traditional way of thinking about these relationships.

While changes were thus underway, the power of the past resulted in considerable path dependency. Notwithstanding formal reforms, an efficient market for corporate control (one where the inefficient management of an undervalued company would be fired after a successful hostile takeover) was virtually absent in Japan. According to some calculations, from the beginning of the crisis in 1990 to the early years of the new century, only four hostile takeovers have been launched, an incredibly low number if one considers the high number of listed companies in the country (more than 3,500). As an acute observer of the current situation in Japanese capitalism has put it, "the main ingredient of a shareholder-oriented corporate governance structure, a market for corporate control, is still virtually absent and unlikely to grow much in the near future" (Witt 2006: 46).

Crumbling industrial relations

Layoffs, under the label of "voluntary departures," were massive. The crisis forced a discussion of all of the fundamentals of Japanese capitalism, including the complex system of industrial relations that had for decades characterized the country's industries. The "lifetime" and long-term employment system was, in some cases, replaced by a system with higher emphasis on meritocracy and efficiency. The job market, particularly for the new generations, rewards flexibility and mobility much more than in the past. These new practices heavily challenged the traditional loyalty-based relationships between the companies and their workforce. In many cases, under the pressure of short-term results, Japanese companies have not backed away from undertaking decisions unthinkable in the past.

In consumer electronics, for instance, one of the sources of the Japanese competitive advantage, global leaders such as Matsushita, Toshiba, and Hitachi started to reduce their size at home. They have done so in part to remain competitive. There are also moves, for instance, to increase their foreign investments in order to diversify risks and reduce costs. As in the case of the corporate finance system, however, the pace, direction, and intensity of the transformation are all far from being clearly established. It would appear that in this instance—as in others—the crisis has not been able to undermine completely the Japanese model of industrial relations with its emphasis on amicable social ties at the company level.

In sum, the legacy of the crisis is not clear-cut. At the very least, the downturn has brought into serious question the main pillars of the once successful Japanese way to capitalist development and international competitiveness. Many transformations have been introduced, even if the structural—and not contingent—results of this process are still uncertain.

What undoubtedly remained untouched to any significant degree are many of the structural features of Japanese industry. During the entire crisis, the country's trade balance remained positive, thanks especially to mid-tech industries. By the early years of the new century, the value-added quota of Japanese high-tech industries was approximately 15 percent of the total, less than half of the US level. This peculiar competitive advantage—in substance not very different from the European situation—continues to be a special feature of Japan's economic structure.

Further reading

M. Albert, *Capitalism vs. Capitalism: How America's Obsession with Individual Achievement and Short-Term Profit has Led It to the Brink of Collapse*, Four Walls Eight Windows, New York, 1993.

B. Eichengreen, *The European Economy since 1945: Coordinated Capitalism and Beyond*, Princeton University Press, Princeton, NJ, 2007.

K. Fogel, *Japan Remodeled: How Government and Industry are Reforming Japanese Capitalism*, Cornell University Press, Ithaca, NY, 2006.

E. Lincoln, *Arthritic Japan: The Slow Pace of Economic Reform*, Brookings Institution Press, Washington, 2001.

H. Schröter (ed.), *The European Enterprise: Historical Investigation into a Future Species*, Springer, Berlin, 2008.

M.A. Witt, *Changing Japanese Capitalism*, Cambridge University Press, Cambridge, 2006.

Appendix

Table 22.1 GDP and per capita GDP: international comparisons, 1991–2003

	GDP				GDP per capita					
	1999 US dollars (billions)				1999 US dollars (thousands)					
	United States	Europe	Japan	South Korea	United States	Germany	Japan	South Korea	United Kingdom	France
1991	6,949.12	6,509.97	2,868.11	468.37	27.41	22.03	23.11	10.82	19.75	21.78
1992	7,180.19	6,594.6	2,890.71	493.84	27.95	22.36	23.21	11.29	19.75	21.99
1993	7,372.11	6,579.59	2,895.76	520.96	28.32	21.95	23.18	11.79	20.17	21.71
1994	7,668.45	6,767.6	2,914.93	563.94	29.11	22.4	23.27	12.63	21.01	22.08
1995	7,860.47	6,927.6	2,963.25	614.24	29.49	22.72	23.6	13.62	21.56	22.37
1996	8,151.33	7,033.26	3,064.21	657.23	30.22	22.83	24.35	14.44	22.1	22.53
1997	8,517.95	7,193.22	3,124.74	687.79	31.21	23.11	24.77	14.97	22.78	22.88
1998	8,873.6	7,384.57	3,097.11	640.65	32.13	23.56	24.49	13.84	23.43	23.58
1999	9,268.4	7,575.21	3,110.34	701.42	33.18	24.03	24.55	15.05	24.01	24.23
2000	9,607.71	7,828.99	3,190.97	760.95	34.02	24.69	25.14	16.19	24.85	25.03
2001	9,656.25	7,948.39	3,188.59	790.14	33.84	24.85	25.05	16.69	25.22	25.42
2002	9,868.04	8,013.37	3,185.77	345.22	34.24	24.85	25	17.74	25.55	25.59
2003	10,176.32	8,062.37	3,265.41	871.16	34.96	24.81	25.59	18.18	26.04	25.58

Source: Adapted from Angus Maddison, *Statistics on World Population, GDP and Per Capita GDP, 1–2006 AD*, http://www.ggdc.net/maddison/, accessed November 10, 2010.

Table 22.2 High-technology share of all manufacturing industry value-added revenue for selected regions and countries: 1990, 2000, and 2005 (%)

	1990	2000	2005
United States	14.2	19.3	23.9
European Union	10.2	12.6	14.1
France	9.5	15.3	17.3
Germany	9.5	11.0	13.5
United Kingdom	13.6	17.0	17.8
Asia	15.6	19.6	22.3
Japan	16.7	18.7	18.6
China	10.6	19.1	28
South Korea	12.7	24.4	25.7
India	6.2	7.2	8.8

Source: Adapted from National Science Board, *Science and Engineering Indicators 2008*.

Notes: High-technology manufacturing industries classified by the Organisation for Economic Co-operation and Development and include aerospace, communications equipment, office machinery and computers, pharmaceuticals, and scientific instruments. Revenue on value-added basis, which excludes purchases of domestic and imported materials and inputs. European Union excludes Cyprus, Estonia, Latvia, Lithuania, Luxembourg, Malta, and Slovenia. Asia includes China, India, Indonesia, Japan, Malaysia, Philippines, Singapore, South Korea, Taiwan, and Thailand. China includes Hong Kong.

23 New protagonists

China and India*

At the risk of bringing this account up to the current day—a move that can be dangerous for an historian—with its dual chronological and comparative focus, a work like this cannot avoid some reflections on the rise of the two Asian giants, China and India. These two nations best embody the world of business in the early years of the twenty-first century. The historian is interested in the phenomenon for two reasons. Principally because, for the first time since the monumental transformation brought about by the First Industrial Revolution, the epicenter of the world economy shifted from the usual areas, Europe and the United States, to Asia. The second reason is related to the first: this groundbreaking shift in international economic history brings us full circle; for in the 2,000 years prior to the eighteenth century, China and India held a much superior position to Europe or its colonies. Today the inhabitants of China and India number 3.5 billion with a much younger population than in the West. Although there are still large pockets of poor and marginalized citizens, these nations are bursting with scientific know-how, technological skills, and cultures friendly to business activities. Moreover, if we consider the size of the "hidden" populations in the countryside (estimated to be about 800 million in China and 700 million in India), we get a better understanding of the enormous potential expected in the twenty-first century: as historical statistics show, for every peasant who starts to work in a factory, productivity increases sevenfold. This advantage, combined with heavy investments by multinationals, should enable both countries to sustain their remarkable business expansion.

India's tale of success is more recent; it started with the economic reforms of the early 1990s. In 1998, with its 320,000 billion dollars of GNP, India was the world's fifteenth largest economy; a decade later—with a GNP of 806,000 billion dollars—it had moved up to tenth place. China, with its 2,234,000 billion dollars, occupies fourth place. China's sprint ahead began in the 1980s when it rid itself of the unbearable weight of Maoism. In the 25-year period starting in 1980, the economy grew at an average annual rate of 9.6 percent. By 2005, China overtook the economies of nations like Italy, France, and Great Britain.

China

It has not been easy for China in the last three decades to develop a coherent model of economic policy to be systematically repeated so as to always obtain well-defined results. Instead, a conceptual buildup of this type was accomplished by mixing some of the keys of the Japanese "miracle" with those of the other Asian "Tigers." The "lessons" were:

a) create a relationship based on a principle of reciprocity between big businesses and the State so that the former were protected via high customs tariffs, helped with *ad hoc* financing or easy access to credit, and often freed of the risks of market fluctuations via a system of price controls. At the same time, large enterprises were expected to compete in the global marketplace with precise export goals;

b) target product areas where a competitive advantage could be secured by staying in fields requiring mid-level technologies that were not too difficult to apply and where the maximum economies of scale could be obtained. These were the so-called "mature" sectors of the Second Industrial Revolution. This option goes hand in hand with a special attention to the production stage—high technical qualifications and social cohesion of workers—as there is a conviction that it is impossible to fully utilize a plant just by purchasing one that is ready to go into operation;

c) provide support for the big groups considered to be the best interlocutor for a policy of rapid growth. These groups were expected to manifest that special ability of overseeing management of the large dimensions of a business in a process of unrelated diversification.

Compared to Japan and other emerging Asian nations, the case of China had some significant differences. The former focused on industries with relatively high capital intensity as they saw the path of competing via low labor costs to be potentially dangerous. China, however, seemed ready to act on all technological fronts and could count on a workforce that was paid at rates far lower than others. While Japan and South Korea kept foreign multinationals out as a way of maintaining their independence, China used a qualified "open door" policy. While the first-comers of industrialization acted on the basis of an economic policy of systematic interventions, of guidelines, and of moral stances (the so-called Developmental State), China focused on releasing the "animal spirits" that had been repressed during the Maoist Cultural Revolution.

Starting in 1978, when Chinese leader Deng Xiaoping launched a program of economic liberalization, extensive new legislation was initiated. More rights were granted to private enterprise while, on the other hand, the weight of State properties was reconfigured. It was in this kind of setting that Schumpeterian entrepreneurs appeared. These were individuals like Ma Yun, the son of two poor workers and himself a mediocre student who succeeded because of his ability to speak English. When the IT revolution was just appearing in the United States, he created a website (Alibaba.com) that became a serious competitor to giants such as eBay, Yahoo!, and Amazon. Each day two million Chinese firms meet up online with seven million importers from 200 nations around the world via Alibaba.com. Then there was Liu Chuanzhi, a military engineer in the People's Liberation Army. Like the pioneers of Silicon Valley, he created Lenovo, a large hardware firm that bought IBM's business in this sector a few years ago. Consider too the case of Li Ka-shing, a big operator in the field of container transportation as well as a major constructor, important operator in the mobile telecommunications industry, and today, via the purchase of the French company Marionnaud, the owner of one of Europe's largest cosmetics and fragrance retailers.

Relations between these entrepreneurs and the government were not always easy; they remind us of those traits of oriental power described by Marx and by Wittfogel. Some of these entrepreneurs, like Ma Yun, followed the Asian tradition of maintaining a very low profile regardless of their notable wealth. Others, instead, maintained connections with the political world, sometimes because of family ties (30 percent of China's entrepreneurs are also card-carrying members of the CCP—the Chinese Communist Party). A few adopted an opposing stance, challenging political harassment as did Sun Dawu, a farmer who became a large food manufacturer and blew the whistle on party leaders who asked for bribes. Sun Dawu was jailed but some in the echelons of government intervened to free him and restore his reputation, due to his popularity. As a result, some other entrepreneurs have used their own wealth to fund local election campaigns and unseat politicians who had held power for many years.

Ma Yun, with his daily earnings of 100,000 dollars, is probably the world's wealthiest Communist. He comes from the province of Hangzhou, an area north of Shanghai where in 2004 industrial production grew by 30 percent (in part due to monthly salaries that on average are the equivalent of 100 euros for workers and 300 euros for managers). Undoubtedly the extremely low salaries are an essential component of the Chinese "miracle," but no less is the nation's policy of openness toward foreign investments, a policy that already started to appear in July 1979 when a law was passed allowing for foreign equity participation in firms. Four special economic zones (SEZs) were created in the provinces of Guangdong and Fujian; their objective was to attract foreign capital by granting tax breaks on profits (taxation would not exceed 10 percent) and by arranging exemptions for customs tariffs. Overall the experience was positive; in 1984 a new zone was added—the island of Hainan—and 14 coastal cities were also opened to international trade and foreign investors.

Over the course of the next decade, tax exemptions and the elimination of duties were revoked. At the same time, the government allowed complete managerial freedom and reconfirmed its promise that firms with foreign equity would not be nationalized and the law imposing a Chinese head on companies made up of mixed capital was revoked. This open-door policy had unequivocal consequences: between 1979 and 1999 China's commercial surplus grew to more than 40 billion dollars. But it did not bring about the nation's economic colonization if we keep in mind that Lenovo acquired the computer division of IBM, Guangdong's Telecom purchased both French television manufacturer Thomson as well as the cell phone division of Alcatel, while a firm controlled by the giant State-owned China National Offshore Oil Corporation made an attempt to take over control of the long-established Union Oil of California by offering 13 billion dollars.

In the end, China was no longer just the world factory dependent on its low labor costs or the exporter of cheap goods. Over time the country had favorably influenced consumers in the United States and other Western nations by transforming into commodities goods that were originally defined by their brands; the transformation affected products such as household appliances, watches, toys, and leather goods. A symbiotic relationship between Chinese manufacturers and the giant American retailer Wal-Mart had taken form. Wal-Mart's competitive advantage was provided by its ability to offer the consumer the lowest prices possible; it made enormous strides in logistics and the resulting drop in the amount of time necessary to load and unload merchandise helped promote Chinese exports. In the furniture industry, for instance, the United States imports about 10 billion dollars' worth of products.

Despite these advances, China still badly needed other Asian nations' exports. This was the path it was obliged to travel in order to cover its growing needs for raw material imports and capital goods. In China there is still a pressing need to create jobs for the enormous number of young people flooding the labor market, for the hundreds of millions of peasants who are leaving the countryside for cities, and for the employees of declining, almost bankrupt State holdings. This impetus explains why today China accounts for 9 percent of world exports; if the number does not seem significant, just remember that in 1996 the percentage was not even 3 percent. In some labor-intensive sectors, China's presence is felt all over the world. In total 70 percent of the world's production of toys, 60 percent of the bicycles sold around the globe, half of the world's shoes, and one-third of the suitcases manufactured come out of its factories. But China's impact on other global industries where labor costs are not a determining factor is just as significant. Some of the nation's most dynamic exports include half of the microwave ovens sold today, one-third of the televisions and air conditioning units, one-fourth of the washing machines, and one-fifth of the refrigerators.

Of course, "Chinese prices" (i.e., the possibility to produce practically any consumer or industrial good at a price about 50–70 percent less than in any Western nation) are an object of concern for many. The United States and other nations have attempted some countermeasures. Increasingly, suppliers and intermediate goods from China are used to keep low final prices on products. Plants have been moved to China or in other areas of Asia and Latin America where labor costs are competitive. New emphasis is being placed on technological innovation and automation as these are two ways to keep labor costs to a minimum in the developed economies.

But economic "fear" over the medium–long term does not seem reasonable. The "China factor" should be beneficial both for demand as well as what is offered by Western nations. Consumers today are able to purchase a range of goods that would have been unthinkable a few years ago. Manufacturing firms have enjoyed drastic reductions in some of the costs of production and many can expect to enjoy new opportunities inside China's growing domestic consumer market. Still, some fears appear to be well founded. For example, there is concern for the impact that China's economic growth might have on the environment and the planet's natural resources. If the Asian giant continues to grow at the current rate, in 20 years there will be 200 million automobiles on China's roads. Another important unknown factor is the political situation; the government is no longer Communist but it also shows few signs of being either democratic or transparent in its decision-making. It is impossible to foresee the future evolution of the contradictory relationships between the economy and politics or how—and with what consequences for international investments—the system might respond in the event of a slowdown in growth.

India

Asia's other giant—India—seems to hold a net advantage over China in terms of political climate. In fact, India is the world's most populated democracy and has been able to tolerate the coexistence of ethnic and religious groups that is potentially explosive. Furthermore, its system of democracy has deep roots even in the presence of strong social imbalances that, in the case of India, are reinforced by its caste system. Still, even the groups that occupy India's lowest caste levels have the right to vote and secure representation in the battle for social mobility and real equality. In this way, the institutional framework around India's impressive economic growth actually helps to soften the West's concerns. Unlike China, India probably will not translate its economic growth into aggressive military power. The country has become a positive example for nations that seek to overcome problems of backwardness and minority conflicts.

Like the nation's extensive—albeit outdated—railway system, India's political system is a part of the inheritance from the British colonial era. The system guarantees rights and individual liberties to all; it is not only based on majority rule but also assures a presence for the minority parties in Parliament and in elections. Life was not easy during colonialism but India, unlike other nations, also recognized the many positive elements introduced under British domination. Perhaps the greatest asset is the language: English is the common language of the middle class and, with more than 350 million Indians who are fluent, the country can boast an English-speaking workforce that is larger than the combined populations of the United States and Canada. This is a powerful advantage that has permitted India to become a global center of business services.

Unlike China, which opted to take advantage of the race of Western nations (especially the United States) toward "offshoring" and hence became the world's factory, India followed a path that used its special resources in services. The former British colony started off with call centers that were manned 24 hours per day and progressed toward advanced service industries such as financial analysis, statistical and actuarial research, legal and financial consulting, medical diagnosis, and scientific support for pharmaceutical firms. These sectors took off in part because the old industrialized areas of India were eager to find new industries based on primarily immaterial assets; the technical and scientific skills that are so intrinsic to these fields were already present in this ancient culture. The actors of this more recent Asian economic miracle were renowned for quantitative skills that could be easily combined with their deep knowledge of the Vedic writings and their ties with the ancient Hindu mathematical traditions.

The fact that India ranks so high in immaterial industries such as software is in good part the result of specific decisions. The Tata family, the nation's biggest and longest-lasting entrepreneurial dynasty, created the Indian Institute of Science (IIS) in Bangalore well before the nation secured its independence. Tata's decision to create a top-ranking technological and scientific center in Bangalore was later reinforced by the Indian government in the 1960s. Governmental policy sought to concentrate on high-tech industries that were potentially important for national defense in geographic areas far from the country's volatile northern borders. So it also decided to build up other industries in Bangalore such as Hindustan Aeronautics Ltd. and the first major telecommunications firm. In the 1980s, then Prime Minister Rajiv Gandhi, especially keen on moving ahead in technical and scientific industries, actively encouraged Sam Pitroda, an Indian who had emigrated to the United States and made a name for himself as an entrepreneur, to return to his homeland. Back in Bangalore, Pitroda created an innovative center of research and development that was described as the "Bell Labs" of India. In this kind of setting, IIS quickly became the world's top-ranking university for IT; the process of admissions was extremely selective for students who could count on a ratio of three students to each faculty member. The world's top software and IT firms quickly understood that their future strategies had to include Bangalore, twin to America's Silicon Valley.

The story of Pitroda is not unusual. The government actively solicited Indian scientists and technologists to return home. Over the course of time, many have in fact done so and this is further proof of the managerial class's farsightedness in not fearing competition from abroad.

India's current situation is characterized by entrepreneurial actions taken over many years, actions deeply interwoven with the evolution of the giant peninsula's economy. For example, the Tata Group, the nation's largest private firm, was created more than 150 years ago by the son of a rich Bombay businessman, Jamsetji Nusserwanji the Tata, who, eager to be a pioneer in many sectors, created an extremely diversified group that included steel plants, electric power plants, textile factories, cement factories, and even a shipping company. Tata's successors continued to pursue this strategy, branching into sectors such as banking, petrochemicals, air transportation, and automobile manufacturing. The Tata Group's history is intrinsically tied with that of the nation, so much so that it lived through a certain decline in the nation's socialist phase under Nehru and Indira Gandhi before experiencing a rebound after the neoliberal reforms introduced in 1991. Under the leadership of Ratan Tata, turnover in the group increased sevenfold to 22 billion dollars and the strengths of the colossal conglomerate extended from steel, automobiles, and industrial vehicles to include tea (Tata is the world's second largest producer), software, tourism, and finance.

Unrelated diversification is a common characteristic in the economies of India and the other newly industrialized countries (NICs). One of the principal reasons, at least in an early phase of development, was that in a limited domestic market it was impossible to adequately take advantage of economies of scale. One way for a company to overcome these limits was by entering the international arena—this is the path chosen by Mittal (today the world's leading producer of steel) or Birla (who, after acquiring the US aluminum manufacturer Novelis, now is the leader in this sector). Still, it was also possible to pursue a diversification strategy of smaller dimensions than that chosen by Tata. For example, Vijay Mallya, owner of Kingfisher, has successfully mixed the manufacturing of alcoholic beverages with air transportation; in the latter industry, Kingfisher has the largest growth of any competitor.

When considering Indian entrepreneurs, one of their distinguishing characteristics is the strong ethical ties that seem to guide their actions. For example, from its very outset, managers of companies in the Tata Group acted under a form of "enlightened paternalism." Housing was constructed for employees who enjoyed 8-hour workdays, assistance for their children, and a form of profit sharing. The model city, Jamshedpur, was designed to honor the group's founder and subsequently declared by the United Nations to be a masterpiece of urban planning. These same ideals are behind Ratan Tata's insistence today that the Indian consumer, with an income still significantly less than most Western nations, should be able to purchase low-priced goods. Even Mukesh Ambani, the affluent petrochemical entrepreneur, wants to give a "soul" to capitalism; his firm stubbornly searches out alternative energy sources. Ambani also sponsors research institutes focused on producing energy from agricultural products that are abundant in rural areas. Vijay Mallya, the colorful tycoon–owner of Kingfisher, also joins in. Upon being elected to Parliament, Mallya became an advocate for poor farmers, securing for them both drinking water as well as electricity. He also speaks up for improved work conditions for the "untouchables" who labor each day in the society's garbage dumps.

Social entrepreneurship appears to be an intrinsic part of India's economy. A good example is Satyan Mishra who created a network of tiny newsstands, each with at least one computer that was linked into a network that reached into the nation's remotest villages. Services of all types, from driving licenses to birth certificates supplied via e-mail, were made available to citizens in any part of the country. Other good examples are Rajesh Jain's company, Novatium, that offered computers at a cost of about 70 euros each or the nonprofit created by Ramalinga Raju, that made the emergency call system for ambulances more efficient. Shalabh Sahai's foray into the nonprofit sector, iVolunteers, with its 9,000 centers, is heroic in its mission of getting young affluent Indians to help the poor by teaching, fighting urban decay, and coordinating emergency assistance during natural catastrophes.

In this setting, even the civil service has its entrepreneurs. Take the country's railway minister, Lalu Yadav, who has embarked on an ambitious plan of privatizing railroads and transportation of goods to include the transformation of train stations into centers for shopping and entertainment. India still faces enormous problems of poverty, social inequality, and environmental pollution (the tragedy of Bhopal occurred not that long ago). It is probably correct that we should be skeptical of forecasts that envision India arriving in the twenty-first century ranking as one of the world's top three economies together with the United States and China. Still, the incredible progress made by India since the second half of the 1990s is an area worthy of future analysis by economists, sociologists, political scientists, and, of course, historians—including historians of business.

Note

* The stories of the entrepreneurs that appear in this chapter are drawn from two useful books, *Il secolo cinese* (Mondadori, Milan, 2005) and *L'impero di Cindia* (Mondadori, Milan, 2006), both by Italian journalist Federico Rampini.

Further reading

D. Guthrie, *China and Globalization: The Social, Economic and Political Transformation of Chinese Society*, Routledge, London, 2006.
T. Khanna, *Billions of Entrepreneurs: How China and India are Reshaping their Futures and Yours*, Harvard Business School Press, Cambridge, MA, 2007.
N. Kumar, P. Mohapatra, and S. Chandrasekhar, *India's Global Powerhouses: How They are Taking on the World*, Harvard Business School Press, Cambridge, MA, 2009.
B. Naughton, *The Chinese Economy: Transitions and Growth*, MIT Press, Cambridge, MA, 2007.
O. Shenkar, *The Chinese Century: The Rising Chinese Economy and Its Impact on the Global Economy, the Balance of Power, and Your Job*, Wharton School Publishing, Philadelphia, PA, 2006.
K. Tsai, *Capitalism without Democracy: The Private Sector in Contemporary China*, Cornell University Press, New York, 2007.

Appendix

Table 23.1 Share of world's GDP

	1973	2001
Western EU	25.6	20.3
USA	22.1	21.4
Japan	7.8	7.1
China	4.6	12.3
India	3.1	5.4
Former USSR	9.4	3.6
Tigers (Taiwan–Hong Kong–South Korea–Singapore)	8.7	13.2
The rest	18.7	16.7
World	100	100

Source: Adapted from Angus Maddison, *Statistics on World Population, GDP and Per Capita GDP, 1–2006 AD*, http://www.ggdc.net/maddison/. Last accessed October 6, 2010.

Table 23.2 The China/West European dichotomy, 1913–2001

	Population (millions)		Per capita GDP (1990 dollars)		GDP (billions, 1990 dollars)	
	China	Western Europe	China	Western Europe	China	Western Europe
1913	437.1	261	552	3,458	241.3	902.3
1950	546.8	304.9	439	4,579	239.9	1,396.2
2001	1,275.4	392.1	3,583	12,256	4,569.8	7,550.3

Source: Adapted from Angus Maddison, *Statistics on World Population, GDP and Per Capita GDP, 1–2006 AD*, http://www.ggdc.net/maddison/. Last accessed October 6, 2010.

Table 23.3 Real sectoral GDP growth rates

	GDP	Agriculture	Industry	Construction	Transportation. communication	Commerce	Nonmaterial services
1992	9.7	4.7	13.1	21	10.5	13.1	6.1
1993	9.7	4.7	13.8	18	14.5	8.4	5.1
1994	10	4	12.9	13.7	11.6	9.5	10.1
1995	15.1	5	26.1	12.4	14.1	7.7	7.9
1996	2.1	5.1	−3.2	8.5	13.6	7.2	4.3
1997	5.3	3.5	5.1	2.6	12.9	10.4	3.9
1998	0.3	3.5	−7.1	9	10.6	7.8	4.3
1999	6.6	2.8	9.6	4.3	13.4	9.1	1.4
2000	9	2.4	14.5	5.7	13.6	10.1	3.1
2001	10.7	2.8	17.3	6.8	11.6	9.3	4.8
2002	12.4	2.9	20.7	8.8	9.9	10	3.7
2003	15.1	2.5	24.9	12.1	8.3	11	4.5
1992–2003	8.7	3.6	11.8	9.2	12.2	9.1	4.9

Source: Adapted from Angus Maddison and Harry X. Wu, *China's Economic Performance: How Fast has GDP Grown; How Big is It Compared with the USA?*, http://www.ggdc.net/maddison/, p. 5. Last accessed October 6, 2010.

24 A last look

This long journey that we've made over the pages of this book was rendered possible by the *weaving* of three elements. The choice of the word is deliberate because in reality the elements are intertwined and each exercises an effect on the others. Still, for analytical reasons and to provide a clear message, let us try to untangle and consider each of them independently.

The first component is the technological system or, better still, its evolution. Technology is a product of human beings and is determined by technical abilities, scientific know-how, and social attitudes. At any given time, all these elements fall into place as a paradigm, an organized system with a value that is greater than the sum of the single components. Of course, the paradigm changes over time and evolves into a newer version. But in our experience, it remains unchanged—at least for a couple of decades—and so we must accept its exogenous being. We have given a name to this cycle of paradigms—the Industrial Revolutions—and seen how they had an impact on globalization. In its basic characteristics, technology is the same around the world. As the Chinese learned first-hand during the era of Mao, it is not possible to make steel in a backyard furnace.

The second component is the protagonist of this book—the firm: a mixture of people and tools of production assembled in a hierarchical fashion. We might say that, although it has always existed, the firm became more visible during the First Industrial Revolution as it relied on a new and "large" production place—the factory. Around 1900, when we entered into what we call the Second Industrial Revolution, our term for the protagonist started to become cumbersome. This is because the evolution of the technological paradigm brought about the birth, and long-term permanency, of giant firms that ended up coinciding with entire industrial sectors. At this point, it was a game of Chinese boxes. The most important segments of the "secondary sector" (industry) were fields such as metallurgy, chemicals, machinery, and electricity. These sectors were dominated by a few big corporations that often were directly tied to the fate of their home country's well-being. Naturally, we do not want to suggest that big business was the only actor. Not all sectors were affected by the Second Industrial Revolution and, in any case, it is also clear that a healthy and flourishing economy counts on a large community of firms—companies that pursue different objectives and that take on different dimensions in the pursuit of their missions. Still, as our work claims to take a global view of the situation, we readily admit that for us the large corporation is the irreplaceable motor of development, the tool by which nations compete for global leadership.

The third element is the local context. Our choice of adjective should not be seen as denigrating. Instead, when we consider the local context, what we are really considering is the *national* dimension. In some cases, even this notion might not be pertinent: for example, in many chapters, we have tended to look at Europe rather than single nations of the continent. It is the local context that brings to the forefront three other variables: (a) markets considered in their entirety (population and per capita income) and distinguished, most especially, by their dynamism; (b) the relationship between political powers and the business world, both regarding regulation of competition, as in antitrust, and that complex set of policy choices made to intervene directly and sometimes even create the "State as entrepreneur"; and (c) culture in the sense of a combination of values such as the attitude to accept an institutional market and the ability to adapt to universalistic rules drawn up to assure the growth of business.

Our walk through business history started with the workshops of the preindustrial era though that period also had some important companies as well as extensive manufactures. But, in the disorder of the economy, these were little islands. The tale became more interesting with the First Industrial Revolution when it appeared in England toward the end of the 1700s. The fact that, as mentioned earlier, the new system called for a centralized place of production, the factory, meant that the firm took on solidity, something that the intellectuals, the politicians, and the writers of the time had to seriously consider. The stake at play, however, became much greater in the last two decades of the nineteenth century. Global supremacy was decided by the performance and future of the firm, of big business.

England, that up until the middle of the 1800s was considered to be the world's workshop, was not able to grasp the more important opportunities brought about by the Second Industrial Revolution and was not able to develop the new integrated steel plants or machinery for continuous mass production or organic chemistry. This was because the country labored under the typical disadvantages of a pioneer—it was too affluent, too urbanized, and often characterized by anti-industry sentiments as well as governed by policymakers who were not interested in regulating competition. Within Europe, England was overtaken by Germany because the latter was thirsty for railroads and urban structures, and hence needed steel, electricity, and chemicals. Germany's answer to British individualistic capitalism was a form of cooperation between banks, firms, and business or professional associations; soon organizations of workers were also added to the equation. But Germany as well as England had to take a back seat to the United States, which, at the outbreak of World War I, was clearly the world's leading industrial economy. The United States arrived at this point as a result of a complex combination of different factors: (a) extremely dynamic markets: between 1870 and 1913, the US population as well as per capita income grew by almost a factor of three while railway lines extended about ten times as far as those of England; (b) *antitrust*, a strict regulation of competition that, in a certain sense, was the American paradox. Antitrust legislation, inspired by idealistic values and concrete interests, came about as a way of halting business growth that was producing the opposite effect: as companies were unable to get together to agree on market control, they began to take on ever-increasing dimensions; and (c) a culture that valued a *"search for order,"* a form of Weberian bureaucratization that crossed over all segments of American society—influencing political parties, labor unions, professional associations, institutions of higher education—in the quest to establish the precise channels of authority and communication that were absolutely essential for launching and then consolidating big business in America.

On the eve of World War I, the American economy gravitated around large industrial corporations that came out of processes of vertical integration and mergers that were far more than the sum of the individual parts. Their increased size foresaw a new way of governing these businesses with a separation between ownership, management, and financial control. The salaried manager came to the forefront, and this tendency was reinforced in the years between the two wars when market saturation and an accumulation of surplus internal resources led big American business to set off on an expansion into neighboring fields (a strategy of correlated diversification). This policy allowed the most innovative companies to translate into an organizational form—the multidivisional firm—that was able to blend long-term decision abilities with operational efficiency on a daily basis so as to be constantly ready to respond to the market's demands. Though less quickly, this was the same path that Europe's most advanced nations, countries such as Germany and Great Britain, undertook.

The situation in Europe had its distinguishing characteristics. There was more active family control and a greater willingness to enter into agreements on market control. In some countries that entered the industrialization "game" with a handicap, a new actor came forth—the State. Nations such as Japan, Russia, and Italy are certainly different from the others, both as regards traditions as well as their individual geopolitical weights. Still, no one intended to quit the game. For nations like these, the crucial problem was the relationship between the State and the market, a market that Soviet power was able to eliminate from the Russia of the late 1920s in favor of a planned economy based exclusively on big business.

At this same time, technology's impact was global; no one was able to avoid the big dimensions it required, even in light of local idiosyncrasies. The image that comes to mind is of two giant cogwheels moving in opposite directions but that have to overlap in the right point: one of the wheels captures all the local customs, practices, and interests, whereas the other represents technology's needs. As the world emerged from World War II, the United States' superiority was increasingly apparent. In the middle of the twentieth century, the United States occupied the same position held by England a century earlier: with only 10 percent of the world's population, the United States produced almost 50 percent of global output.

But history doesn't stand still. The competitive scenario changed in the 1960s: thanks to pension and investment funds, stock ownership expanded, a new kind of management (convinced that it was possible to manage any company operating in any sector) came forth, and antitrust legislation acquired a new orientation and was likely to punish size as well as collusion. All these factors pushed American big business toward unrelated diversification. It was the dawn of a new form of business, the conglomerate, and the beginning of a management style based on financial reports (christened "management by numbers") and focused on short-term results.

That situation put some of America's big businesses (giants such as Radio Corporation of America [RCA], US Steel, Singer, and International Harvester) into an uncomfortable predicament. Some disappeared entirely, together with whole segments of the American economy. Surprisingly, the country that almost overtook America was not the giant nation that had presented itself as the antidote to American capitalism—the Soviet Union. Even though the USSR had achieved great results by the early 1960s, that nation, too, entered into an unavoidable decline because of the absolute rigidity of the "Plan" and the lack of a community of competitive companies. This time the victorious challenger that took on the United States was Japan, with its groups based on stable ties, a long-term perspective, workers deeply connected with their firms, and a certain *do ut des* between State and big business: the former subsidized, protected, and even eliminated some market fluctuations, but in exchange, it insisted that business embark on a radical plan of productive rationalization and, most especially, that business competed on a global basis. This policy was more or less the one pursued by most newly industrialized countries (NICs), including the Asian Tigers: South Korea, Taiwan, Hong Kong, and Singapore. These nations showed that it was possible to escape underdevelopment not by simply substituting imports but, rather, by combining that type of control with a big push toward exports.

Did the United States experience a decline like the "Victorian syndrome" of England? No, history doesn't always repeat itself, as can be seen by the story of the last two decades. Unstoppable globalization after the fall of the Berlin Wall and especially the diffusion of new technologies for information and communications—for example, the Internet—have penalized the neo-mercantilistic capitalism of Japan and the other Asian Tigers and given a new life to the United States, the nation that has best understood how to ride the wave of the latest technological paradigm, the Third Industrial Revolution. This new technological revolution has shrunk space and communication times. It's a dramatic process in which we now see shareholders taking back the reins of power wherever management becomes "fat and happy." It's also an era of deconglomerations, a return to core businesses, and, most especially, a remorseless application of new technologies of information technology (IT) and communications inside firms. Re-engineering cost millions their jobs and restructured the multinational firms in country after country.

Of late, too, we see signs of the victory of "animal spirits," of the market, and Schumpeterian entrepreneurs. On the horizon, we see signs of new and threatening rivals whose advancement is intertwined with the serious financial and industrial crisis affecting the Western world since the summer of 2008. These rivals include nations such as China and India, both of which have been thrown by the Industrial Revolution into new roles in the global economy. Vast countries like these will, however, have to wade through some deep contradictions as they grow—but perhaps the fact that they are rich in ancient cultures and technical know-how will help them move ahead without the conflicts and tensions generated and resolved in all of the nations of the developed world. We'll see...

Index